# The Revolt of Snowballs

*The Revolt of Snowballs* unpicks a rare and turbulent protest and investigates the meaning behind it. On 27 January, 1511, the island of Murano was the scene of an exceptional collective action, when the representative of Venice, exercising power in the island on behalf of the Serenissima, was hunted by the inhabitants under a shower of snowballs and to the sound of hostile clamour. This book uses microhistory techniques to examine the trial records of the incident and explores the lives of Murano's inhabitants at its heart.

The book begins by providing a detailed introduction to life in Murano during the sixteenth century, including its political framework and the relationship it shared with Venice. Against this context, the political skills of Murano's inhabitants are considered and key questions regarding political action are posed, including why and how people chose to protest, what sense of justice drove their actions, and what form those actions took. The latter half of the book charts the events that followed the revolt of snowballs, including the inquest and its impact on Murano's society.

By putting Murano under the microscope, *The Revolt of Snowballs* provides a window into the cultural and political world of early modern Italy, and is essential reading for historians of revolt and microhistory more broadly.

**Claire Judde de Larivière** is Senior Lecturer at the University of Toulouse and Honorary Research Fellow at Birkbeck, University of London, UK. Her previous works include *Naviguer, commercer, gouverner. Économie maritime et pouvoirs à Venise (XVe-XVIe siècles)*, 2008; "'Le peuple est la cité'. L'idée de popolo et la condition des popolani à Venise (XVe-XVIe siècle)", *Annales HSS*, 2013, n°4 (with Rosa M. Salzberg); and "The Urban Culture of the Ordinary People. Space and Identity in Renaissance Venice (Fifteenth-Sixteenth Centuries)", *Medieval Urban Culture*, ed. by Andrew Brown and Jan Dumolyn, Turnhout, 2017.

# Microhistories

*Series editors:* Sigurður Gylfi Magnússon and István M. Szijártó

The *Microhistories* series is open to books employing different micro-historical approaches, including global microhistories aimed at grasping world-wide connections in local research, social history trying to find determining historical structures through a micro-analysis, and cultural history in the form of microhistories that relate directly to large or small scale historical contexts. They are interesting stories that bring the everyday life and culture of common people of the past close to the readers, without the aspiration of finding answers to general "big questions" or relating them to the grand narratives of history. The series is open to publishing both theoretical and empirical works but with a focus on empirical monographs, which can communicate stories from the past and capture the imagination of our readers.

Published:

**The Revolt of Snowballs**
Murano confronts Venice, 1511
*Claire Judde de Larivière*

Forthcoming:

**A Tale of a Fool?**
A Microhistorical Study of an 18th-Century Peasant Woman
*Guðný Hallgrímsdóttir*

**Roman Tales**
A Reader's Guide to the Art of Microhistory
*Thomas V. Cohen*

**Who Killed Panayot?**
Reforming Ottoman Legal Culture in the 19th Century
*Omri Paz*

# The Revolt of Snowballs
## Murano confronts Venice, 1511

Claire Judde de Larivière
*Translated by Thomas V. Cohen*

Routledge
Taylor & Francis Group

LONDON AND NEW YORK

First published 2018
by Routledge
2 Park Square, Milton Park, Abingdon, Oxon OX14 4RN

and by Routledge
711 Third Avenue, New York, NY 10017

*Routledge is an imprint of the Taylor & Francis Group, an informa business*

© 2018 Claire Judde de Larivière

Translated by Thomas V. Cohen

*British Library Cataloguing in Publication Data*
A catalogue record for this book is available from the British Library

*Library of Congress Cataloging in Publication Data*
A catalog record for this book has been requested

ISBN: 978-1-138-06606-9 (hbk)
ISBN: 978-0-429-50433-4 (ebk)

# Contents

# Preface

Let me say here a few words, to lay out the scholarly and editorial project that shaped the writing of the original *La révolte des boules de neige*, which came out in 2014 with the Paris publishing house, Fayard. The form and content of my book owe a great deal to an intellectual project and editorial mission proper to its land of origin. In France, publishers have fostered a substantial body of writing that, all the while it looks to serious research, reaches out to a broader public. I wanted to join that undertaking by furnishing a piece of original research on a little-explored topic, while making it accessible to general readers who care for history.

That meant that I had to keep several complementary goals in mind. On the one hand, the inquiry into the Revolt of the Snowballs allowed me to analyse the forms of everyday politicization, and the way non-nobles contributed, in so many ways, to the political construction of their communities. So, I could use a rather dramatic event to show the importance of everyday political practices for communities' institutional and political organization. On the other hand, I wanted to bring to the fore Murano's social density and lay out the nature of the place's *popolo*, as the island is an exceptionally well-documented place for an historical study of ordinary people. It was a world at once big enough to support a great variety of social interactions, and yet small enough to allow a scholar to identify the actors and, sometimes, to trace their life stories. These two conditions – variety of actions and precision of the record – are essential if one wants to study the *popolo* well, without falling back on threadbare generalizations that stunt analysis.

These two objectives required of me an authorial stance that took very seriously the persons whose history I hoped to write. I had no wish to compile an erudite, compendious monograph about Murano. Given the variety and abundance of the documents I collected, I could indeed have done so. But I chose instead to use this surprising tale of the Revolt of the Snowballs as a device to tell a story that embodies the histories of both individuals and collective groups. So my process of writing could in no way be sundered from research I had done. It fell to me to make my choices, boil matters down to essentials, bring good details to the fore and, step by step, trace the histories both of the trial and of the islands' inhabitants. That editorial choice persuaded me to keep my footnotes simple, mostly just archival references, while I placed my historiographical comments and bibliography at the end of the work, organized by theme. Despite the light touch, nothing written in this book is made up or imagined. Rather, every contextual remark, anecdote or action comes straight from the archival papers.

*The Revolt of Snowballs* is thus the fruit of complementary desires and goals, at once methodological, analytic, and stylistic. In its form, rhythm, and deliberately modest bulk, it reflects the scientific and methodological preoccupations that marked its drafting and production.

As I moved to English, Tom Cohen's translation marked for me an exciting new intellectual stage. It was his idea to translate the work, and I am deeply grateful for the hard work he put in and for the quality of the translation, for he, like me, is alert to the play of the writer's craft, long so central to his own work. The translation put us both to a double task, as we not only consulted carefully on the movement from French to English prose, but also returned to the archival sources to bring them faithfully into a new language.

The deconstruction of analytic categories is, for historians, a necessary first step, and the passage from one language to another is an exercise particularly fruitful for debate about the sense of words, their pertinence, and their range of meaning. The translation project was a very stimulating effort, as it forced me to reflect on my original linguistic and analytic choices, the better to respond to Tom's questions. The exchanges between us were endless, and our discussions on concepts and ideas and on how to translate them helped the translator to pick best words and phrases. They also pushed both author and translator to return to their own thinking, keeping in mind the comparison with Rome, where Tom is a specialist. His familiarity with the Roman world alerted me to some of the Lagoon's particular traits, and his questions and suggestions sometimes brought to light blind spots in my own analysis; meanwhile my Venetian findings helped him think through Roman problems on his hands.

This English edition is coming out in a new series dedicated to micro-history. As a method, research strategy and mode of writing, microhistory emerged in Italy in the 1970s and, as a historiographic current with flexible boundaries, it has since those years inspired several generations of historians of many sorts and varied fields. Microhistory has inspired work and kindled debates over how scale makes a difference, around how focus shifts and plays, and about the lessons, if any, of "the normal exception" (something strange that has assorted normal traits) and, in that connection, about how to guarantee that a single study of any quirky thing can represent any wider pattern outside its own odd self. Meanwhile, discussion of a history's best shape and voice has also been central to microhistory, and, most recently, microhistorical analysis has been pertinent to the new fields of connected history and global history. So the method is a rich one; while it rests on a set of shared traits that are trenchantly heuristic, setting models for historical practice, microhistory is open-spirited enough to lend itself to many fields of historical inquiry and to serve researchers with a great variety of paths of inquiry and goals.

It is indeed an honour to be able to participate in the first steps of this book series, and I hope that this work, conceived and written in the French language, for a French public, will have the art to address an English-speaking public that approaches it with different assumptions, skills, and knowledge, but which shares with France a love of history.

*November 2017*

# Acknowledgements

The research for this work enjoyed the support of Labex SMS (ANR-11-LABX-0066).

I wish to express my gratitude to the personnel of the Archivio di Stato di Venezia, the Archivio storico del patriarcato di Venezia, the Biblioteca del Museo Correr and the British Library for their helpful support. Marco Toso Borella and Alberto Toso Fei shared with me their knowledge of Murano; Marina Schenkel, Francisco Leita, Sergio Volpe, and Anna Pizzatti were, over the years, wonderful guides to Venice; Patrick Boucheron agreed to read and reread this book and offered valuable suggestions; Antoine Lilti welcomed the French edition into the Fayard series that he edits, and his comments, both critical and suggestive, helped this history to take shape; István Szijártó and Sigurður Gylfi Magnusson generously welcomed the English version into their book series; and with Julien Weisbein, Rosa M. Salzberg, and Paolo Nelli, I was able to share my thoughts and discuss the book's evolution from start to finish, as they read and reread it and commented with insight and intelligence.

And finally I must express my great gratitude to Tom Cohen, who proposed translating this work into English, and my express sincere appreciation for his splendid translation. This English version of *La révolte des boules de neige* owes a good deal to his intellectual involvement in the project, to his suggestions and comments, and to the dialogue that he helped carry on between us.

# Abbreviations and comments

AC          Avogaria di Comun
ASPV       Archivio storico del patriarcato di Venezia
ASVe       Archivio di Stato di Venezia
b.           *busta*
BL          British Library
BMC       Biblioteca del Museo Correr
MP         Miscellanea penale
PM         Podestà di Murano

In the book, in accord with current usage, the names of Venetian patricians appear in their Italian form. The spelling of names of inhabitants of Murano and of places has been standardized in accordance either with Venetian or with standard Italian, depending on the more common form they take in the sources.

Although the old Venetian calendar starts the year with 1 March (in Latin: *more veneto*), all dates in the book follow the modern habit, with the year beginning on 1 January.

Coinage:
One ducat is worth 6 *lire* and four *soldi* (124 *soldi*).
One *lira* is worth 20 *soldi*, or 240 *denari*.
One *marcello* is worth half a *lira*.

All quotes from the trial of the Snowball Revolt are extracted from ASVe, Avogaria di Comun, Misellanea Penale, busta 142, n° 17.

- Murano, 4 February 1511: fol. 1–1v Nicolo di Blasio; fol. 1v–2 Gasparo Furlan; fol. 2–2v Angelo Zeloxo; fol. 2v–3 Vincenzo di Murano; fol. 3–3v Domenico di Andrico; fol. 3v–4 Domenico Rizo; fol. 4–4v Domenico Bertoluso; fol. 4v–5 Pietro Zorzi; fol. 5–5v Tommaso Paliaga; fol. 5v–6 Zuan Rizo.
- Venice, 26 February 1511: fol. 7–8v Antonio Malcanton; fol. 8v–9 Jacopo Cagnato; fol. 9v–10 Bernardin Bigaia; fol. 10–10v Zuan dall'Aqua.

- Venice, 27 February 1511: fol. 11–11v Andrea dall'Aqua; fol. 11v–12 Pietro Bigaia.
- Venice, 12 March: fol. 12–12v Paolo Contarini di Pietro; 15 March, fol. 13–13v Alvise Contarini di Francesco; fol. 14 Polo Contarini di Bortolo; fol. 15 Domenico Contarini di Matteo.
- Murano, 24 February 1511, unnumbered document, Giacomo Suriano.
- Venice, 26 March 1511: fol. 16 Jacopo Cagnato; fol. 16v Bernardin Bigaia; fol. 17 Andrea dall'Aqua; fol. 17v Zuan dall'Aqua; fol. 18 Pietro Bigaia; 28 March, fol. 18v–19v Sebastiano Bellencito.
- Venice, 29 March–10 April 1511: fol. 20–22, sentences.

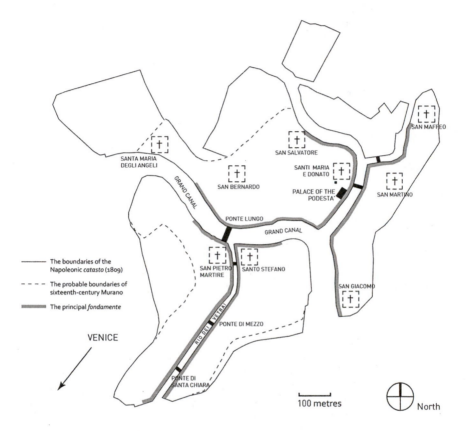

Murano in the sixteenth century
Source: Pietro Belli and Claire Judde de Larivière

# Introduction

It is Monday morning, 27 January 1511. The furnace men of the Murano glassworks are coming off the night shift. They step from their warm workshops into the icy wind blowing down the Rio dei Vetrai. Since last evening, the snow has not let up. The oven of Nicolo and Maddalena, German bakers, fills the air with the scent of warm bread. Servant girls duck into the nearest glassworks to fetch fire to light the hearth. The spice merchant Zuan Rosso claps shut the little wooden cages behind his shopfront lest his ducks and chickens freeze. Already the women are astir; they carry off the snow that overlies the quays. Jacopo Cagnato, a fisherman, steps out briefly to assure that his boat is staunchly moored to the *riva*. No fishing today; the weather is dreadful! And he would have to be back by evening to welcome the new podestà, Giacomo Suriano, the Venetian official charged with the island's governance. That's what Antonio Malcanton has on his mind; Antonio had long sold fruit and vegetables, but, for the last few months, he has been town crier. For the first time ever, it will fall to him to orchestrate the ritual that passes power from one patrician holder to another.

The most recent podestà, Vitale Vitturi, has had a hard time, thanks to the Italian Wars, with Venice faced off against a powerful coalition. The inhabitants of the Venetian Lagoon have suffered for this war, paying ever-higher fees and taxes and shouldering campaigns inside the Venetian state. Vitturi has been loathed; news of his departure sets tongues free. For several days now, children have frolicked through the streets, jibing at "the dog who has ruined Murano". Meanwhile, at the glassworks, workers have taken up, heartfelt, a ditty reviling the man "who has gulped down Murano's poverty".

Early in the afternoon, after the midday meal, the inhabitants gather in front of Santi Maria e Donato, the church where the ceremony will take place. Across the way, the palace of the podestà dominates the *campo*. In its majesty, the building symbolizes Venice's power. Vitturi takes his place on the ground floor, under a covered gallery facing the square. He stands by a fire lit by the town crier to warm him while he awaits his successor's arrival. The snow still falls. The master glassmakers and their workers, the fishermen and peasants, the artisans, the merchants, a few servants all gather for the ceremony. Meanwhile, the children scamper, shouting on the *campo* and excited by the solemn day's festivity. Some adults shush them; others just egg them on.

When Giacomo Suriano docks at the quay, folk fall silent to look the new podestà over as he climbs from his boat. He has an escort, a squad of Venetian patricians, shouldering power's robes and colours and, by gesture and posture, flaunting high position. Vitturi, quitting the loggia, marches towards the canal's edge. Around him cluster Murano's better folk – glassmakers and furnace-owners, no less dressed up than the others for the event. Ranged behind the crier, it is a solemn procession that heads to Santi Maria e Donato. Then, inside the church, the ceremony runs its course; meanwhile, most townsmen linger on the *campo*. The church houses Byzantine mosaics, among the Lagoon's most ancient. Under their glowing auspices, Vitturi passes to Suriano the staff of authority that symbolizes rule over the island and, by that act, formalizes the new podestà's entry into office. The priest oversees this well-paced ceremony, repeated like clock-work over the centuries to advertise Venice's power. Now that Giacomo Suriano has been installed, Vitturi can return to the capital, free of these Muranesi, who are as eager as he himself to see him off and gone.

According to the rules, the ceremony requires that the cortege escort an out-going podestà to the canal's edge, and, as if in a mirror, that his successor accompany him to the watercraft that will ship him back to Venice. So the procession duly reassembles, the crier up front, followed, in order, by the two podestà, the Venetian patricians, and Murano's leading townsfolk – those who have enjoyed the privilege of witnessing, inside the building, power's passage from hand to hand. Carefully, the parade makes its way out through the church's portals, and there meets the crowd, whose usual job it is to cheer their community's new chief and show their joy and enthusiasm for Venice's representative. But, in fact, the anticipated clamour and gestures greeting the procession turn out far less jubilant than expected. Instead, a great barrage of snowballs slams the two podestà, mixed with hallooing shouts that strike them dumb. The children, fishermen, and workers bombard them. Hurtling snow fills the air, balls sailing across the square from the far side, pelting the procession. Yells, whistles, and laugher smother the shouts of the crier, who strives in vain to quell the brawl. From atop the bell tower, a clutch of men barrage the podestà and set the bell to hectic ringing. Meanwhile, in unison, up floats a chant:

> *Surian Surian*
> *Caccia via questo can*
> *Che ha ruinato Muran*

> Surian, Surian
> make this dog run
> who has ruined Muran

The parade founders in confusion. Vitturi, doing his level best to cover himself with his cloak, scurries for his gondola. A clutch of youngsters lurches his way shouting ever louder insults against "this dog". The podestà's companions, Venetian nobles and Murano citizens, hesitate to step on board with him. It had been the plan to keep him company to Venice, a floating parade. But, given the melee, they fear a capsize or another ambush along the canal. Rumour has it that the glassmakers are lying in wait all along the Rio dei Vetrai, by their shops and workplaces. With ammunition piled and ready, they too are primed to sing out loud the scornful refrain that, for days already, they have been humming. So it is with a paltry escort that the patrician leaves the community that, for sixteen months, he governed. He opts to depart via the Lagoon, not by way of the island canals. Relieved that at last his mission is over, Vitturi would still far rather have left Murano without these jeers and projectiles. But, at least, flying snow beats a hail of rocks.

In Venice, by evening, news of this sorry departure is probably making the rounds. Like the city's commoners, the patricians might take offence, or laugh to hear the tale; they would shop the rumour around, in their gatherings on the piazzas and at the Rialto markets, and at the fine dinners and dress balls laid on to celebrate Carnival season. Marino Sanudo, Venice's compulsive chronicler and recorder of city doings, mentions the affair in his *Diaries*. On February 28, summing up the month's events, he records:

> Yesterday, Ser Giacomo Suriano, son of the late Ser Michele, made his entry as podestà of Murano. The podestà before him was Vitale Vitturi, who is disliked by the people of Murano, because he had dealt with them badly. So, when the new podestà arrived at Murano, they began to shout, "There's come Surian, who is chasing out this dog, who has ruined Muran." So this morning the aforesaid Ser Vitale went to the Signoria complaining of this. And the case was entrusted to the Avogaria, and they have had arrested some persons from Murano, against whom this podestà has launched a formal grievance.

Sanudo is one of the rare Venetians to have left a record of the event, as the public archives are mostly mute. Still, a trial is swiftly launched by the Avogaria di Comun, the institution that serves as an appeal court for Venetians and handles conflicts between Venice's government and its subject people. Although the trial survives in Venetian archives, the whole affair is now quite forgotten. To this day, no historian has studied it.

And there we have it! That's what draws us to Murano. It is an event as strange as it is trivial, a "revolt" that smells of charivari, a happening that would have gone unheeded in Flanders or in Tuscany, places inured to armed clashes and popular uprising. But the Lagoon is different: there, violent demonstrations against patrician authority are so rare that this 1511 power-transfer merits our attention.

In these years, Murano is under Venice's dominion. For a great long time, glass-making has been its industry and, in Italy and in Europe, its glassmakers have enjoyed a solid reputation. Good rich histories have laid out the economic organization of this industry, its technical processes, and the organization of its workshops. But the historians have contented themselves with that; we know very little about all the other Muranesi who, in these years, inhabit the island, the glassworkers and apprentices labouring in the workshops, the other artisans, the shop-keepers, the fishermen, the peasants, the domestic servants – in short, the men and women who came to watch the handover. This book is devoted to them: the *popolo*, Murano's community and society. It is still a tricky question: what, at the end of the Middle Ages, did it mean to be a *popolano*, a man of the people? This collective category, the *popolo*, which often shades into "the poor", covers the majority of the inhabitants, both the wealthy artisans and workers of much lesser means; it includes folk who are well ensconced in the community and others with a perch more wobbly. In Murano, as in Venice, and as in just any Western city at the advent of the modern age, just who and what constitutes urban society's fabric?

Neither patricians nor statutory citizens (*cittadini*) of Venice, the *popolani* of the Lagoon have no formal political power. Nor do they head the most profitable economic enterprises, in international commerce. Nor do they own the palaces that, today still, so embellish Venice. Nor do they write the papers that fill the archives. But they are not poverty stricken and excluded, nor are they banished to society's margins. They do not live off low crime and petty theft, nor do they dwell in makeshift lodgings or scuttle from city to city. These ordinary folk are the town. They constitute and create community. They fill the streets and quays with their activities and talk. Their actions and their thoughts give shape to the Lagoon's world, space, and history. But they are no clear group, all uniform inside and sharply drawn, and the *popolo* has no formal existence, save in the discourse of the patricians who rule the city. Meanwhile, inside the community, hierarchies set inhabitants off from one another, and values sort them, and help shade and nuance the complex society we will be exploring.

Our encounter with the Muranesi takes place on 27 January 1511, when, gathered on Campo Santi Maria e Donato, they show their rancour against podestà Vitale Vitturi. For historians of the Middle Ages and early modern times, such tumults represent one of the principal means of expression for populations cut off from other recourse. Since small folk take little or no part in institutions, vote no laws, run no courts, and do not rule their city, what are their weapons, their means to win a hearing? What catches our scholarly eye are their violence and shouting, riot and sedition. But in this early modern scheme of things, Venice barely figures. From the commune's foundation, in the twelfth century, down to the Republic's fall in 1797, patrician power has almost never been contested, and no popular protest ever made the Serenissima's solid foundation quake. So the Snowball

Revolt is a rare moment, a clash between the inhabitants of the Venetian Lagoon and their rulers. But what is it exactly? Is it a moment of festive excess, a civic ritual that for a brief moment slips out from under rulers' control, a carnivalesque uproar against a little-loved podestà, or an explicit political critique in rebellion's guise? One job of this book is to pin down the event's precise nature.

But first we must figure out who are the actors here, and what is the community to which they belong. Now, to write the history of glass blowers, fishermen, labourers, and servants from the sixteenth century, persons who left few papers of their own in the archives, is no easy task. Tracing ordinary petty lives, often nameless, in documents they themselves very seldom penned, leaves us with some intellectual choices.

First off, how to conceive society? It seems fruitful to see it as the result of a multitude of everyday interactions on its constituents' part. Society is not some rigid, static infrastructure into which individuals fit themselves, slotted tidily into categories, hierarchies, or groups. It is, rather, a moving conglomeration, made up of configurations that shape-shift in response to the locus, the situation, and the movements of social actors. In street, workshop, or dwelling, on the public square, or before a court of law, these people fashion and form society by word and action. From their talk, and their dealings, and their relationships and quarrels – with their peers and neighbours, employees and masters, tenants and landlords, subjects and rulers – a social and political space emerges, complex and dense. There they play out their lives.

To grasp these fluctuating patterns, and to explain them, and to understand how they form society, the historian faces a second decision, this time about narration. If the *popolo* does not figure, except in words that elites bring to bear on it, how then to write its story? It is by reading in the archives, as closely as one can, that we can get there, by chasing down details, reality's minutest motes, those tiny facts that give shape to concrete, everyday experience. Touch by touch, one must fill out the picture of Muranese society, the spaces and landscapes in which the inhabitants live and move, and the words and objects in common use. These hints, albeit tiny, are never lacking: in the trial at Venice, after the Snowball Revolt, in the judicial sentences of podestà Vitturi and the deliberations of the Council of Thirty, the proclamations of the town crier on the island bridges, the accounts of the chamberlain, the debates in guildhall by glass blowers and gondoliers, in all these places things turn up. That is what archives are made of, heaps of inventories, decisions, debates, anecdotes, little meetings – details that *a priori* count for little, flimsy indicators, vague evocations. Just like the chancellors who first made the documents, we too must draw up lists of names, of things, of goods, of places. We must heap up testimonies and stories, in order to write the history of the common folk of Murano at the beginning of the sixteenth century, and of the society that they form. It is not our job to do them justice, nor to pity their precarious lives; rather it falls to us to take seriously the way in which they contribute, day to day, to configuring their society.

The third choice that has guided this book is to "repoliticize" social history. Our exploration of the Muranese community, in tracking the Snowball Revolt, traces the actions and words by which the island's denizens join the collective construction of society's frameworks, and it lays out their roles inside institutions and their capacity to set communal action rolling. Working out the meaning of the deeds of the Muranesi gathered that day on Campo Santi Maria e Donato forces us to rethink their riot in its general political context. For, when we scan the archives, the event seems in fact just one proof among many of the inhabitants' capacity for action. The island is a social and political space that in no way boils down to a simple dichotomy – the power of the dominant, on the one hand, and the resistance of the dominated, on the other, or the authority of the Venetian patricians here, and there the submission of Murano's *popolo*. The inhabitants' everyday practices, their interactions with the podestà and with judicial institutions, their professional and neighbourly relationships, all reveal their integration into a myriad of institutions and social settings. Murano society is run by usages, by codes, and by a kind of order, all of collective origin. The denizens continually intervene in the public spaces, albeit less spectacularly than on 27 January 1511, but far more effectively. They are led to debate with their fellow islanders and take decisions with an eye to communal interests, and also to gloss the social order and assess the structures on which that order rests. Some Muranesi collaborate directly with the regime and contribute to the island's governance; they hold office and shoulder administrative burdens. Others take part in everyday construction of the economic, social, and political scaffolding that supports and organizes society.

A tight community, a finite chronology, and a well-bounded event, between them, let us identify and follow the persons involved, recapture their biographies, and study their social interactions, all properly situated and placed in context. But if Murano is our chosen terrain of inquiry, we wager that the processes brought to light here will pertain to other places, and that our conclusions will resonate with other histories. A reader who knows microhistory well will find here a method that, ever since the 1970s, has inspired many studies. Other works consecrated to Murano and to Venice, to the people of medieval and early modern cities, to popular revolts and to forms of politicization, have inspired this book. But they won't be summoned up here in the writing; rather, the bibliography will discuss them. Turn there for this book's historiographic and methodological framework.

After having discovered Murano and its inhabitants, and then analysed their relationship with Venice, we shall return to the ritual passing of power and to its strange outcome on 27 January 1511. Then we will put the event into context, especially that of the Italian Wars. After that will come the analysis of the trial held in Venice in the weeks that followed to examine the procedure set up by the Venetian magistrates and the relationship between the inhabitants and the machinery of justice. With all that done, we will be in a position to assay the meaning of the Snowball Revolt and to judge its eventual political impact. A history of Muranese society at the end of the Middle Ages, an inquest into the Snowball Revolt, and an analysis of the forms of action open to the *popolo*'s members: these are this book's three goals.

# 1    The island of Murano

## Glass and gardens

At the beginning of the sixteenth century, any stroller walking the north-side quay of Venice might see the smoke rising from Murano's glass furnaces and, with the wind right, the stroller might hear the bell at Santo Stefano when it calls the glassmakers to mass. Twenty minutes, by gondola, suffice to carry one across the channel that separates the two islands to land on Murano's south shore, the Fondamenta and the Rio dei Vetrai (the Glassmakers' Quay). To the locals, it is just *the* Rio, and their expression *in Rio* subsumes the rest. The *bora* and the *greco* sweep it readily – these cold winds down from the Alps carry off the furnace smoke, guaranteeing Murano pure clean air.

The glass making craft has been a Venetian trade since the twelfth century. The raw material comes from a mix of silica (sand from the Lagoon and the nearby rivers) and soda (contained in ash imported from Syria, made by burning Mediterranean seaweed). Cooled in the Lagoon's briny water, the glass is extolled for its exceptional quality. The glass industry feeds the prosperity of Venice's artisanal sector, stimulated in turn by the maritime commerce that assures the city its Mediterranean hegemony. But, to hedge the risk of fire and to remove pollution and smoke that is hard on breathing, the government decides to shunt certain activities to the city's edges and to the islands: furnaces for glass, or brick, or mortar, soapworks, tanneries, and abattoirs. On 8 November 1291, the Maggior Consiglio, the Republic's main legislature, decrees the destruction of the glass furnaces in Venice itself and orders them placed anywhere else in the Lagoon. Over the next few years they disappear from the capital, although certain operations that imitate precious stones with glass do receive the right to stay, provided they keep their distance from neighbouring houses.

The inhabitants of Murano, thanks to a favourable reading of this decree, make sure that the furnaces are installed on their own island; from then on they enjoy the monopoly on production. The invention of transparent crystal, in the fifteenth century, and then the multiplication of glass varieties – painted, raised, and gilded – and of enamels and varnishes allow the workshops to blossom and wax rich. Their fame finds its way to Italian courts, where princes and Renaissance art collectors become great lovers of Murano glass.

The artisans make objects of all sorts: tableware both crude and refined – bottles and flasks, glassware for official wine measures at inns, low-end cups and bowls, stem glasses and precious chalices, drinking bowls, goblets, candy-dishes, small cups and carafes, wine jugs and plates. The glass is gilded, blue, turquoise, red or milky-white, marbled, striped, mottled or polychrome, transparent or opaque, adorned with rosettes, patterned or slyly striped like chalcedony. There are, meanwhile, chandeliers, inkbottles, knife handles, saltcellars, flasks for alcohol and vials for holy water, musical instruments, hanging lamps, rosary beads, and smooth flat glass for windows and for mirrors. And pearls, and false gems, and plaques painted with holy images, plus glass razors for barbers and ampoules for alchemists. The Murano glassmakers also have the knack for decorative arts: coloured fruit, model galleys with glass-wire mooring cables, and miniature animals. And, finally, the island is famous for its production of eyeglasses – it even claims to have invented the frame that holds the lenses – and of the lenses that would someday let Galileo observe the heavens.

Murano is one of the obligatory stops on visits organized for merchants, pilgrims, ambassadors, and princes, all come to discover the Serenissima's splendours. The usual tour begins at the very heart of Venice, at the spectacle of the gold in Saint Mark's basilica, followed by a climb up the hundreds of steps of the campanile; from the top, one can peer straight down onto the mosaic of roofs and the tangle of passages and canals, and, looking outwards, scan the Adriatic to the south, the snow-clad Alps to the north, and then catch Murano, a small spot so close in that it seems to brush up against Venice. But, to go there, first you have to make your way through the Mercerie, past the displays of Italian silkworks, perfumes, and spices from the Orient, leather goods and pewter, holy images, packs of cards, and works now out in print. The taverns at the Rialto serve out sweet Greek Malvasia (Malmsey wines), with a side dish of marinated sardines with onions. On the Rialto Bridge, street singers hawk the latest scuttlebutt on courtesans now in fashion or dish out news of the most recent twists of the Turkish wars. Once across the bridge, the great market thrums with the cries of victuallers – bream and clawless slipper-lobsters, cheeses from the high Dolomites, lamb's heads, fresh *finocchio*, Sicilian oranges, and fruit of the jujube tree. After luxuriating in such abundance, for expiation, the visitor can tour the city's churches to pay a call on the holy relics – Christ's miraculous own blood, the arm of Saint George, the head of Saint Eustace, the hand of Saint Martha, and Saint Martin's foot. The visitor, at the east end of the city, can pay homage to the world of work, gazing at the carpenters and ship builders at the Arsenale, who boast that, keel to mast, they can build a galley in just a few hours. And, finally, off one rides to Murano, "where they make the glass" (*dove si fa veri*).[1]

Ambassadors, travellers, and authors of treatises on geography report their bedazzlement when they behold the glassworkers' talent. The German Dominican Felix Faber visits the island in 1483 before setting out on pilgrimage to the Holy Land. He admires the "very fine craft" of the glassmakers, who have no equal "in the entire world".[2] A few years later, Pietro Casola, an Italian priest also heading towards Jerusalem, reports "all the beautiful glass *vasi* that are sent out across the world".[3] Queen Anne of Hungary, in August 1520, and the son of the Marchese of Mantua, in May 1517, figure among the prestigious guests, sovereigns, art lovers, cardinals, and *condottieri* who come to watch the artisans blow and shape the glass.[4]

On the shopfronts, placards identify the workshop.[5] These signs appeared in the first third of the fifteenth century and then, with time, they multiplied. The Fondamenta dei Vetrai is a veritable bestiary (At the Rooster, The Eagle, The Dolphin, The Dragon, The Mermaid, The Bear, The Golden Lion, The Phoenix, The Little Dove). And there are images inspired by the heavens (The Moon, The Star, The Two Seraphs) and earthbound objects (The Golden Apple, The Three Crosses, The Silver Chalice). Some shops are more spiritual (At The Three Saint Marks, The Jesus, The Angel, The Flowering Faith, The Holy Spirit) and others have a human guise (The Golden Head, The Moor, The Turk's Head, The German). These shop signs, often sources for the glassworkers' family names, to locals and visitors alike are points of reference. They shape the imagination and organize the sense of space for an age when images, not yet abundant in public and private space, buttress information.

Renaissance Venetian painters also honour Murano glass. In Giovanni Bellini's "Agony in the Garden" the striated landscape has the wavy striped look of chalcedony glass. In Titian's "Pastoral Concert", the Muse pours water from a transparent carafe. In Veronese's "Wedding at Cana", there are elegant stem glasses and small dishes heaped with treats.[6] The letters of poets, from Francesco Colonna to Pietro Aretino, play with glass's diaphanous transparency, or its unique colours, to enliven their metaphors and verses.[7] Technical treatises such as *De Re Metallica* of the learned German Georgius Agricola, and geographical works like Leandro Alberti's essay on islands in his *Descrittione di tutta Italia* (1561), laud the quality of this glass, which surpasses, says Alberti, "all the others made of the same material across the world". Alberti recounts the fabrication of "a miniature galley as long as an arm, with all its gear made to measure, and to my eye it seemed impossible that they could have been able to fabricate a thing so well-proportioned using such material. I also have seen a little organ of which the pipes were made of glass . . . and if one blew into it and if expert players touched its keys, one heard the pipes play very sweetly".[8]

The workshops' owners are among Murano's richest and most influential inhabitants. In the second decade of the sixteenth century there are some twenty of them.[9] Some still practice the craft themselves; others are merely owners who oversee the glassmakers' labour. The workshops, or *fornaci*, some of them installed on several stories, have one or several furnaces, each with assorted apertures, the "mouths" (*bocche*), five or six on average, but sometimes up to twelve. Each mouth has its master, who every year renegotiates his contract, and, if better conditions surface, quits one workshop for another. Masters specialize in the fabrication of one type of product and command a squad (*piazza*) of three or four labourers who work with them.

In the laws and rules that he puts out, the podestà Vitale Vitturi addresses the "glassmakers", but his term covers a multitude of men and functions: the furnace owners, the masters who direct the work and stage the operation; the workers and *serventi* who take part in manufacture, who blow down the glassmaker's tube and shape the molten glass; the *bufadori*, specialist blowers who work large-scale pieces; the *conciatori* charged with concocting the chemical mixture before the melting; the *garzoni*, who function like apprentices, assistants, and servants; the *stizadori* or fire-lighters, who feed wood to the ovens and keep the heat even; the young serving folk who do all those little jobs requisite for the workshop's upkeep and who serve the masters. Thus the craft imposes internal hierarchies and distinctions that shape and order the whole society. The women take full part in this hierarchy, if less visibly to us now, thanks to the documentation's gaps and silences.[10] They work with their husband, their father, their brother, or their son. Take Maria, the widow of the first witness at the trial launched after the revolt, Nicolo de Blasio. She inherits the workshop from her husband, and specializes in the production of alembics and of bottles used by chemists (*boze da partir*).[11] A few years later, Elena dell'Urso appears among the twenty-one furnace owners convoked by the podestà, along with other inhabitants, to agree on financial outlays to pay to renovate the island's chief bridge.[12]

As remarkable as it is, the glass industry is not the only thing to give the island its reputation; rich Venetians also appreciate the beauty of its gardens and the sweetness of greenery that, in the capital, has vanished. Palm trees, fruit trees, flowers, and edible plants make Murano's villas cool and pleasant. "Flourishing gardens, as charming as almost anywhere in Italy", boasts the Venetian man of letters Francesco Sansovino at the century's end.[13] Murano even becomes the terrain for the experiments of the patrician Andrea Navagero, who, in the 1520s, creates there one of Italy's first botanical gardens.[14]

The splendour of the palaces contrasts with the modest condition of most of the island's folk. In the Renaissance, rebuilding and new construction enriches further this patrician architecture, visible still today in the Palazzo da Mula, near Ponte Lungo, or in Palazzo Contarini, on the Fondamenta dei Vetrai. The Venetians also invest in houses, shops, workshops, and fishponds, all then rented out to the inhabitants of Murano.[15] They are the owners, but also the masters, as they hire some locals as serving men to keep up their gardens and repair their palaces.[16]

In summer, Murano lets one escape the confusion of the capital's streets, the heat of its stones, its canals blocked up for lack of water, and its stench. The doges often come out for excursion, as do high churchmen and papal legates, who sojourn there in the company of rich Venetian landowners.[17] Andrea Calmo, poet and polygraph, pours endless praises on the isle. He was, he says, "brought up in the net-boats and in the Lagoon, nourished among the fish-boxes and trained to go catch fish, a descendant of the good old denizens of Torcello, just, brave, and attentive to their legal rights". Calmo makes deft use of the "idiom of the old days of these marshlands of ours" (*la idioma de l'antighitae de sti nostri paludi*) to honour the "noble, worthy, odiferous, great, power-laden and honourable city of Venice." For him, Murano is a "true paradise" with its "gardens full of perfumed herbs, and the canal, so clear and pure, with its pretty houses, so well aired", and is a "place of nymphs and demigods".[18]

Talented glassworkers and agreeable gardens – that is what Venetians and foreigners think of Murano. But, when the last visitors have departed, the Rio dei Vetrai and the streets of the isle still bustle with the activity of the masters and their apprentices. The fishermen set out their nets and their boxes drying all along the quay. The peasants tote back their tools and put their livestock in the stalls. The women workers finish off their tasks and the artisans shut their shops. Women drop by at the shop of Zuan Rosso to buy vegetables, a bit of fowl for the stew pot, and oil or *pancetta*. Servants go to the German bakers on the Rio to fetch bread. The men go off for a glass of wine at the *osteria* called Salvàdego (the Wild Man) or stroll in the evening cool to discuss the day's work or to recount the latest news from Venice.

## Glassworkers and fishermen

In order to govern the community of Murano, Vitale Vitturi has had to understand how it works, and to decipher this society at once so close to Venice and yet so marked by its particular quirks and traditions. That is the job of the podestà, elected from among the Venetian patricians to administer justice and to apply the *Statuto*, the set of laws that regulate the place, just recently renegotiated with the Venetian authorities.[19]

When he arrived at Murano, Vitturi encountered a lively island, especially around the Fondamenta dei Vetrai. Night and day the furnaces keep burning; they are only quenched in summer months when the air grows too hot to breathe.[20] The rest of the year, one feeds them wood unceasingly, to keep them hot enough to make glass. Around the Rio dei Vetrai, the hurly burly never stops. The socializing, the fights, and the quarrels that surface in the archives play out here; often enough someone tumbles into the canal and the fight gets soaked. On the day that power passes from Vitale Vitturi to Giacomo Suriano, as on other days, nobody puts out the furnaces. Some glassmakers stay in their workshops and miss the ceremony. But word of the snowball fight spreads fast, and Vitturi is constrained to quit the isle via the Lagoon, rather than make his way along the Rio dei Vetrai. Word has gone around that the glassworkers are waiting for him there, with more ammunition and, doubtless, more insults.

The intense activity of the Rio made it necessary to build three closely-placed bridges: the Ponte di Santa Chiara, the Ponte de Mezo (Middle Bridge), and the Ponte di San Pietro Martire, to link the two embankments. The Middle Bridge is one of the principal places for the Town Crier's proclamations. The unceasing to-and-fro along the Rio dei Vetrai makes the zone a fine place for the circulation of information, to trade news and rumours. It is there that the rich glassmakers and the humbler workers, the German merchants and the Friulian serving women listen to the story-tellers, comment on the wartime defeats and victories of Venetian arms, assess the policies of the podestà, and grouse about the rising price of grain. It is one of the island's liveliest public forums.

The Fondamenta dei Vetrai is perpetually encumbered with tonnes of wood, ash, silica, and pigment to feed the glassworks, with packets bundled by the *ligadori* (tie-up-men) and shouldered and hauled by the *caricatori* (loaders). From the furnaces issue, in their hundreds, straw-filled boxes, neatly packed with serried cups and flasks. Central to all this traffic are the porters and haulers, *fachin* in Venetian, often Bergamask in origin (to the point that *bergamasco* is synonymous with 'porter'). They load and unload boats, and scurry along the quays and streets, with baskets and packets atop their heads or heaped on little hand-drawn carts.

Children and young folk, too, are out in number, in the workshops and commercial shops. In the glass trade apprenticeship starts early, between ages eight and fourteen, and lasts up to eight years, a longer stint than in most trades. Sons of a master can debut young at full apprentice work; other youngsters start with lowly tasks, cleaning up the shop and laying out the tools, rummaging the floor for fallen fragments, and plying the workers with water and wine. They learn by serving and observing, picking up work's rhythms and workshop hierarchies, watching the craft's actions and tricks of hand. *Robar co l'ocio* – steal with the eye – the expression was still current in the twentieth century.[21] In other crafts as well, apprentices start young. So, though they may be young, the children who chant on the ritual's eve, and who revel in the song while awaiting Suriano on Campo Santi Maria e Donato are already well ensconced in the island's economic and social life.

All along the Fondamenta are ranged the glass shops, but there are also the workshops of Maestro Antonio the tailor and of Maestro Jacopo the shoe-maker, and the shops of Zuan Rosso and of the bakers Nicolo and Maddalena, plus the meat and fish markets, not to mention the outlets of "sellers of fruit, of grain and of fish, dry-goods sellers, sausage-makers, venders of fat and of oil".[22] All along the quay, also, roam the strolling peddlers, Venetians hawking sausages and Muranesi with Lagoon oysters on offer.[23]

With Venice so near, one can furnish and buy spices and sugar, and the sweet wine and candied fruit of the eastern Mediterranean, plus clothing and shoes – both in the latest fashion – pewter tableware, linen cloth, paper, candles, assorted nostrums to cure congestion, soap. . . . But the Muranesi are not dependent on Venetian output. The island is populous enough to justify making goods of many sorts. If one reads the archived papers of Vitale Vitturi and the other early sixteenth-century podestà, one runs into tailors, tanners, wool workers, dyers, shoe-makers, weavers, and the fashioners of chests, and barrels and also masons, carpenters, shipyard workers, makers of boats and oars, and smiths who forge the blow-tubes, prods, pinzers, and scissors used by the glassmakers, the millers, and the wood workers whose task it was to sculpt the moulds inside which one blew the molten glass, also a mortar-maker and a wax blancher, plus wood merchants, shop-keepers, sellers of spices and drugs, small goods dealers, a comb-maker, a goldsmith, and, atop all that, a physician and several barber-surgeons.

Many of these artisans work with their wives or daughters; some widows in their own name shoulder a late husband's business. Almost all women have a trade, even if, in the archives, they are harder to trace, and their place in Murano is less conspicuous.[24] Some of them get by with a boost from prostitution, either main income or supplement, though we should beware the hasty epithet *putana*, so quickly slung to lambast many a woman living on her own.[25]

And finally, in service of the artisans and glassworkers, and the clergy and the podestà, there is a swarm of domestics and servants, valets and bespoke boatmen, nurses and serving maids, many of them young and often immigrants from the Venetian mainland, or Friuli, or Dalmatia, or Greece, come to scrounge a coin or two beyond their room and board. Also, there are slaves – some of them labelled *saraxin* (Saracens, Muslims) – Africans or Turks, who serve as private boatmen or domestic servants, and who once set free keep their slave name, or take that of their final owner.[26]

The denizens of the island's southern part, tied to artisanal production and the glass trade, belong to the parish of Santo Stefano. The church, no longer standing, sits at the end of the Rio, on the eastern bank. It is one of Murano's fourteen churches in that time. The isle is well known for its monasteries and its convents.[27] Across the way, on the Rio's other bank, is the monastery of San Pietro Martire, renovated in a major way in the first decades of the sixteenth century; the campanile houses one of Murano's first clocks.[28] In the environs are hospitals and hospices to house the poor, the homeless, and the solitary women who have no one. Santa Maria delle Grazie, for example, founded in the fourteenth century, shelters a dozen widows.[29] If less numerous, doubtless, than in Venice, beggars beseech passers-by for alms in Murano's streets and at the portals of the churches. Note for instance Zuan da Piave, "who is in such poverty that his father goes begging for the love of God, scrounging to get by".[30] In the next century, Francesco Luna, a Murano glassmaker who for many years kept a journal – one of the few such to have survived in Murano – tells how, as the plague raged, the poor who begged in the streets of Venice became so numerous that the hospital *dei mendicanti* (of the beggars) could no longer house them: so then they brought "a great quantity here to Murano, to San Cipriano, where there was an Academy of nobles run by the Most Illustrious Patriarch".[31]

To arrive at the church of Santi Maria e Donato, where the passage of power takes place, the parishioners of Santo Stefano must cross the Grand Canal that cuts the isle in two. The canal has such a current that on the bank the inhabitants built a mill, and they take their grain there to grind it into flour.[32] The Ponte Lungo (or Magno), made of wood, was rebuilt just before Vitale Vitturi arrived, thanks to a subsidy from more than two hundred islanders.[33] Like the Rialto bridge at Venice, it is the only bridge to span Murano's Grand Canal, so people have to use it and it is very busy. It is the other chief place for public cries, so Antonio Malcanton goes there for his proclamations. The shops around it are many: Zorzi Rosso from Parma the barber, the baker Matteo Padoan, as well as several little shipyards (*squeri*). The Fontego della Farina, an entrepôt where they store the grain, stands close by the mill.[34]

The Rio dei Vetrai, running south to north, and the Grand Canal, lying west to east, plus three other major canals divide the islets that make up Murano. Dozens of *bragozzi, peate* and *burche* – sailboats or rowing craft of assorted sizes, with one or two masts for sail or with oars, glide across the waters of the island and jam the navigable spaces. Some belong to the Muranesi; others come from Venice or the mainland. These watercraft arrive with grain and flour, wood for the fires, and raw materials used by artisans. They sail back laden with glass, fish, fruit, vegetables, and the local island wine. These boats are the principal tool of many inhabitants, for fishing, hauling merchandize, and carrying passengers. As busy as the quays, the canals swarm with activity, the boatmen moving from craft to craft, the hubbub of accents and dialects, with tricky dodges on the water as boats jockey and bicker for position.

Nevertheless, most inhabitants move about on foot, along the streets, passageways and quays. On the island, one almost never goes on horseback; the Lagoon is one of those rare places, in medieval times, where horse culture has little footing. A few mules and donkeys, and perhaps a horse or two, carry raw materials and baskets of fruit harvested in the orchards of the island's northern part. Distances are short. All it takes to cross the island from south to north is thirty minutes; less than an hour suffices to go around the whole of it. Quays, called *fondamenta*, are especially plentiful on Murano; they let a person pass easily, access the shops, and reach storage places and watercraft, but they also let one settle in to work. A workshop can spill out to the canal's edge. Maestro Marco, dyer, soaks his vests in barrels of dye aboard his *burchiello* (oversized gondola), moored right in front of his shop.[35] We can imagine that women and old folk bring out their chairs to work there by daylight. Children still too young to learn a trade play amidst the dogs, and the cats prowling after rodents.

Once across the Ponte Lungo, one is in the island's north, a place for fishermen, wood merchants, market gardeners (*ortolani*), and peasants (*villani*). The latter work the gardens, orchards, and fields that feed the people of the Lagoon, in an epoch when, in Venice, agriculture has almost vanished, as it has in most other great cities of the West. In the capital, there have been almost no cultivated plots since the middle of the previous century. But Murano is still a mixed space: both a city, relatively populous, where urban infrastructure is not lacking, and a rural space where piles of manure and hay fill the streets and squares with their odours. Between the fields and hedges, amidst the stables and wooden houses with roofs of thatch, one raises chickens, cows, and goats. A special privilege allows each Murano family, tax exempt, to buy and raise its yearly piglet.[36] The animal has to remain cooped up; it cannot roam "in the streets, the squares, the holy spaces".[37] And, one more thing, people practice *oselàr*, the hunt for sea birds and ducks, sometimes in the company of patricians who fancy themselves as hunters, on the model of the old feudal nobility.

The islands of the Lagoon, especially Murano, are very fertile thanks to the local mud, rich in limestone. The peasants cultivate vines and make wine, and they harvest vegetables and garden crops: onions and shallots, cabbages, lentils, beans and other pulses, salad greens and arugula, marrows and melons, with perhaps a few artichokes. And if, as some say, the first maize plant ever cultivated in Italy was on Murano itself, nevertheless there are, at the start of the sixteenth century, neither tomatoes, nor potatoes, nor string beans, nor pimentos nor other peppers now typical of Italian cuisine.[38] The Statutes control production and protect the peasants, punishing persons who "enter to steal the fruits and other things in the gardens" and those who steal "the chickens, the ducks, or the geese", and the "pigs and other beasts . . . lambs, kids, or similar animals".[39]

So, it is the island's north where live most of the fishermen, traditional members of the Lagoon economy. In the sixteenth century, some fishermen from Venice are still an autonomous community, clustered around the parish of San Niccolò, west of the town, where, according to Marino Sanudo, they use their own dialect, "a certain ancient Venetian speech called *nicoloto*." The chronicler also evokes fishermen

> from assorted *contrade*, like Murano, Burano da Mar, Torcello and also Chioggia [at the Lagoon's southern end], who come with their fish to sell them here in Venice at the fish market. . . . And they can bring as many fish as one desires each day, and in the evening, nothing of it remains.[40]

The Murano fishermen exploit the natural basins (*valli*) that form between the *barene*, sandbars that form and vanish at the beck of the tides. They also range across the waters of the Lagoon and to the Adriatic. Fish and shellfish abound – sea perch, Peter's fish, sardines, scallops, *moeche* (little softshell crabs in molt). Murano oysters have a reputation for being succulent, as, a few decades later, the English traveller Thomas Coryat recounts in his famous *Crudities* (1611), "Here did I eate the best Oysters, that ever I did in all my life. They were indeed but little, . . . but as green as a leeke, and *gratissimi saporis & succi* [of the loveliest flavour and juice]".[41]

"Let no person dare steal fish in the nets, the boats, or the baskets, under pain of a fine of twenty-five *lire*, of the rope, or of reimbursement for the damage"[42]: so warn the Murano Statutes, which uphold and oversee the activity of the fishermen. It is also the podestà's function, and Vitale Vitturi deals out plentiful sentences against the Venetians who come poach in island waters. In July 1510, Vittorello Sbisia and Nicolo Can, of San Niccolò parish in Venice, are arrested and prosecuted for fishing near Santa Chiara in Murano.[43] In August, it is the turn of Nicolo di Stefano from Burano (an island north of Murano); then in September comes the trial of Andrea di Zuan Forner, who defends himself by explaining that he came fishing at the request of gentlemen.[44] But Vitturi is also an officious podestà against Muranesi fishermen, stirring up a wealth of votes on laws to regulate their activity. He sets in motion many trials against their fishing practices, contesting the size of catches taken, the types of nets and gear, and the places where fishermen go. During the podestà's mandate, fishermen are dealing with him daily; on 27 January 1511, having tied up their boats for these days of snow and intense cold, they are probably as many on the *campo* as are the glaziers. Illiterates, most of them, often poor, and probably easily marked thanks to their tanned visages and dress, fishermen figure among the revolt's accused, suspected of having targeted the podestà with their icy projectiles.

Fishermen and peasants, whose work permits them, in a pinch, to feed their families, live in the parishes of Santi Maria e Donato, San Martino, and San Salvatore, the island's poorest and shabbiest. At the end of the sixteenth century, when the bishop of Torcello sends a representative to Murano for a pastoral visitation, as decreed by the Council of Trent, the little fishing parish of San Salvatore is a sorry spectacle. The holy precinct around the church that serves for a burial ground has no enclosure, and dogs come there to rummage in the earth for bones and then roam the quarter with their booty between their jaws.[45]

Fishermen leave their mark on Murano's landscape. The banks and canals swarm with small craft and the moorings along the quays are taken by fishing boats. No designated port surfaces in the sources; everybody keeps his boat near home and at night some sleep aboard. Nets, mooring cables, and sails heap up in the streets, and on the bridges, walls, and banks, where they are laid out to dry. In February 1510, Vitturi commands the public crier to proclaim to the fishermen that it is prohibited to lay out nets and sailcloth on the Cà Maran bridge, and Ponte Longo, and Ponte San Donato; he pushes back against this habitual encroachment on public space.[46]

The glassmakers to the south, the fisherman in the north: the opposition defines Murano's society, and the podestà slips it into his language. A mobilization order put out by crier Malcanton a few days before power changes hands is addressed to "all the men of Murano, glassmakers and fishermen alike, and all the other inhabitants of this *terra* of Murano, of whatsoever condition".[47] In the middle of the sixteenth century Leandro Alberti still reflects: "Murano is well populated, and the greater part of the inhabitants are merchants, glassworkers, or fishermen".[48] This social and geographic structure sometimes kindles antagonism between the two groups. See for instance a dispute, in 1510, between Francesco Barovier and a man with the name of Polo. The former belongs to one of the oldest, best regarded glassmaker families; the latter is a domestic servant who lives in the island's north.[49] Early one evening Francesco Barovier is crossing northwards the Ponte Lungo to stroll among friends towards Santi Maria e Donato when Polo crosses him, armed and menacing. "Why couldn't one go walk this way," Francesco asks him. "Doesn't this bridge belong as much to glassmakers as it does to fishermen?" As often in Italian towns, the quarter nourishes a sense of identity. Space feeds group formation.

Belonging to a parish, or to one of the island's two parts, does not nevertheless undermine the community, unified and loyally united. Reading the trials Vitale Vitturi administered reveals a multitude of interlocking networks between glassmakers, artisans, fishermen, and labourers. They come together in the shared spaces, weave lines of friendship or business, and intermarry. Insularity and subjection to Venice reinforces the sense of belonging to the same community. So it is that many fights and brawls of the period set the Muranesi against Venetians or "foreigners". When that happens, the inhabitants of Murano know full well how to defend their interests against outsiders.

One of the principal places where the inhabitants gather and socialize is the *osteria* of the Salvàdego. They go there to drink a glass of wine, watered as is the custom, to buy "strong and good" vinegar, or to eat soup or other simple fare.[50] There is an establishment with the same name in Venice, near Piazza San Marco, perhaps because it has the same shop sign, "The Wild Man".[51] At Murano, the Salvàdego "tavern, wine-cellar, and inn" is situated in the northeast of the island, near the monastery of San Maffeo. The place belongs to a Venetian, Ferigo Contarini, and to his brothers.[52] The right to sell wine is a public concession auctioned off to an inhabitant for a fixed term, usually one or two years. The innkeeper pays a rent to Contarini and also pays the Muranese and Venetian authorities a portion of the profits and of the taxes levied on the wine trade he controls for the whole island. Pietro Amado in 1508, his partner Nicolo Molena, and then in 1511 Domenico Orobon (sometimes called Antonio in the documents), and one Sebastiano and Zaneto Crayna the following year – they are the innkeepers in these years.[53] Those men aside, nobody is allowed to sell wine beyond a pint in local measure (a *mezaruola*). There may be other *osterie* and points of sale, but the archives are unclear about them. Given the size of the population, a single inn seems not enough, especially if we have in mind that at the beginning of the twentieth century, Murano had some fifty drinking places.[54]

The Statutes are strict about the quantity and quality of wine one may sell, and about closing hours: "after the second hour of the night in winter and the first hour in summer" (about 8pm in the first instance and 10pm in the second, as back then one calculated the hours from sunset).[55] One could always buy wine or food after closing hour, but only with the door closed, through a window, and the client could consume nothing at the place of purchase. Two months before the Snowball Revolt, Pietro Amado is accused of serving food after the closing hour. But Donato Stocho and Angelo Franzoso, two clients served that evening, declare under oath that, as Pietro's invited guests, they had paid nothing.[56] Franzoso does concede that he has handed over a ten-soldo coin (a *marcello*), not for his dinner, but because he lost at gambling. Muranesi, in fact, are devoted to games of all sorts; the archives are full of them. Children and adults alike play ball games in assorted places around the island, before the monastery of San Bernardo or in the *Corte Nuova*, on the east bank of the Rio dei Vetrai. They also play at dice and cards, but betting in silver above a certain sum is banned.[57] They play *mora*, an elaborate form of rock, paper, and scissors, where one has to guess the number of fingers players will throw forward, and shout louder than the other contestants.[58] Play, an everyday pastime, is one form of the sociability that structures the life of Muranesi, both fishermen and glassworkers, both priests and domestic servants.

Among the spaces shared by all the islanders, above all, are the main square (*campo*) and the church of Santi Maria e Donato, places that belong to all and that give the community coherence. The *campo* represents the heart of political, religious, and public life. Near the church stand the palace of the podestà, close to the houses of the policeman (*cavalier*) and the public crier. Off to one side is the third bridge onto which Antonio Malcanton must go to make his proclamations, and where, on 27 January 1511, the inhabitants stand waiting for Suriano to arrive. The *campo* is the theatre of Murano's chief rituals, among them the transfer of power and the annual great religious rites. Not far off stands one of the island's two public latrines (*necessario*); the other is at the end of the Rio dei Vetrai, near Santo Stefano. These public latrines permit the faithful to relieve themselves without soiling the sacred character of the *campo*.[59] The church, sometimes called the *duomo* or cathedral, shelters the body of San Donato, a Greek saint of the fourth century.[60] It is decorated with mosaics as precious and refined as those at San Marco, a reminder of past Byzantine influences. San Donato's priest, like the others of the Lagoon, is chosen by the inhabitants. But, while the others are picked by their parishioners alone, as is usual, here the priest is elected by all the property holders on the island as he is considered the chief of all the other churches.[61]

## Insularity and community

The nature of Murano is complexly layered: it is a town endowed with many urban infrastructures – bridges, wells, a communal square, but it is also a largely agricultural island, with gardens, orchards, fields, a mill, salt pans, and many fishponds. Thanks to glassworks and artisanal production, fishing, and market gardening, Murano is one of the most prosperous and densely-populated communities of the Lagoon. In the absence of reliable censuses and of parish registers before the end of the sixteenth century, it is hard to estimate the number of inhabitants, but a pastoral visit in 1591 gives us precious information.[62] If we can trust the information collected by the priests, there are then around 7,400 inhabitants on the island: more than 4,150 in Santo Stefano (the parish of the glassworkers and fishermen), 2,000 in Santa Maria e Donato, and 1,250 in San Martino and in Santissimo Salvatore between them (parishes of fishermen and market gardeners). The inhabitants are doubtless less numerous at the time of Vitale Venturi, before the Lagoon's great sixteenth-century demographic growth (we estimate that Venice passes, between 1500 and 1570, from 100,000 to 170,000, before the great plague of 1575–1576). We can wager that Murano has, in our time, between 5,000 and 6,000 inhabitants. It is a modest community, if contrasted with its hulking neighbour, but it is substantial vis à vis other cities, such as Grenoble, Nîmes, or Saint-Malo, which, at the beginning of the sixteenth century, have a similar population. In the middle of the century, Bari has only 8,000 inhabitants, and Siena around 13,000. The new port at Livorno does not reach 4,000 at the century's end.[63] In England, meanwhile, Norwich and Bristol, the largest towns after London, were a bit bigger than Murano, but less than twice its size.

Murano, meanwhile, is a community more closed than others. In the Middle Ages and in early modern times, the demographic growth of towns is due mostly to immigration, as with Venice, which has welcomed wave after wave of migrants. Murano is harder to access, especially because the protection of the secrets of glass manufacture and the production monopoly both limit, indeed forbid, foreigners to work in the glassworks. Decisions inside the glassmakers' guild and laws put out by the podestà and by Venetian institutions, at least in theory, ban all foreigners. But, all the while the rules do purport to ban them, they also regulate their labour, imposing a residence requirement, conditions for participation, and exceptions to the rules.[64] In reality, the glassmakers adapt their recruiting policy to their needs, favouring up-take of workers during expansion, and limiting it when the market plunges.

When, in December 1509, Vitale Vitturi vets fifteen workshops to see what foreigners are there, he gathers names of one hundred *laboratores* and sixty-five *famulos* (workers and servants).[65] Among them he turns up innumerable Vicentini and Bergamaschi (especially among the *conzadori*), as well as Dalmatians. All the others are labelled "from Murano", but their patronyms often reveal immigration, whether old or recent (Padoan, Bergamasco, Trevisan, Greco, Tedesco, Sarasin ...). Workers keep on arriving, generation after generation – just like the servants and domestics – coming from Italy and the Mediterranean, and keep joining the Muranese community. In this closed space, new blood is always needed.

With a population of around 5,000, Murano remains below the threshold where one loses track of people. Thanks to its insularity, and to how few of its inhabitants move town, one can know and recognize most residents. Even if one cannot pin down the name or trade of every fellow citizen, one knows them at least by sight. Vitturi often hears witnesses say they do not know such and such a foreigner, or resident newly settled in, but most identify their peers with scant trouble. In Venice, on the other hand, long already, one is known only among neighbours or fellow parishioners, or among fellow craftsmen or confraternity brothers. Beyond those familiar bonds, it has become impossible to be familiar with the tens of thousands who people the city. In Murano, however, it remains difficult to be anonymous and to fake things: one acts and speaks under the surveillance of peers, friends, and neighbours. Social control is all the stronger.

"Public voice" and reputation (*fama*) are the measures and means of knowledge and of the construction of opinion. In all the medieval West, rumours and hear-say are considered legitimate means of knowledge. In matters before courts of justice, common knowledge is mobilized by witnesses and by suspects, alongside other sorts of knowledge. In Murano at the beginning of the sixteenth century, whether the matter on the docket is a minor brawl or some graver crime, inhabitants fall back on "one knows that", "all the world knows that", "all the world says that", to relay the common knowledge that circulates on the island. In November 1509, the priest Jacopo di Zuan da Spalato (Split), lodged at the hospital of Spirito Santo, brings complaint that he was assaulted while returning home. But Alvise Stola, his asserted attacker, defends himself by saying that the very opposite happened, explaining that the priest is "half mad and sometimes drunk", a fact "manifest to all".[66] In October 1510, amidst an affair that set many members of one family at odds, one disputant affirms to the podestà that "Angelica is the daughter of the aforesaid Ser Domenico Nicheto: I know it by true knowledge (*scientia*) and one can ascertain it by public voice and *fama*".[67] One must mistrust such floating rumours, which can lead to accusations, as a member of the Murano government explains;

Sebastiano Bellencito expected to be summoned by the court because, says he, there circulated "here, in Murano, gossip (*zanze*)" about him.[68]

This diffuse knowledge is a source of information for the authorities. At the time, births and deaths are not yet registered by priests, nor have the state's procedures for identification been sharpened. To determine if a given resident is a native of the Lagoon or a foreigner, to establish genealogies and connections, the rulers have to trust local knowledge. As happens in 1518, when an inhabitant of Murano, Andrea di Matteo dell'Urso, speaking to a Venetian tribunal, invokes other inhabitants of the island. About a Francesco Moliner, he says, "Francesco is not a native of Murano, but rather he was taken in by one Ser Greguol as an adopted son (*fio de anima*), outside Murano, a thing I remember as if it were now, for he was four years old when he arrived at the mill in Murano". Andrea then adds,

> And also Bernardin Torcellan, who was taken at the house of one Antonio Torcellan, called Antonio Piacentin, who lived here at Murano. I do not know where he came from, but I remember that he was a child, and that he was not born at Murano. And I affirm he same thing for Vincenzo Rombolo . . . who is not born at Murano but at Venice and is come to Murano after the death of his father, who was in Venice and was a carpenter.[69]

The inhabitants see, listen, appraise, and judge, and official power banks on this shared knowledge. Justice, in particular, takes seriously the talk that comes from the population. Collectively, the Muranesi participate in the elaboration and construction of a sort of knowledge about society.

## From Murano to Venice: the *traghetto*

To have Venice so close by has a profound effect on Murano's life. Giant, cosmopolitan, swarming, and rich, the capital sets the balance of the Lagoon's forces. It sucks in and spews back the Lagoon's inhabitants, it weaves them into a community of interests, it dominates them with its sovereignty and sheer sway. It is quick and easy to go from place to place, thanks to a communication network set up by Venice. Plentiful navigation lines link it to Murano, Chioggia, Padua, and other towns of the Venetian hinterland. Boats big and small carry passengers at a fixed rate. There is ferry service for crossing (the *traghetti*) all along the Venetian Grand Canal, as there still is today, that at strategic points lets one go over without having to use the Rialto bridge.

The *traghetto* between Venice and Murano has been there since the ninth century.[70] In Vitturi's day, some forty gondoliers, half of them Venetians, half Muranesi, offer their services and assure, day in day out, the connection between the embarkation place behind the church of San Canciano, on Venice's north side, and the Rio dei Vetrai. They adhere to a professional association, the *scuola*, that lets them regulate their activities and set their number. They hold meetings in the cloister of the monastery of San Cristoforo, a snug islet south of Murano, next to the monastery of San Michele, where, at present, lies Venice's cemetery. Ex-servants, freed slaves (Africans or Turks), migrants come in from Italy, Dalmatia, or Greece, or natives of the Lagoon, these *barcaruoli* are sometimes hard to identify ethnically. Their name might point to a geographic origin difficult to interpret. Are a Martin Saraxin necessarily a Muslim or ex-Muslim and a Jacopo Trevisan from Treviso? Or did they inherit their name from an old ancestor?

The Lagoon's configuration makes their services essential, especially to keep links to the capital. Still in the eighteenth century, the *traghetto* is the main way to arrive at either island and even Casanova mentions them, more than two hundred years after the business of our book. In the summer of 1753, the seducer, then twenty-eight years old, falls passionately in love with two young girls locked away in the monasteries of Murano. He choreographs an incessant ballet between the two islands, making the Lagoon crossing sometimes several times in one day to go join C. C. and M. M. in his *casino*, the little palace he rented to enjoy their charms. In the end he decides to buy his own boat and conjure himself a boatman, because he cannot rely on the *traghetto*. As he tells it, one morning at dawn, he wants to go back home to Venice.

> I go running to the ferry, hoping to find a gondola, and don't find any. According to the police laws of Venice, that cannot ever happen, for at any hour every ferry station has to have at least two gondolas ready to do public service; in spite of that it does happen, if rarely, that there is none. As then. There was a sea wind, as strong as could be, and the boatmen, out of boredom, seemed to have gone off to bed. What could I do at the end of the quay, an hour before daybreak, almost entirely naked?[71]

The *barcaruoli* assure the circulation of both persons and information, for they are held to advise their passengers of the decisions taken by the government. For the diffusion of new laws, they are a powerful network, one that the Venetian state cannily exploits. Moving from one island to the other and working their way up and down the canals of Venice and Murano, they are up to date on the hottest gossip and on the most alarming shreds of news. The evening of 27 January 1511, while Vitturi mulls over, bitterly, the day's events, and the patricians who had come to take part in the ceremony tell about the scandalous spectacle played out before their eyes, the gondoliers who fetched them back to Venice may be already at table in the Rialto taverns, or at the Salvàdego, regaling ears with the whole story of the snowballs and relishing the cutting song, *Surian Surian, Caccia via questo can, Che ha ruinato Muran*.

## Notes

1  Marino Sanudo il giovane, *De origine, situ et magistratibus urbis Venetae ovvero La città di Venetia (1493–1530)*, ed. Angela Caracciolo Aricò (Milan: Cisalpino-La Goliardica, 1980), 46–8, 62.

2  Quoted by Luigi Zecchin, *Vetro e vetrai di Murano*, 3 vols. (Venice: Arsenale Editrice, 1987–1990), vol. 1, 59.

3  *Viaggio a Gerusalemme di Pietro Casola*, ed. Anna Paoletti (Alessandria: ed. Dell'Orso, 2001), 98.

4  Marino Sanudo, *I Diarii*, vol. 4, col. 298, 5 August 1502; vol. 24, col. 298, 26 May 1517.

5  Zecchin, *Vetro e vetrai di Murano*, vol. 1, 185–95, 206–9, 213–17, 222–6.

6  Giovanni Bellini, *Agony in the Garden*, ca. 1465, London, National Gallery; Tiziano Vecellio or Titian, *Pastoral Concert*, ca. 1509, Paris, Louvre Museum, sometimes attributed to Giorgione; Paolo Caliari also known as Veronese, *Wedding at Cana*, 1563, Paris, Louvre Museum. Quoted by Paul Hills, *Venetian Colour. Marble, mosaic, painting and glass, 1250–1550* (New Haven, CT & London: Yale University Press, 1999), 109 ff.

7  Francesco Colonna, *Hypnerotomachia Poliphili*, eds G. Pozzi and L. C. Ciapponi, 2 vols. (Padua: Editrice Antenore, 1980 [1499]), vol. 1, 311; Pietro Aretino, *Sei Giornate. Ragionamento della Nanna e della Antonia (1534)*, ed. Giovanni Aquilecchia (Bari: Laterza, 1969), 14.

8  Leandro Alberti, *Descrittione di tutta l'Italia & isole pertinenti ad essa . . .* (Venice: Gio. Maria Leni, 1576 edition), 2nd part, *Isole appartenenti alla Italia*, 95v.

9  Two *Isolari* published in the sixteenth century affirm that they numbered 23 or 24 (respectively: Benedetto Bordone, *Libro . . . de tutte l'isole del mondo* (Venice, 1528), XXX verso, and Leandro Alberti, *Descrittione di tutta Italia*, 95v). One can establish the following list of owners for the years 1509–1511: Zuan Ballarin, Angelo Barovier (owns two glassworks), Zuan Andrea Barovier, Nicolo Barovier, Nicolo de Blasio, Alvise Blondo (*gastaldo*, i.e. the head of the guild, from February 1511), Vettor Blondo (*gastaldo* from 1509), Nicolo Bocapicola, Sebastiano da Chadamestre, Domenico Caner, Gasparo Capello, Rugiero Cavograsso, Jacopo Corona (owns two glassworks), Zuan Corona, Pietro Cortiner, Bernardin detto Rizo Dracan, Tommaso Dracan, Andrea Angelo dal Gallo, Andrea Grasetto, Pasqualin Marcozane, Nicolo Moro, Zuan di Nicolo, Zuan Sclabone, Gregorio Stella, and Pietro Trevisan (ASVe, PM, 44, 8 Extraordinariorum 1, for 7 December 1509; 20 Criminalium 2, for 20 November 1509 and 10 December 1509; BMC, Mariegola dei Fioleri, 26, fol. 56, for 17 February 1511).

10  See for example the different chapters of the Statutes of the glassmakers of Murano which mention both men and women, for instance BMC, Mariegola dei Fioleri, 26, fol. 11v (*fante over fantesca*).

11  Zecchin, *Vetro e vetrai di Murano*, vol. 2, 176. See also Zecchin, "Maria Barovier e le 'rosette' ", *ibid.*, vol. 2, pp. 211–14.

12  ASVe, PM, 203, Descrizione abitanti, a list of contributors for the restoration of Ponte Lungo (1523–4).

13  Francesco Sansovino, *Delle cose notabili della città di Venetia* (Venice: Appresso Felice Valgrisio, 1587), Libro primo, 72.

14  *Lettere di XIII Huomini illustri*, Venice, Per Francesco Lorenzini da Turino, 1560, letters of Andrea Navagero to Giovanni Battista Ramusio. Mentions of his garden at Murano: 665, 5 May 1525; 675 (paginated in error as 975), 12 September 1525 and 20 February 1526; 676–7, 12 May 1526; about fruits coming from America, 684, 12 May 1526.

15  See the declarations of the Venetian and Muranese owners in ASVe, Dieci Savi alle Decime, 1514, busta 82, Murano. The proprietors declare their goods in the parish where they reside. Most of the mentions of property on the island are found in other bundles in the series. See for example ASVe, Dieci Savi alle Decime, 1514: busta 15, Sant'Angelo, no. 11, Pancrazio and Alvise Dolfin di Dolfin; busta 49, Santa Maria Zobenigo, no. 44, Andrea Giustinian di Onfrè (his brother is podestà of Murano in 1504); busta 62, San Samuele, no. 11, Leonardo Contarini di Marco.

16  See for example, ASVe, PM, 44, 22 Criminalium 4, for 6 May 1510.

17  The chronicle of Marino Sanudo has abundant mentions of their visits to Murano. See for example Marino Sanudo, *I Diarii*, vol. 3, col. 41, 26 October 1499; vol. 8, col. 558, 26 July 1509; vol. 26, col. 52, 21 September 1518; vol. 32, col. 205, 4 December 1521; vol. 46, col. 379–80, 16 December 1527.

18  *Le lettere di messer Andrea Calmo riprodotte sulle stampe migliori, con introduzione ed illustrazioni di Vittorio Rossi* (Turin: Loescher, 1888): Introduction, v, ix; Book III, 170, letter 5, to M. Marco Gussoni di Andrea; Book III, 173, letter 7, to M. Giovanni Francesco Prioli di Francesco; Andrea Calmo, *Le bizzarre, faconde et ingegnose rime pescatorie*, ed. Gino Belloni (Venice: Marsilio, 2003), Sonetto XLII.

19  "Statuto de Muran del 1502", ed. Monica Pasqualetto, in *Statuti della laguna veneta dei secoli XIV-XVI* (Rome: Jouvence, 1989), 207–87.

20  Mentions of night work are abundant. See for example ASVe, PM, 44, 20 Criminalium 2: 2 January 1510, against Francesco Butario *et socios*; 19 January 1510 testimony of Francesco son of dona Lucia Grande. See also BMC, Mariegola dei Fioleri, 26, fol. 10v: *ancora che i fioli di patroni possa lavorar cussi de di como de nocte per caxon de imparar larte*.

21  *La memoria del vetro. Murano e l'arte vetraria nelle storie dei suoi maestri*, ed. Andrea Tosi (Venice: Marsilio, Scuola del Vetro Abate Zanetti, 2006), 120.

22  "Statuto de Muran", book III, ch. 32, 278.

23  BMC, Mariegola dei luganegheri, 2, fol. 20, ch. 47; ASVe, PM, 44, 22 Criminalium 4, for 20 June 1510.

24  See for example ASVe, PM, 43, Extraordinariorum 1, dated 5 July 1508, among the list of contributors for the restoration of the Ponte Lungo: Dona Barbara and son, Vincenza calegera (shoe-maker), Maddalena forner (baker), la Ferandina.

25  ASVe, AC, MP, 410, no. 14, 1517, about Franceschina and Meneghina Guriano.

26  See for example the mention of Martin saraxin in the list above, or Caterina saracena, servant of Pietro Marcello, ASVe, PM, 44, 22 Criminalium 4, for 6 May 1510.

27  Marino Sanudo il giovane, *De origine*, 201; Bordone, *Libro . . . de tutte l'isole*, XXX verso.

28  ASVe, PM, 236 bis, fol. 26v, for 25 September 1533.

29  Vincenzo Zanetti, *Guida di Murano e delle celebri sue fornaci vetrarie* (Venice: Stabilimento tipografico Antonelli, 1866), 70. See the hospital accounts for the beginning of the sixteenth century: Archivio Parrocchiale San Pietro Martire di Murano, Varia 1, Libro XI, fol. 7 ff.

30  ASVe, PM, 212, documents 1509–19, 25 January 1511, inventory of dona Lena, at the hospital of San Giovanni Battista; ASVe, PM 212, documents 1545, for 16 March 1545, for Caterina Padoana, mention of Zuane da Piave.

31  *Diario di Murano di Francesco Luna, 1625–31*, ed. Vincenzo Zanetti (Venice: 1872), 76, for November 1630. Francesco Luna belongs to the glassmaker family called Molino or Moliner. See Zecchin, *Vetro e vetrai di Murano*, vol. 1, 181–5.

32  ASVe, PM, 44, 20 Criminalium 2, for 9 January 1510, against Vincenzo son of dona Lazarina, and 11 January 1510, *defensio*.
33  ASVe, PM, 43, Extraordinariorum 1, for 25 June 1508, 5 July 1508, and 3 September 1508.
34  About the Fontego: "Statuto de Muran", book I, ch. 6 and 11, 242, 248; ASVe, PM, 44, 22 Criminalium 4, for: 5 March 1510, Zuan Rosso of Parma; 6 March 1510, Bernardin di Sebastiano of Bergamo.
35  ASVe, PM, 44, 22 Criminalium 4, for 20 April 1510, against Zuan Maria son of Andrea Moliner, and 26 April 1510, testimony of Marco tintor.
36  ASVe, PM, 236 bis, fol. 22, copy dated 1589 of a law of 1445 inscribed on a stone tablet; see also fol. 25, 10 December 1524. See the copy of the privilege: ASVe, PM, 203, 1445.
37  "Statuto de Muran", book III, ch. 35, 279.
38  Andrea Navagero, on a diplomatic mission in Spain in the 1520s, reports on the maize recently arrived from America, which he hopes to plant in his garden in Murano. *Lettere di XIII Huomini illustri*, Venice, Per Francesco Lorenzini da Turino, 1560, letter of Andrea Navagero to Giovanni Battista Ramusio, 684, 12 May 1526.
39  "Statuto de Muran", book III, ch. 15–17, 274.
40  Marino Sanudo, *Cronachetta*, ed. Rinaldo Fulin (Venice: Visentini, 1880), 48.
41  Thomas Coryat, *Coryat's Crudities* (Glasgow: James MacLehose and Sons, 1905 [1611]), vol. I, 387.
42  "Statuto de Muran", book III, chap. 13, 273.
43  ASVe, PM, 44, 24 Criminalium 6, for 23 July 1510, against Vittorello Sbisia and Nicolo Can.
44  ASVe, PM, 44, 25 Criminalium 7, for 11 September 1510.
45  ASPV, Diocese of Torcello, Pastoral Visitation of 1594, fol. 144v, 26 May 1594.
46  ASVe, PM, 44, 1 Proclamatione, 25 February 1510.
47  ASVe, PM, 44, 12 Extraordinariorum 5, for 1 January 1511.
48  Alberti, *Descrittione di tutta Italia*, 95v.
49  ASVe, PM, 44, 22 Criminalium 4, for 10 March 1510, against Francesco Barovier.
50  "Statuto de Muran", book III, ch. 28, 277. The Statutes distinguish the inn (*hostaria*) from the wine depot (*magazen*).
51  Giuseppe Tassini, *Curiosità veneziane* (Venice: Filippi Editore, 1990 [1863]), 571.
52  ASVe, PM, 43, Extraordinariorum 1, for 29 January 1509; ASVe, PM, 44, 12 Extraordinariorum 5, for 17 January 1511; ASVe, PM, 212, documents 1509–1519, February 1511; ASVe, PM, 45, Extaordinariorum 2, for 16 February 1512.
53  ASVe, PM, 44, 23 Criminalium 5, for 8 July 1510, against Pietro innkeeper; 25 Criminalium 7, for 3 December 1510, against Pietro Amado; ASVe, PM, 229, 2, Cassa fontico di Murano, book 1, fol. 27, for 12 February 1511.
54  Silvia Ramelli, *Murano medievale: urbanistica, architettura, edilizia dal XII al XV secolo* (Padua: Il Poligrafo, 2000), 107, for mention of an inn at Santo Stefano in the sixteenth century. On Murano inns in the twentieth century, see *La memoria del vetro*, 46.
55  "Statuto de Muran", book III, ch. 27–28, 277. The schedule is made more flexible in 1511: three hours in winter and two in summer, ASVe, PM, 212, documents 1509–1519, for February 1511.
56  ASVe, PM, 44, 25 Criminalium 7, for 27 November 1510, against Pietro Amado.

57 ASVe, PM, 44, 1 Proclamatione, September 1509, where, at his arrival, Vitturi sends out a proclamation that it is forbidden to gamble for more than 40 *soldi*. See also ASVe, PM, 212, documents 1509–1519, for February 1511. "Statuto de Muran", book II, ch. 29, 268.

58 ASVe, PM, 43, Criminalium 5, for 31 July 1509 (*e molto me stimolo che zugasse*); ASVe, PM, 44, 22 Criminalium 4, for 4 April 1510, against Jacopo da Brescia, 5 April 1510, *defensio* (*in corte nuova a veder a zogar ala bala*); ASVe, PM, 44, 20 Criminalium 2, for 7 January 1510, against Sebastiano Bellencito (*zugando mi ale carte*); ASVe, PM, 44, 20 Criminalium 2, for 2 June 1510, against Apolonio a Gallo and his friends, *defensio* of Zaneto Padoan (*zugavemo a le tazolle*); ASVe, PM, 44, 1 Proclamatione, 2 April 1510; ASVe, PM, 45, Criminalium 2: for 16 November 1511, against Andrea Becher; 24 November 1511, testimony of Zorzi Rosso (*io viti che zugava ala mora*).

59 ASVe, PM, 44, 12 Extraordinariorum 5, for 31 December 1510. Their bad condition incites the Trenta and Vitturi to vote unanimously that they be remade. So "the citizens and inhabitants of this *terra* often find themselves at divine services in the churches and they have no other place to see to their bodily needs than the *campi* and the public streets, as do the foreigners, with little decorum and honor for this community".

60 Marino Sanudo il giovane, *De origine*, 159.

61 ASVe, PM, 43, Extraordinariorum 1, for 25 July 1508.

62 Silvio Tramontin, "Caorle e Torcello: da diocesi a parrocchie", ed. Bruno Bertoli, *La chiesa di Venezia nel Settecento* (Venice: Ed. Studium cattolico veneziano, 1993), 187–220, here 206 (in ASPV, Diocesi di Torcello, Visite pastorali, reg. 1, 1591).

63 The figure of 30,000 inhabitants that circulates in the literature on Murano dates from the 1920s, when Murano was resisting the project of annexing it to the commune of Venice. The communal councilors build the myth of the glorious origins of the city, writing in their legal plea in the hearing of 21 November 1923 that "in the fifteenth and sixteenth centuries Murano arrived at the high point of its prosperity and its glory, with a population of 30,000 inhabitants", Sergio Barizza, Giorgio Ferrari, *L'archivio municipale di Murano, 1808–1924* (Portogruaro: Nuova dimensione, 1990), 24. For the comparison with other cities: Philip Benedict, "French cities from the sixteenth century to the Revolution: an overview", in *Cities and Social Change in Early Modern France*, ed. Phillip Benedict (London: Unwin Hyman, 1989), 7–68: Nîmes has 6,000 inhabitants in 1510 and Saint-Malo 5,000 in 1540 (p. 9); Grenoble numbers 6,000 inhabitants in 1550 (p. 25). For Italian cities: Christopher Black, *Early Modern Italy. A Social History* (London: Routledge, 2001), 218–20 and Daniele Beltrami, *Storia della popolazione di Venezia dalla fine del secolo XVI alla caduta della Repubblica* (Padua: CEDAM, 1954), 65.

64 BMC, Mariegola dei Fioleri, 26, among others fol. 12r-13v, 18, 19, 33, 59v. See also the many references cited by Zecchin, *Vetro e vetrai di Murano*, vol. 2, 79–84.

65 ASVe, PM, 44, 20 Criminalium 2, for 10 December 1509.

66 ASVe, PM, 44, 20 Criminalium 2, for 30 November 1509, against Alvise Stolla.

67 ASVe, PM, 44, 1 Proclamatione, 4 October 1510, testimony of Domenico Rizo.

68 ASVe, PM, 44, 20 Criminalium 2, for 7 January 1510, against Sebastiano Bellencito.

69 Archivio Parrocchiale Santi Maria e Donato, Fabbriceria, Atti generali, Prima serie, busta 6, processo no. 18 (Avogaria di Comun), fol. 9v, for 3 May 1508.

70 Elisabeth Crouzet-Pavan, "Murano à la fin du Moyen Age: spécificité ou intégration dans l'espace vénitien", *Revue historique*, 268/1 (1982), pp. 45–92, here page 55; Marino Sanudo il giovane, *De origine*, 55.
71 Giacomo Casanova, *Histoire de ma vie* (Paris: Bouquins, 1993), tome I, vol. 4, ch. VI, 776–7, our translation.

# 2   Murano's political community and Venice

Every sixteen months, Murano is the theatre of a well-structured ritual, during which the patricians pass the baton of command. Vitale Vitturi makes his entry (*intrar*) in September 1509. Giacomo Suriano comes to replace him on 27 January 1511. As podestà, they assure the connection between the community of Murano and Venice. Nevertheless, the island has negotiated the conditions of its submission and maintained relative autonomy. It does, of course, belong to Venice's political space, but it has its own laws and institutions, which frame its inhabitants' public and private life. Like many Italian urban communities and villages, it conserves at the local scale a margin of manoeuvre in running its affairs, even if it is subordinate to a higher authority with which it shares a political culture shaped by the fragile, hostile configuration of the territory to which it belongs – the Venetian Lagoon.

## The political space of the Lagoon

Already inhabited in Roman times, the Venetian Lagoon acquired stable settlements in the sixth century. To the north, Torcello, Burano, and Murano were the first places to receive pioneers, who came to exploit the little islands of sand and mud, going by boat to fish, hunt, and farm, and to harvest the salt of the vast saltmarshes. Further to the south, the Rialto and the islands clustered around it offer the best conditions for urban growth, and, swiftly, most of the inhabitants settle there to battle the dubious tides and storms, and the risks of silt and flooding. At this improbable spot Venice is born, to become one of the greatest cities of the medieval world. Freed from the tutelage of Byzantium at the end of the eleventh century, Venice becomes an independent city state, capital of its Duchy (Dogado), the territory subject to the doge and Venice.

Benedetto Bordone in his *Isolario*, in 1528[1], writes

> That Lagoon, on the side where the sun is born, is defended from the tempestuous fury of the sea by a dike, or Lido (as the inhabitants call it) produced by nature, and the Signoria, to ward off the tempestuous

fury of the sea and to keep the anger of the sea from breaking it, spends every year a huge amount of money.

The *lidi*, long sand beaches, indeed do protect the Lagoon from the Adriatic Sea and gird the Venetian lake, like natural walls. Two principal openings let one come in, the "mouths of the port" (*bocche di porto*), though which come and go, in the hundreds, the roundships and galleys that sail to the Italian shores, the Mediterranean, and the Atlantic coasts.

At the beginning of the sixteenth century, the islands of the Lagoon still harbour communities, more or less important. Some of them flourish in the shadow of their prestigious neighbour, while others gradually fade away. All of them participate in a general economy dictated by Venice, obeying its desires and needs. Sant'Erasmo, Certosa, Le Vignole, and Murano are places for agriculture, fishing, and salt; Murano, Burano, and the Giudecca are centres of artisan production and commerce. La Giudecca, south of Venice, hosts polluting activities (the preparation of hides, dying, soap-making, brickworks). At Murano, one makes glass, and at Burano, a few kilometres to the north, they make lace. Thus, each island shoulders an economic function assigned by the capital, and shares in its prosperity.

But the Lagoon also receives the sick, who cannot stay in Venice. The city, as crossroads of Mediterranean and European commerce, often falls prey to epidemics. Hardly a week passes that a ship coming from Greece, the Middle East, North Africa, or Italy does not unload men and mer-chandise in the markets and warehouses. In 1423, the little island of Santa Maria di Nazareth, near the Lido, becomes the mooring for ships suspected of plague, who must stay there for forty (*quaranta*) days, "in quarantine". So there appeared the first *Lazaretto* (plague hospital); the name is a Venetian deformation of Nazareth, and the word, in many countries, became a synonym for the medical establishment where one took care of victims of plague and other contagions. After 1468, the Lazzaretto Nuovo, near Sant'Erasmo, and not far from Murano, replaces it. The dead also find their final dwelling out on the Lagoon. Regularly, the corpses that encumber Venice are unloaded on the island of Sant'Ariano, a vast open-air ossuary. The Venetians divert the decomposed remains that overload the cemeteries beside their parish churches, *campielli dei morti* (little squares of the dead) and *campi santi* (holy grounds); the city's layout still shows their traces. Whenever the ground can no longer absorb the heaped up dead, especially when a plague is raging, bones and skeletons join the Sant'Ariano cortège.

The many little islands also offer that isolation and solitude that so well suits the men and women who, in the face of the troubles of the age, seek salvation and remedy in monastic life. One says that Saint Francis of Assisi, back from Egypt, once stayed on Sant'Erasmo and that he founded a community of Friars Minor on the island, called San Francesco del Deserto. Other islands, La Certosa, San Giorgio, San Clemente, San Lazzaro degli

Armeni, were among the places of retreat and spiritual life, where clutches of the faithful, warded by the waters, fled the world and its temptations.

After Venice, the two most populous islands are the Giudecca and Murano, very close but still separate. They belong to the city's territory but are not quite part of it. Word circulates that the piece of iron that ornaments the bow of the gondolas (*ferro di prua*), with its six horizontal fingers in front and one behind, stands for the six quarters of Venice (*sestieri*) and for the Giudecca. During the debates, early in the sixteenth century's second decade, about where to put a district for the Jews, the Giudecca and Murano are proposed. While some Jews have lived in Venice or the Veneto for generations, others have been arriving since 1492, when royalty expelled them from Spain, and soon after, from Portugal. Their stay in the Lagoon, in theory, is curtailed to a few days, and many rules strive in vain, half-heartedly, to prevent their staying longer; meanwhile, as everywhere in Europe, the Venetians impose the wearing of a distinctive mark. In 1515, when Venice proposes the Giudecca, as Marino Sanudo notes down, the Jews protest that they fear they will be attacked by soldiers; they prefer Murano.[2] In the end, neither island is chosen, and the next year the northerly quarter of the old foundry, called *ghetto* in local dialect, is appointed for the Jews' confinement.

In the Middle Ages, Venice's political space laps against the Dalmatian coast, Greece, and the islands of the Aegean. From the end of the fourteenth century, it reaches too across the Veneto hinterland and part of Lombardy (the Terra Ferma). When that happens, political domination over the cities of Padua, Treviso, Vicenza, and Verona, as well as their countryside, shifts the regime's balance of forces. From then on, the Venetian *dominio* has three divisions, the Duchy, the Stato da Terra, and the maritime Stato da Mar. This reconfiguration touches on the fate of Murano and other subject towns, without erasing some of their particular traits. The cities and countryside of northern Italy, the seaports and coasts of Dalmatia, the islands of the Aegean, and the Mediterranean territories are lodged under the authority of podestà and captains, but they conserve their own system of justice, and local nobilities keep their social and political sway. But this does not hold for Murano, where there is no other justice or nobility than the one in Venice.

The Muranese protest against Vitturi is just one of the hostile displays that governors encounter in the subject territories. Local political arrangements, relative antiquity of the link to Venice, and distance from the capital all shape how communities sometimes resist central authority and its podestà. It is always hard to map the boundary between banal violence and hostility to the Signoria, between agitation and real sedition. That is the judges' task after the Snowball Revolt: is it the expression of indignation vis-a-vis Vitturi's conduct, or profound resentment against Venice? The magistrates of the Avogaria di Comun know their procedure well; such cases have become all the commoner since the outbreak of the Italian Wars, as local nobilities have been tempted to shrug off Venetian tutelage and have incited seditions. The Republic must be on its toes.

## A community of risk

The Lagoon was a precarious place; its risks made it easier for Venice to impose its choices on communities there and to have its officials accepted. Like other "rectors", the podestà of Murano belonged to a political apparatus that aspired to control the capital's subjects, their institutions, and natural resources. The Duchy's inhabitants should make shared use of the Lagoon's spaces, its canals for navigation, its unstable grounds for building houses, its dykes to ward off the Adriatic's incursions. The artisans, the fishermen, and the peasants, accustomed – like the monks and nuns with their works of mercy – to the floods, carried on the work of city building started by their ancestors, laying down quays, draining marshes, and maintaining the canals. Gradually, an equilibrium emerged, with Venice its guarantor.

The natural conditions have shaped the inhabitants' common culture, their shared ways of dwelling, moving about, exploiting the environment, and protecting themselves from it. To domesticate this landscape has required collective, concerted management of resources, and collaboration in the control and exploitation of its spaces. Ecological constraints have shaped arrangements. The Muranesi know that they are under the thumb of Venice precisely because they are among the first to be targeted by such laws.

The coherence of the environment reinforces the sentiment of belonging to a Lagoon community. On the night of 9 March 1502, "an enormous storm come from the West, with rain, wind and snow" crosses the Lagoon, as Marino Sanudo reports in his chronicle. All the fishermen, and others too, "saw the campaniles of Venice, Murano, and Torcello, that looked as though they were on fire".[3] At Venice, storms could be dramatic. In the middle of the century, Andrea Calmo, in a letter to a friend, plays on the caprices of the weather, recounting the tempest that, the day before, has taken the Lagoon over:

> I can say that, almost in an instant, there came the flood's ambassador, pushed by the anger of the Greco wind from the East ... the water rising in less than three hours over the top of all the Lido, from one end to the other, sinking ships and barks, breaking the pilings, carring off the huts, killing the birds and drowning the fish in the fishponds, the water rising so high that in all of Venice one went wading, three arm's lengths above the quays, ruining the shop-keepers, flooding the grain-stocks, and, in the end, wrecking every sort of creature ... Chioggia trembled in fear that it would be sucked all the way to Altino [well north of the Lagoon] by the current: Pellestrina stripped down to its undershirt to swim to a safer place; Malamocco climbed on a pile of

baskets to save itself; Povaglia put on boots to escape among the canals; Murano put its zucca squashes in its armpits [as floats] and began to bargain for a treaty with the Tessera coast [on the mainland]: Mazzorbo, Torcello, and Burano, with legs akimbo on boats, armed with harpoons, went to take refuge towards Grassaga [well inland]; Jesolo ran to save itself on the tower of Sant'Erasmo.[4]

So, perforce, it is necessary to learn to share this little inland sea, so fragile, thanks to its natural conditions. In October 1535, the podestà of Murano receives precise instructions, after high tides (*acque grande*) have carried off boats, oars, oarlocks, decks, bailing buckets, and other wooden gear, strewing them all around the Lagoon.[5] He is required to make a public proclamation, at Murano: the wood does not belong to those who find it; bring all pieces to the Savi alle Acque (Water Officials) within two days. A shared natural space does not imply goods in common.

When the *scirocco* blows from the South it pushes the Adriatic tides, and the waters pile up. If rain falls atop them, *acqua alta* (high water) invades Murano's streets, lapping against the foundations of the houses, which seem to melt into the canals. In October 1625, Francesco Luna, in his diary, records a frightening spectacle:

> In the evening, the canal water rose higher than the quays, almost an arm's length and damaged many wells, and the workplaces and glass shops here at Murano also suffered. The water started rising around midnight, and rose until the seventh hour of the night [ca. one in the morning], with a great wind storm. And it was a dark night, so that it was very frightening to behold. There has not been such high water since 1600, which then lasted three days, but without wind. I went by boat as far as San Bernardo, by the streets. One also went above the quays in boats and ships, into the warehouses.[6]

As if in paradox, the Lagoon is threatened by rising waters, as it is by the silting and clogging of its canals. The heat of summer dries up the wetlands around the *barene* (sandbanks), endangering navigation. One must make every effort, explains the Veronese architect Michele Sanmichieli, who works in Venice in the 1530s, to assure that "these marshes not silt up, or, to put it better, that their silting up be held off as long as possible".[7] The Venetian government keeps on putting out regulations condemning the behaviour of certain inhabitants who, for their own convenience (*commodo particolar*), throw their trash into the canals, threatening to sand the Lagoon up even more "around our city, the Giudecca, the monasteries, Murano, and the Lidos".[8] The silting of the canals is "a very grave harm" targeted by a specific chapter in Murano's Statutes: "That one cannot throw detritus in the canals".[9] The inhabitants must bring it to the gardens, and access cannot be denied to anyone. But it is sometimes hard to accommodate the contradictory rulings of the Venetian authorities. In 1537, a certain Gasparo d'Anzolo, whose job it is to maintain the canals (*cavacanali* is his title) is ordered by the authorities to clean the San Cassiano canal in Venice and to dump the surplus mud and sand that block it in a marsh near Murano, although the podestà has just proclaimed the prohibition on dumping waste.[10]

These natural dangers integrate the Lagoon's inhabitants into a community defined by risk. Venice's authority is better accepted because it does good environmental service. The ecology of the Lagoon sets the conditions for political rationality, which is nourished by the collective work of the inhabitants to tame a space they have managed to make fertile. Ecology also favours the politicization of some professions, the fishermen and gondoliers, who are recruited by the government whenever it is necessary to take steps to protect natural resources: the fight against silting, the protection of the navigation channels, the preservation of the fish ponds, for example. Although it is in some ways different, the link between Venice and Murano is reminiscent of those ties that Italian cities entertain with their *contado*, the adjacent agricultural zone linked by fate with its capital. Recruiting ground for manpower and future residents, source of food and of artisanal products, place of refuge when plague hits, and zone for exercising power, justice, and taxation, the *contado* is the territory held under political and economic sway that, all the Middle Ages long, let the cities flourish. But, in the Lagoon, water gave this relationship a special shape, and the chronology of settlement permitted communities to conserve their relative autonomy.

## A shared fragile space

To its subjects, both on the Terra Ferma and in the maritime empire, Venice signalled its sovereignty and presence via many symbols and images – lions made of marble, paper, or wax – deploying them wherever its power surfaced. At Murano, they turn up, assorted: little statues and bas reliefs adorning buildings and wells; the image flapping on the banner above Campo Santi Maria e Donato; miniatures or sketches scattered across the podestà's legal papers. But, because they are so close, the Muranesi share with the capital a landscape, easily sensed, that reinforces their knowledge that they belong to a shared space. The Lagoon creates a paradoxical space: it brings its inhabitants together all the while, as a natural border, it separates them. No bridge or quay or wall has ever allowed Venice to write in stone, concretely, its mastery over the islands around it. Nevertheless, the Muranesi are aware, daily, of their attachment to the capital, because they can see it, hear it, and feel its gravitational pull. On a clear day, one sees far. One need only contemplate the *Vedute* painted by Canaletto early in the eighteenth century; it is as if one could touch Murano from the north side of Venice, where the painter set up his easel.

That state of affairs called for policies to match. In June 1500, the *provveditori* of Health, tasked with hygiene and the control of sickness, send a message to the podestà of Murano à propos of the annual *festa* of Sant'Erasmo, an island less than thirty minutes by gondola to the east, under Murano's rule.[11] The festivities usually attract a crowd from assorted places, among them the folk of Chioggia. But now cases of plague have just turned up, and the festivities must not occasion new contamination. Sant'Erasmo is near the Lazzaretto Nuovo, and several ships are now there in quarantine. "If one made this *festa*", the *provveditori* explain, "the crews, when they hear the sound of flutes, will not be able to refrain from debarking at Sant'Erasmo, and there could therefore easily arise some new cases of plague". One can imagine the enthusiasm and excitement grabbing men beset by boredom and worry in the Lazaretto. All the podestà can do is ban the *festa*, and he must do so as fast as possible, lest the "poor inhabitants" spend their money in vain.

The community of Sant'Erasmo, largely devoted to agriculture, is one of those most isolated from power's centre. Contacts with the outside world are rare, and the arrival of foreigners even rarer. But it faces on one of the port's mouths, linking the Adriatic to the Lagoon, and enjoys a wondrous prospect on the ships, passing some way off, as though they are floating above the fields and vines. Isolated and confined, the inhabitants witness daily the spectacle of sails flapping in the wind and hear from afar the cadence of the rowers as they head out toward other shores of the Mediterranean. The space of experience defines a space of belonging. To see, feel, and hear the neighbouring communities: these things participate in the acceptance of the Signoria's tutelage.

Consent to Venice's political and fiscal domination over the Duchy is the condition for continued membership in this unified territory. So, one must give in to the podestà's control.[12] Vitale Vitturi oversees economic activity and the traffic of the Lagoon, as have his predecessors. The Terra Ferma is not far away. It is tempting to go there to sell the island's ducks, geese, and chickens, and its glass jugs, avoiding the commercial taxes. In November 1509, Vitturi proclaims a decision that recalls that, in the Lagoon, traffic in meat and livestock is subject to authorization, and that it requires documents that the Venetian chancery centralizes and verifies.[13] One month later the crier announces a similar decision concerning wood bought in Venice or Murano.[14] In these years, these statements multiply: *bollettini*, *lettere*, little notices, little papers that the officials deliver to the inhabitants, and that, in swelling numbers, fill the archives.[15] In 1537, still keen to steer the island's trade, the podestà has repeated, in Murano, a decision of the Council of Ten in Venice, made a century earlier, against the "many acts of smuggling committed by the ships that come to Venice with wine or provisions, to the harm and prejudice of our fiscal income ... Any ship, big or small, that will come to Venice" with such provisions is obligated to enter the Lagoon by the port of San Niccolò, or those further to the south, so as to pay its taxes.[16] If the repetition of these rules proves their inefficacy, they remain, for all that, manifestations of Venetian power.

The inhabitants of the Lagoon are well aware of the riches hidden in the ships that arrive in Venice and stay in the know about their comings and goings. No sooner does a ship arrive at the Lido port or pass the Punta della Dogana, at the entrance of the Grand Canal, than it must be unloaded, to store the bales of wool or spices, the tonnes of salt or wood, the cases of pewter or gold, to register the names of the owners, and to ready the list of taxes to be paid. The ship is then reprovisioned in water and wine, in flour, biscuits, and salted cheese. The bureaucrats, the porters, the prostitutes, the tavern staff, and innkeepers therefore make inquiry to find out when the boats are coming, for how long, and to learn what profits they can expect to extract from them. The oarsmen, the sailors, the pilots, and the porters depend on this traffic to make their living, and keep an ear out for rumours, gathering news to figure out how to make some money for the next few days.

An affair before the Venetian courts in 1512 testifies to the inhabitants' capacity to be alert to maritime activities and profit from the opportunities they offer.[17] Jacopo di Natale, an oar-maker from Ragusa (Dubrovnik) domiciled at Murano, is questioned by the judges and recounts how, urged by Stefano Dragessa, a Venetian from Castello (the Arsenale quarter at the city's east end), he took a pleasant outing to the Lido. That evening, at Vespers, they headed towards the port with two companions, one called Domenico Parga, and the other unknown to him. A caravel moored next to San Niccolò catches their eye. They come closer. Jacopo tells the story: "Stefano asked the sailors, 'Have you anything?' And the officer answers, 'We have some casks of wine and if you are willing to carry them off, we will pay you.'" In exchange for a commission, they would have sold the wine without paying a foreigner's custom fees. Jacopo and his cronies make off with "three or four casks" to Stefano's house and promise to come back in the morning for a packet of tanned skins and cordovan leather. "And so, the next morning, when we went to Piazza San Marco to hear the publication of the League [the anti-French alliance signed in October 1511], Stefano told me, 'So let's go a bit on our boat to see if we can make a little money', so all four of us went off to that same caravel." Smuggling is standard practice, and even the patricians are often tried for it. But the government keeps a watchful eye, as the revenues from its ordinances are the lifeblood of the Republic. To the eyes of the Lagoon's folk, and Murano's, such fiscal imposts, even when indirect, are the clearest signs of their subjection to the power of Venice and its patricians.

## The law of the podestà

At Murano, the first podestà was installed in 1275.[18] Later, legitimating language would explain the decision by blaming disorders and troubles that had set the community at odds.[19] At the beginning of the sixteenth century, in the Duchy, the podestà are eight in number: among them are those of Murano, Torcello, Malamocco (Lido), and Chioggia, all places on the Lagoon.[20] In the Middle Ages, many Italian cities have recourse to a podestà, a political figure whose functions vary from place to place. Usually these men are foreigners (from another city), administrators chosen for their competence and neutrality. Putting their fates in the hands of a man outside local quarrels, the ruling families hoped for social peace; they banked on the podestà's impartiality amidst local factions' conflicts.

But the Venetian podestà are not neutral; they are charged with defending Venice's interests in the subject lands, be they the Lagoon's islands, the cities of the Terra Ferma, or the Mediterranean colonies. The posts figure among the seven hundred political offices that, each year, patricians parcel out and share. At the onset of the sixteenth century, the patricians number some two thousand, who all take part in the Maggior Consiglio, where they are appointed for relatively short terms of office (in general one year or two), to the positions of senator, councillor, judge, procurator, *provveditore* of Health or of the Comune, captain or podestà, ambassador or consul.

To be podestà of Murano is not the most prestigious job. To govern a small community of glassworkers and fishermen, to unscramble spats of neighbours, keep the lid on glass trade secrets, and chase down the backyard theft of ducks, for a young patrician, is political apprenticeship: paltry stakes, no zest. For an administrator who is inured or older – Vitale Vitturi is, on election, more than sixty – the post, probably, is a bore. But it is the lesser of two evils: better this nearby island than some outpost on the Peloponnese.

The patrician chosen to be podestà of Murano governs not on his own account, but as holder of the public authority the Signoria confers when it commissions him. So, as a Venetian nobleman, he embodies double domination, that of Venice over the subject lands, and that of patricians over the *popolo* of the Lagoon. That is why the event of 27 January 1511 cannot go unpunished; it targets both a regime and a Venetian nobleman, public authority and the patrician elite. "You have sworn the profit, utility, and honour of the *comune* of Venice" – so say the podestà's marching orders, which go on to admonish him to do credit to his mission and to respect the community he rules.[21] The text of this *commissio* is cut from a familiar cloth. It mixes precise instructions with general objectives shared by all Venetian emissaries. It restricts the podestà: he should respect Murano's 1502 Statutes, render justice, receive and run the taxes, bar smuggling, assure the security of persons and of commercial goods, keep an eye to the borders, and guarantee the territory's good order. He is also responsible for the link between the capital and the community, serving the former the better to control the latter. So, the podestà of Murano, like governors of other possessions, covers a vast terrain. It is all in the spirit of patrician power: the rotation of offices undercuts any specialization, and magistrates must cope with matters of every kind.

A podestà's salary depends on the context of his mission. It is cobbled from the fines he levies and the taxes on the butcher shops and on the wine trade.[22] The Venetian authorities fret about conflicts of interest and corruption; in the *commissio* they stress the probity that the podestà and his official household must evince.[23] At the end of his term of office, he is held to show his books and archive his papers with the Venetian chancery.[24] The Venetian archives, today, hold hundreds of podestà registers, from the thirteenth to the eighteenth century. Compared with most binders, Vitale Vitturi's really bulge, as if, as administrator, he was busily officious. Sadly, those of his successor, Suriano, are gone; we cannot compare the two. But those of Suriano's brother Agostino, who oversaw the island from September 1511 to February 1512, are much slimmer than Vitturi's.[25]

The podestà resides and rules in a palace, now vanished, next to the church of Santi Maria e Donato. It is the equivalent of the communal palaces of Italian cities and looks rather like a princely castle. The *palazzo del podestà*, also called the *palazzo della Raxon* (literally, "palace of reason", meaning of law or of justice), is Murano's central place for power. It was built in 1334, probably replacing a smaller structure. In 1555, it is partly destroyed by fire, and then rebuilt.[26] Four stories tall, the building looms over a covered loggia that offers a passage between the regime's palace and the public piazza. Some podestà choose to install their families in Murano; others prefer to stay in the capital and come four days a week, as stipulated by their commission.[27] They must also be sure to be on hand for "solemn holidays" and for the main days of the religious and civic calendars.[28] Vitturi sets up house on the island with his wife, the daughter of Tragnaco Contarini di Polazzo; she dies at Murano during his term of office.[29] They have at least two servants, a valet named Alessandro and a house-keeper, Caterina.[30] The town crier, Antonio Malcanton, stands in as personal gondolier whenever, as often happens, they traverse the island.[31]

Like all those who held the job before him, Vitturi has had to test the boundaries of his zone of jurisdiction, to clinch his sovereignty over the inhabitants, and to exercise authority in easy alignment with the usages established by his predecessors and by Murano's habits.[32] He embodies a political role that each patrician who holds the post helps to fashion and define, by deeds and words, acting in a way that makes his political mastery clear to all. The *commissio* and the island's Statutes trace the contours of this role, and they lay out some material conditions – the ritual of passage and the baton of command – that permit the podestà to embody his job and authority. There are also some surviving old seigneurial rights. One privilege reserves for the podestà certain cuts of beef (called *lomboli* or *nomboli*) that the island's butchers can sell to none but him "as has always been observed by ancient custom".[33] Moreover, the custom of *regalia* constrains the community to regale him with gifts at annual celebrations: sausages from the salami shops in Carnival, and, from the bakers, *focaccia* on Saint Martin's day.[34]

Just as the doge, in certain rituals, distributes little medals (*oselle*) to the Venetians, the podestà hands them out to the Muranesi, to reward fidelity.[35] These tokens, paid for by the community, are of meagre worth, but, on the island, they serve for petty purchases. So, for instance, in December 1510, a party of friends gathering at the Salvàdego *osteria* pay for wine "with some *oselle*".[36] The podestà's open hand buttresses his authority with the people, as Vitturi knows. A few days before his departure, he puts a law to council, raising the tax on flour. To make up for the decision, he proposes, local funds permitting, that "the magnificent podestà, his judges and his four deputies, or their majority, will spend ten ducats, and give them to the needy poor of this *terra* of Murano, as they see fit".[37] These practices evince the paternalism that Vitturi and the other podestà foster on the island.

## Citizens and Muranesi officials

The Muranesi do not heed the podestà's rulings solely; they have their own institutions. As a whole *popolo*, they constitute a general assembly, the *Concio* or *Arengo*, which in theory has the power to deliberate. Such an institution, arising in the medieval communes in the eleventh and twelfth centuries, very often assembles the adult men of free condition to decide collectively their community's fate independently, out from under the power of the lords who at the time still dominate the towns. But, historically, the more urban populations swell, the harder it becomes to call the general assembly. At Venice, the *Arengo* lives on until 1423; it is convoked after each ducal election so that the people can show its acceptance of the decision taken by the nobles. Nevertheless, with a population burgeoning past 100,000, the body becomes less a political institution than a notional ideal, as it is materially impossible to assemble all the inhabitants. For Murano, documents from the early sixteenth century still cite the *Arengo* or the "public *contio*", though it has by then evolved into an assembly restricted to the wealthy.[38] In the eyes of law, the rest of the Muranesi constitute the "community" embodying the common good, a coherent group that defends shared interests. In political rhetoric, as in law, "the *comunità*" is pregnant with meaning, but no longer is its own institution.

From the later Middle Ages, a process of internal distinction has imposed new hierarchies. In light of their trade, their greater autonomy in the glass business, and their own wealth, certain inhabitants have claimed the title of "citizen", the equivalent of the French *bourgeois* and the English "burgher" in the word's old sense. "Citizen of Murano" first surfaces in the 1480s. A few years later, at the time of the Snowball Revolt, between fifty and one hundred residents lay claim to this still-vague title of *cittadini*, sometimes also designated no more sharply as "good men" (*boni homeni*). There is the notion that only they can be addressed as Ser, even though Ser's usage remains rather random in public records. Sometimes Vitturi and the chancellor apply it to members of the Council of Thirty and the masters of the glassworks. At other times they attach it to most inhabitants.[39]

What sets Murano citizenship off is its reliance on the exercise of a manual trade, and its emergence from a tacit, collective recognition of the social superiority of certain artisans, the glassmakers. Meanwhile, in Venice, the status is reserved to commoners who do no work with their hands. Merchants, bankers, and officials thus win recognition for their legal superiority to artisans and manual labourers and became *cittadini* by birth or grant. They constitute a mid-group between patricians and *popolo*, for they practice a profession not thought lowly. But, at Murano, the citizens are the best artisans, and with time the practice of glass-making becomes the very condition for the rank.

At the beginning of the sixteenth century the citizens dominate Murano's regime and collaborate with the podestà. They form the Council of Thirty; the Statutes call the body "the thing most necessary to the needs" of the island, and sometimes it still goes by "*arengo*". Semantic slippage has assimilated this restricted body to the island's general assembly of the same name.[40] Its members debate, vote, and pass laws submitted by the podestà. Every five years, a complicated election process renews the Council, ensuring that the leading families have fair representation. Everyone is held to vote "according to his conscience"; family members may not nominate one another. The procedure reflects the wish of ranking Muranesi to share power among themselves. On Sunday 30 September 1509, soon after he arrives on the island, Vitale Vitturi convokes the Thirty, then twenty-four in actual number, and has the chancellor, Pietro de Vielmo, read aloud all Murano's Statutes.[41] So begins a collaboration; it will last sixteen months.

To smooth decision making, five magistrates (two judges, two economic magistrates, and a chamberlain) are elected from within the Thirty to form a *banco*, a subcommittee to assist the podestà in matters of greatest weight. On 9 September 1509, the Council elects the *banco* that will govern with Vitturi.[42] The two judges (*zudexi*), Domenico Rizo and Domenico Bertoluso, take on penal justice. They make an oath "with good conscience to counsel the podestà as he will ask of him, not to do service to anyone, nor to take vengeance on anyone at all".[43] The two economic magistrates (*iusticieri*), Sebastiano Bellencito and Lazaro Maroza, are concerned with civil justice, and, in particular, with economic matters.[44] The chamberlain (*camerlengo*), Zuan Rizo di Domenico, is the treasurer and "cashier of this community".[45] He keeps the books, and pays out money in the presence or with the knowledge of the podestà, to whom he has to show the books at the end of his own term of office. He keeps the island's budget and pays the salaries of the other magistrates and officials, thanks to taxes raised via the sale of wine and flour. The members of the banco act like a princely court and, accordingly, they have to receive the podestà when he enters into office, to keep him company, and to remain at his side so long as he holds office.[46] On 27 January, they are indeed present on Campo Santi Maria e Donato when Suriano makes his entry.

Some of the inhabitants have more specific missions. Two Procurators of the Churches (*procuradori dele ghiesie*) are named at each parish church to watch over its property and keep the books.[47] The four Deputies for the Needs of the *Terra* (*deputati per li bisogni dela terra*) meet when summoned by the podestà, especially when the fiscal situation calls for special measures – i.e. new taxes.[48] The chief of the flour entrepôt (*soprastante al fontego dela farina*) oversees the wheat supply and the quality of the grain. The podestà himself keeps a sharp eye on the matter, to ward off hunger riots and to evade hard times that could rock the community.[49] The magistrates receive a salary that also means that they have to attend the councils.[50] Seeing to these public tasks costs them time otherwise devoted to their trades, although some of them, like the glassworks owners, are wealthy and live easily off their revenues.

A number of officials also help the regime. The chancellor is the community's secretary and notary.[51] He is chosen from among Venice's *cittadini*, to register laws and handle private legal papers (wills, legacies, contracts, real estate transactions). In the time of Vitale Vitturi, Pietro de Vielmo drafts and conserves the podestà's papers, the Thirty's minutes, Malcanton's public proclamations, judicial sentences, and fiscal rolls. He also archives the inhabitants' wills, drawn up "by the notaries of Venice, according to the Venetian rules", locking them in a coffer with two keys, one held by him, the other conferred by him to the podestà.[52] The registration of political decisions guarantees the continuity of power and the stability of the laws. Thus is conserved memory, from one patrician to the next, of things done and said. Power passes not only via legitimate violence and public authority, but also via the control of civic discourse and political memory. Venice keeps its hand in, requiring that the chancellor be chosen from among its *cittadini* and by insisting that, at the end of their mandate, podestà hand in their laws and books.

The second officer is the town crier.[53] When Vitale Vitturi arrives, the job is held by Matteo da Brescia, soon replaced by Antonio Malcanton, who is a central figure in the ritual of 27 January 1511, when he organizes power's passage, and at the trial, where he is among the principal defendants. The crier must proclaim the decisions of the podestà and of the Council of Thirty, and assure, inside the community, the circulation of information and the publication of laws. He summons inhabitants to court and transmits the podestà's commands. He also collaborates with three officials (*caradori della comunità*) in charge of provisioning wood, a commodity without which the glassworks would founder.[54] The four must verify that enough wood has come to keep the furnaces going and also must tax the trade. They also work with a third official, the *cavalier*, the island's only real policeman in charge of public order. A new chief arrives with every new podestà, usually straight from Venice.[55]

Finally, as circumstances and needs warrant, certain inhabitants are summoned to other public roles. Murano's innkeeper participates in levying the wine tax (he is *conductor del dazio del vin*). And he oversees the wine trade, turning to his "officers and men, on land and on the water, to inquire into those who do not pay the official tax".[56] When plague flares up, the citizens are ordered to follow good public health procedures. The boatmen, often, are sent to see it done.

So, alongside the podestà, there are magistrates, officers, and inhabitants – privileged citizens and common folk alike, whose everyday activities are needed for the smooth functioning of the institutions, the circulation of news, the maintenance of economic rules, and respect for public order. As elsewhere in Italy and in Europe in the early sixteenth century, the inhabitants take part in power. The application of decisions taken by noble elites depends on the actions of subaltern agents. These men are neither peripheral, nor informal, nor secondary. Rather, they are the indispensable links that make the political order work. If, at Murano, the exercise of power is still under the eye of Venice and of the podestà, by and large it is shouldered by the inhabitants of the island, acting as public persons, bearers of the authority conferred at once by the state of Venice and by their own community of Murano. They know that they represent a higher jurisdiction and that they are summoned to defend the state's common good as well as the local interests of their community. The complex electoral procedures that install them are designed to recruit the best men; they reveal the Muranese mastery of a system that combines voting with selection by lot.

For their sophistication, Muranese institutions owe a great debt to Venice's political culture, from which they draw their collegial sense of power and the density of their own politics. Thus, the island constitutes a complex political space, and the authorities put it on display at the ritual of power's passage. It is a visual declaration that inculcates at once the islanders' submission to Venice and their autonomy. From their earliest years, everyone absorbs the lesson, like those youngsters crowding the *campo*, for whom the splendour and the solemnity of the moment heighten the event's intensity.

## The participation of the people

The Muranesi, *cittadini*, and other inhabitants, contribute by many other devices to the social and political framework that enables their little island society. The management of the urban facilities, for example: the maintenance of the quays, bridges, and public infrastructure all require everybody's cooperation and sharing of resources. In December 1506, it comes time to repair the bell tower at Santi Maria e Donato; the bishop of Torcello insists on it.[57] The members of the Thirty are invited to donate, on the model of the bishop himself, who, to whip up their zeal, offers to throw in ten ducats. Twenty-four citizens, among them the crier Matteo da Brescia, take up the collection, contributing in all more than forty ducats.

Two years later, in June 1508, comes the turn of Ponte Lungo: it needs repairs, urgently, and once more the community is asked to help. The inhabitants turn to the *provveditori di Comun*, the Venetian magistrates in charge of urban planning. But they make it very clear that "it is not possible to give money, because there is no money at all".[58] In the midst of the Italian Wars, Venice is devoting its efforts to the defence of its territories, and, it stands to reason, some sectors will suffer. So, it will fall to the inhabitants to finance the works, each paying "in accord with his status and wealth". A list is compiled: 190 persons, to which they add the glassmakers, the porters, and the monasteries as entities who pay collectively. Each furnace master owes one ducat (six *lire* four *soldi*), the same sum owed by Venetian nobles who own a house at Murano. From the masters, workers, and *garzoni* at the glassworks, they ask the equivalent of one day's pay. The wood porters, collectively, owe one ducat, and it falls to them to apportion the burden among their number. The fourteen *ligadori* each pay in a half-ducat. Certain citizens and inhabitants contribute a considerable sum, but most put in between a half-lira (ten *soldi*) and a lira.

For comparison's sake, note that at the time a worker at the Arsenale, at the start, makes six *soldi* a day (a little more than a ducat a month) while a well-trained carpenter receives on average thirty (five to six ducats a month), and an employee in a shop brings in sixteen to eighteen *soldi* (about three ducats a month). Meanwhile, a loaf of bread in times of dearth, or a mackerel, costs two *soldi*; a pound of oil or wax, or a visit to the barber, come in at four *soldi*. For half a *soldo* one can buy the little printed pamphlets on the war of the League of Cambrai.[59] As for the glassworkers, we know their salaries for the next century; they vary hugely according to the workshop, the type of production, and the level of training. In the seventeenth century, masters bring in between three and sixteen ducats a week; the workers make between five *soldi* and six ducats.[60]

In September 1508 comes the turn of the other half of Ponte Longo.[61] A new loan is organized, among "those who, as fairly as possible, can take part, without involving in any way the smaller folk (*popolo menudo*)". This collective effort gives the repair work a swift start. The same system of contributions permits the installation of the clock atop the campanile of San Pietro Martire, at the end of the Fondamenta dei Vetrai.[62] Once more, adjusting the grant to each man's means reflects Murano's ability to think of the community as a collective whole, in solidarity.

Many other moments, and institutions, embody this collective culture; there are the guilds and confraternities (*scuole*), professional and devotional groups that allow the inhabitants to meet, both to regulate their professional lives and to exercise their piety in collective rituals. In the Lagoon, guilds do not sit in city councils, unlike those in Florence or Flanders. But, for all that, they are no less nodes of political action, places for an apprenticeship in the forms of collegiality and of decision making. Murano's artisans cannot, it seems, join the *scuole* in Venice.[63] But three crafts, on the island, have their own institutions: the glassworkers, the fishermen, and the *traghetto* boatmen. These three groups are out on Campo Santi Maria e Donato in January 1511 and they engage regularly with Vitale Vitturi, with Murano's regime, and with Venice.

Murano's glassmaker guild (*Scuola de fioleri de Muran* – *fioleri* was an early name for glassmakers), founded in the first half of the thirteenth century, allows the owners of the furnaces and the master glassmakers to negotiate the trade's rules and to set work conditions.[64] It soon becomes an institution to reckon with whenever economic matters are up for discussion. The members take on matters beyond production; it is they who, in the sixteenth century, promote a new status of "citizen of Murano". They also work to define what it means in Murano to be a foreigner, as the Venetian statutes, concerning the lower classes, offer little guidance.

The fishermen also take part in Venetian politics, for the regime recognizes their expertise in the management of natural resources. Better than any others, they know how to cruise the Lagoon's waters and to tame the environment. In 1536, for example, the Savi alle Acque ask the fishers' guilds of San Niccolò and Sant'Agnese, both at Venice, and of Murano, Burano, and Chioggia to elect representatives. At Murano, the podestà is to supervise the election, organized by the *scuola*. The Sunday after the publication of this decision, all fishermen thirty-five or older are summoned. They take an oath to choose their delegates, for a two-year term, among "the most senior, competent, and experienced".[65] Across the whole Lagoon fishermen are chosen, so that "when one treats of problems concerning the Lagoon, they might speak up, to have their opinion and agreement about the matter on the table".

For a very long time, the pragmatic foundation of Venetian political culture has persuaded the rulers to resort to the inhabitants' practical knowledge and technical competence. In the sixteenth century, the practice is widespread, as a new culture of experience diffuses in the elites, who feel humanism's influence. Knowledge, now, is based on empiricism, attention to facts, and observation, with growing heed to experimentation. Murano's fishermen, almost all excluded from the status of *cittadino*, nevertheless collaborate with the regime to protect the Lagoon, a central plank of Venice's policies. The election of their delegates, the discussions and debates on the nature of the propositions to put forward, and on the zones where they think action is required – legislation on the size of fish, the upkeep of canals and banks, the dredging of the basins – all these interventions touch the general interest. If the documents available to us have rarely conserved traces of these exchanges, it still pays to keep these things in mind to grasp how the fishermen on the *campo* conceived of themselves and understood their role in the day's ritual.

The political expressions of the inhabitants of Murano spring from their familiarity with the collegial nature of the Venetian institutions, all the more readily learned because the place is fairly small. Fiscal contributions levied with an eye to incomes, collective institutions, respect for principles of representation, regular sessions of assemblies and debates – all these things shape the political socialization of the inhabitants. Meanwhile, elsewhere in Europe, other hamlets, villages, and towns are also familiar with political and institutional systems based on the inhabitants' daily participation.

Murano is on the inner outside. It belongs to the territory of Venice, but the Lagoon sets it a bit apart. Its streets, canals, and quays look like the capital's, just minutes away. Nevertheless, the two communities remain profoundly different. Murano is not Venice, and Muranesi not Venetians. One imagines that their accents differ, even if, in the sources we possess, it is very difficult to discern. There are even the physical traces of their activities: faces etched by the sun or by the furnace fires, hands battered and callused, clothing soiled by the earth or singed by molten glass. Even in our day, the residents of the Rio rag the island's northerners, whom they call *zalòti*, evoking their yellow (*zalo*) complexions.[66] There were so many stigmas, attached to bodies and gestures, to words and accents, things that historians today can barely trace. But these signs, surely everywhere, laid down essential distinctions between the folk of Murano and those of Venice.

At the beginning of the sixteenth century, the fishermen, glassworkers, workers, and domestic servants prosper, at the doors of Venice, one of the world's most dynamic, rich, and cosmopolitan cities. Hundreds of merchants pass through, Italians, Germans, or Turks; the market for luxuries flourishes, and the new architecture of the Renaissance renews the urban fabric and burnishes the city's appearance. From their windows, if they look south, the people of Murano can see the beating heart of the city whose fate they share.

## Notes

1 Bordone, *Libro . . . de tutte l'isole*, XXVII bis.
2 Marino Sanudo, *I Diarii*, vol. 20, col. 138, 23 April 1515.
3 Marino Sanudo, *I Diarii*, vol. 4, col. 244, 10 March 1502.
4 *Le lettere di Messer Andrea Calmo* book III, 218, letter 28, to Bortolamio de Salis.
5 ASVe, PM, 187, Lettere al podestà, 4 October 1535, Collegio savi alle Acque.
6 *Diario di Murano di Francesco Luna, Diario di Murano*, 20, for 23 October 1625.
7 Paolo Selmi, "Politica lagunare della Veneta Repubblica dal secolo XIV al XVIII", *Mostra storica della Laguna Veneta, Catalogo della mostra* (Venice: 1970), 105–15, here 106 (reproducing ASVe, Consiglio dei Dieci, Deliberazioni segrete, reg. 4, fol. 43v, 25 January 1535).

8  Archivio di Stato di Venezia, *Laguna, lidi, fiumi. Cinque secoli di gestion delle acque, Mostra documentaria*, 1983, 44, document 74, decision of the Collegio savi alle Acque, 26 June 1531 (reproducing ASVe, Savi ed esecutori alle aque, reg. 334, par. 5).

9  "Statuto de Muran", book III, ch. 37, 280.

10  ASVe, PM, 187, Lettere al podestà, 28 May 1537, letter of Giacomo Barbarigo to Marco Querini, podestà of Murano.

11  ASVe, PM, 187, Lettere al podestà, 3 June 1500: letter of the *provveditori* of Health to Giovanni Francesco Bragadin, podestà of Murano. Concerning Sant'Erasmo, "Statuto de Muran", book I, ch. 15, 253.

12  For the surveillance of smuggling: "Statuto de Muran", book I, ch. 13, 252.

13  ASVe, PM, 44, 1 Proclamatione, 8 November 1509.

14  ASVe, PM, 44, 1 Proclamatione, 3 December 1509.

15  See for example, on the wood trade and the *boleta*: "Statuto de Muran", book I, ch. 14, 252. See also book II, ch. 3, 261.

16  ASVe, PM, 187, Lettere al podestà, 29 May 1537, letter to Marco Querini podestà of Murano, with a reference to the law of the Council of Ten of 25 June 1407.

17  ASVe, PM, 212, documents 1509–19, 4 March 1512.

18  ASVe, Maggior Consiglio, Decreta, 2 December 1275, quoted by Zanetti, *Guida di Murano*, 185.

19  Crouzet-Pavan, "Murano à la fin du Moyen Age".

20  Marino Sanudo il giovane, *De origine*, 71.

21  ASVe, PM, 200, *Commissio* of the doge Agostino Barbarigo to Francesco Barbarigo, podestà of Murano, 26 February 1493, ch. 52.

22  ASVe, PM, 200, *Commissio* of the doge Agostino Barbarigo to Francesco Barbarigo, podestà of Murano, 26 February 1493, ch. 5; ASVe, Collegio, Formulari di commissioni, reg. 8, 1533, fol. 99; "Statuto de Muran": book I, ch. 24–5, 256; book III, ch. 10, 272.

23  ASVe, PM, 200, *Commissio* of the doge Agostino Barbarigo to Francesco Barbarigo, podestà of Murano, 26 February 1493, chs. 7 and 21.

24  ASVe, PM, 200, *Commissio* of the doge Agostino Barbarigo to Francesco Barbarigo, podestà of Murano, 26 February 1493, chs. 6 and 14.

25  ASVe, PM, 44, Acts of Vitale Vitturi; ASVe, PM, 45, Acts of Agostino Suriano. The podestà Giacomo Suriano takes part in military operations during the summer of 1511 and dies. The Senate agrees that he should be replaced by his brother Agostino, even though the man is still young (Marino Sanudo, *I Diarii*, vol. 12, col. 549–50, 19 September 1511). As for the volume of his papers, see for comparison's sake the extremely abundant papers of Vincenzo Zantani, podestà of Torcello in the same period: ASVe, Podestà di Torcello, 140.

26  Zanetti, *Guida di Murano*, 132; Richard J. Goy, *Venetian Vernacular Architecture. Traditional Housing in the Venetian Lagoon* (Cambridge: Cambridge University Press, 1989), 186.

27  ASVe, PM, 200, *Commissio* of the doge Agostino Barbarigo to Francesco Barbarigo, podestà of Murano, 26 February 1493, ch. 18.

28  ASVe, Collegio, Formulari di commissioni, reg. 8, 1533, fol. 99v.

29  ASVe, Miscellanea Codici, Storia Veneta, Genealogie Barbaro, vol. VII, busta 23, fol. 279.

30  ASVe, PM, 44, 4 Testificationum, 17 July 1510.

31  ASVe, AC, MP, 142, no. 17, fol. 7.

32  In their order, the early sixteenth-century podestà of Murano were: Gabriele Venier in August 1501, Giacomo Antonio Marcello di Fantino in January 1503, Lorenzo Giustinian di Onfrè in May 1504, Cipriano Contarini di Bernardo in

September 1505, Giovanni Alvise Pisani di Bernardo in January 1507, Pietro Morosini di Francesco di Andrea in May 1508, Vitale Vitturi di Andrea in September 1509, Giacomo Suriano di Michele in January 1511, and his brother Agostino from October 1511, Giacomo Antonio Tiepolo di Michele in June 1512, Alessandro Michiel di Pietro in October 1513.

33 "Statuto de Muran", book III, ch. 26, 276.

34 ASVe, PM, 229, 2, Cassa fontico di Murano, book 1, fol. 19, for 15 October 1510; ASVe, PM, 236 bis, fol. 39v, late 16th century, *Regalighe*.

35 Edward Muir, *Civic ritual in Renaissance Venice* (Princeton, NJ: Princeton University Press, 1981), 255.

36 ASVe, PM, 44, 25 Criminalium 7, for 3 December 1510, against Pietro Amado.

37 ASVe, PM, 44, 12 Extraordinariorum 5, for 31 December 1510.

38 "Statuto de Muran", book IV, ch. 8, 287 (*convocata la publica contion*).

39 See for example ASVe, PM, 44, 10 Extraordinariorum 3, for 18 May 1510.

40 "Statuto de Muran", book I, ch. 2, 238.

41 ASVe, PM 44, 8 Extraordinariorum 1, for 30 September 1509. During the tenure of Vitturi the members of the Thirty are: Zuan Ballarin, Angelo Barovier, Nicolo Barovier, Zuan Barovier, Sebastiano Bellencito, Andrea Bigaia, Vettor Blondo, Domenico Bertoluso, Domenico Caner, Vincenzo Caner, Zuan Corona, Polo Forner, Francesco Fuga, Bartolomeo Gabano, Lazaro Maroza, Salvator Moro, Sebastiano da Mestre, Antonio Moliner, Domenico Rizo, Stefano Rombolo, Zuan Rosseto, Pietro de Slave, Pasquale Torzelan, Pietro Trevisan. Other lists also include the name of Andrea Angelo dal Gallo.

42 ASVe, PM, 44, 8 Extraordinariorum 1, for 9 September 1509.

43 "Statuto de Muran", book I, chs. 3, 4, 20 and 21, 240–1, 255. Just before Giacomo Suriano, Andrea Angelo dal Gallo and Zuan Ballarin di Zorzi replace these men: ASVe, 12 Extraordinariorum 5, for 31 December 1510.

44 "Statuto de Muran", book I, chs. 5–7, 241–2. Their successors are Vincenzo Bertoluso and Salvator Moro: ASVe, 12 Extraordinariorum 5, for 31 December 1510.

45 The person in question was the son of the judge Domenico, ASVe, PM, 44, 8 Extraordinariorum 1, for 21 October 1509. For the function of the chamberlain, "Statuto de Muran", book I, ch. 8.

46 ASVe, PM, 236 bis, fol. 26, for 11 April 1531.

47 "Statuto de Muran", book I, ch. 1, 238.

48 "Statuto de Muran", book I, ch. 9, 244. In 1509–10, Andrea Angelo dal Gallo, Angelo Barovier, Vettor Blondo, Bartolomeo Gabano hold this position of deputy: ASVe, PM, 44, 8 Extraordinariorum 1, for 9 September 1509.

49 "Statuto de Muran", book I, ch. 11, 248.

50 For details of the salaries received in Vitturi's term, see "Statuto de Muran", book I, ch. 2, 240.

51 "Statuto de Muran", book I, ch. 10, 245.

52 "Statuto de Muran", book I, ch. 17, 254.

53 "Statuto de Muran", book I, ch. 12, 249–50.

54 "Statuto de Muran", book I, ch. 14, 252–3. ASVe, PM, 44, 10 Extraordinariorum 3, for 6 June 1510: the *caradori* are Antonio a Cancelario, Zorzi dalla Vecchia and Martin Saraxin.

55 See "Statuto de Muran", book I, ch. 13, 250–1.

56 ASVe, PM, 212, documents 1509–19, February 1511.

57 ASVe, PM, 44, 12 Extraordinariorum 5, for 13 December 1506.

58 ASVe, PM, 43, Extraordinariorum 1, for 25 June 1508 and 5 July 1508.

59 For these salaries and prices, Rosa M. Salzberg, *Ephemeral City: Cheap Print and Urban Culture in Renaissance Venice* (Manchester: Manchester University

Press, 2014), 20. For carpenters' salaries, Franco Rossi, "L'Arsenale: i quadri direttivi", *Storia di Venezia. Dalle origini alla caduta della Serenissima*, vol. V, eds. Alberto Tenenti and Ugo Tucci, *Il Rinascimento. Società ed economia* (Rome: Istituto della enciclopedia italiana, 1996), 593–639.

60  Francesca Trivellato, "Salaires et justice dans les corporations vénitiennes au XVIIᵉ siècle: le cas des manufactures de verre", *Annales. Histoire, Sciences Sociales*, 1 (1999): 245–73, at page 250.

61  ASVe, PM, 43, Extraordinariorum 1, for 3 September 1508.

62  Elisabeth Crouzet-Pavan, *La mort lente de Torcello. Histoire d'une cité disparue* (Paris: Fayard, 1995), 175.

63  BMC, Mariegola dei Fioleri, 26.

64  BMC, Mariegola dei Fioleri, 26.

65  ASVe, PM, 187, Lettere al podestà, letter of Lorenzo Giustinian and his colleagues, procurators of San Marco and Alvise Gritti and his colleague savi alle Acque to Antonio Diedo, podestà of Murano, 7 September 1536.

66  *La memoria del vetro*, 39.

# 3   A tottering ritual

We have set the scene. A small island, densely populated, and thoroughly structured, both institutionally and politically. A powerful capital that imposes its sovereignty and law. A podestà whose task it is to represent that capital to a community of glassworkers and fishermen who, gradually, have negotiated the nature and forms of autonomy. The Campo Santi Maria e Donato, on a cold winter afternoon. On stage, the star protagonists are two Venetian patricians come to pass the baton as head of the island's institutions and to take part in a political ritual often replayed ever since the *podestaria* of Murano first saw the light of day. The secondary players are many: the members of the Council of Thirty, the magistrates, the officials, and the town crier. The bit parts are without number: Venetian patricians, Muranese *cittadini*, islanders – men, women, and children who came to see the solemn show.

## Ritual politics

The passage of power is an essential moment in Murano's political calendar. The ceremony is called *intrar*, the entry – that is to say the new podestà's taking on his tasks. And that is what the witnesses and the accused will call it at the trial put on by the Avogaria di Comun. The *intrar* marks the enthronement of the new rector and the old one's departure, but it also allows Murano's society and political structure to walk the boards, on stage. Sometimes the new podestà takes advantage of the occasion to show off his largess: gifts, food handed out, *feste*, balls and banquets, fine speeches lauding him; these demonstrations Venice does rein in, to ward off patronage and favouritism.[1] The passage of power obeys its "codes" and it has a "grammar", to borrow terms from social scientists who study the structure of political ritual. The participants, to be understood, must follow rules and employ symbols easily grasped by the public: images, gestures, and sounds that say what power is and who holds it in his hands.

Across the Lagoon, it is at Venice that ceremonies are most splendid. They draw their power from repetition of the actions that give them structure; these, often, are anchored in texts called "*ceremoniali*". In

Venice, the grand rituals follow the Christian liturgical calendar, which meshes with another calendar that commemorates the Republic's historic and mythical events. Because they dwell inside Venice's political space, Murano's people take part in some of these rituals, which batten off tales of victory against the Ottomans, or of the Wedding of the Sea. They loan their own boats or the *traghetto* and join Venice to marvel at power's grand gestures, to take part in the Ascension's ceremonies and fair, or in the Corpus Christi procession, a foreign prince's visit, or the celebration of an international alliance.

When a new doge is elected, the glassmakers are obliged to come celebrate in Venice. The island's boatmen are also recruited when foreign princes or ambassadors pay a call; they are to swell the gaudy fleet that receives the guest at the Lagoon's entrance, cruising splendidly to proclaim Venice's wealth and maritime strength.[2] The Republic knows well how to impress visitors and inhabitants alike: it sets its confraternities parading across Piazza San Marco, in ceremonial dress, with banners flying and gilded reliquaries aglow, sounding their drums and trumpets. The ceremony is performative: to public eyes the spectacle both represents and creates the power. The regime constructs, and reinforces, its hold on its subjects by making its political and social superiority visible, embodying it in deeds and words deployed for the occasion.

If they are somewhat simpler, Murano rituals are in no way lacking. The weekly meeting of the Council of Thirty and Antonio Malcanton's proclamations have their ritual side. But the great promoter of ceremonies is the church: baptisms and weddings, Christmas and Easter mass, the Palm Sunday procession, the Stations of the Cross, the representation of the Resurrection. The community's account books register Vitale Vitturi's expenditures for the Corpus Christi of May 1510, with particular attention to the flutes and trumpets.[3] In May 1525, after many rainless days, the inhabitants rig up a procession to procure some better weather. As if the heavens heeded, on 8 May a storm brings the Lagoon high winds and rain, overdoing it a bit, as, at Murano and on the Lido, many gardens come off the worse.[4]

In the Lagoon, as in all Italy, many popular rituals stage games, violence, and war. Youngsters, especially, take part in jousts and war games, throwing rocks and other projectiles. On the bridges of Venice, battles set residents of rival quarters against each other. One fight is the famous "War of the Fists" that musters the fishermen of the city's west end against the Arsenale workers of the east. For Carnival, as for other festive occasions, the inhabitants take part in games that sometimes tip over into violence, and the Snowball Revolt fits easily into these well-known forms.

More solemn political and civic rituals serve to bolster Venetian authority and help build up domination through the use of well-calibrated rhetoric. The crimson velvet and cloth-of-gold of the magistrates, the torches, the baldaquins, and banners that adorn the buildings, the roar of the crowd, the chants and acclamations, all of them, heighten the performance. The participants' emotions are the ritual's guarantee: the hair-raised tingle and stirred feelings all feed belief in power's legitimate hand.

## The theatre of society

Ritual is one of the rare opportunities to see, all assembled, the community so often evoked in public discourse, to give it form, to affirm its solidity, and to reawaken the sentiment of belonging. Community, in general, is only theoretical and rhetorical, and power's passage offers an occasion to embody it, to see it on the ground and in action. But the ritual also puts on display the hierarchies that crosscut the community; it displays all the many layers and allots to each precise roles and tasks. One's place in a procession obeys rules of rank; the closer to the podestà the greater the prestige. Some folk follow the procession into the church while others content themselves with awaiting its return to the *campo*. The ceremony, then, acts as a discourse that becomes reality, and functions as a prescriptor of social order.

The folk who come to take part in the *intrar* know that, in the ritual, the Venetian patricians are the principal actors. According to old usage, some of them accompany the two rectors, both the one leaving and the one stepping in. As Marino Sanudo reports a few years later, in January 1525, "Messer Giovanni Trevisan di Vincenzo made his entry as podestà of Murano, dressed in crimson velvet, with many companions and kinfolk dressed in scarlet, to the sound of drums and flutes, with Mantuan flute-players who play admirably".[5] The Serenissima is always keen to trim the outlay and tamp down the splendour of these celebrations, and it sends out strict instructions: the podestà cannot be escorted by more than six patricians, and only women from their own families are allowed. No musicians, no buffoons, and keep those banquets simple![6]

27 January 1511: no mention of flutes or players, but many patricians, friends, and kinsmen turn up for the spectacle. Those who own a palace at Murano also come, to show support to the two podestà. They wait in clutches, on the *campo* or with Vitturi under the loggia. They do not belong to Murano's society, but they participate that day in its thoroughly fashioned order. Easily recognizable, thanks to their dress and headgear, the nobles inhabit their social superiority, their body language, their fashion of speech, and their social skills. Murano's *cittadini*, who dominate the island hierarchy, are also richly dressed, but to a cut remarkably different from that of the patricians. They can enter the church with them to see the passing of the baton of command – it is a mark of rank. All around the church, in front of the palace of the podestà, along the canal, on the bridge that spans it, swarm the other inhabitants, chatting with friends, neighbours, and acquaintances, waiting for Suriano to come.

Each inhabitant on the *campo* sees, after his own fashion, the visual discourse the ritual puts on display. The depositions taken by the *avogadori di Comun*, in February and March, betray two contrasting versions: the patricians' on the one hand, the islanders' on the other.[7] The four patricians called to court mention "those who were in the campanile", "a multitude of people", "these Muranesi, that is children, youths, and certain vulgar persons", "these plebeians", "those who work in the furnaces", "the crowd" (*la brigata*), assorted vague expressions to designate the *popolo* and the common folk. Inside this vast group, they nuance not at all.

The denizens of Murano, before the judges, are far more precise. There was a great crowd, "all the *popolo* of Murano", "the whole *terra*", certainly, but they distinguish between the glassworks owners, the glassworkers and the fire-lighters, the fishermen and the gardeners, the physicians, and the sellers of fruit and vegetables. And there are many children and youth – *puti* and *fantolin*, small children and a "*zovenastro*" or adolescent. Some are from Murano, but one is from Friuli, another from Venice. There are quite a few *cittadini*, and some "gentlemen", and even most of the island's magistrates and officials.

Where the patricians could do no more than gesture at a few indistinguishable plebeians, the inhabitants of Murano are well able to recognize and name a complex, dense social world, crosscut by hierarchies and distinctions. For the nobles, it suffices to know that the *popolo* is present – this faceless crowd, this nameless *hoi poloi* who look just like all the others, who enjoy no official station and work with their hands to make a living. The patricians' testimony reflects their indifference towards the persons of the *popolo*, in distinct bad odour for their reputed rough ways and brawls.

But for the inhabitants of the island, the categories *popolo* and plebeian have no great sense; they are in no way useful. In their practices and daily interactions, the locals recognize handily the many social distinctions that crosscut their world. They mingle readily, work side by side, trade rumours and opinions, but they also pass judgement, assaying others, thanks to how they talk, dress, and act. They gauge accents, spot place of origin, size up wealth, measure competences and professional reputations, reckon influence, and sniff out the resilience of networks. On the *campo* on 27 January 1511, the people know who they are, what is their position in Murano society and, accordingly, what should be their place at the ritual of power's passage.

The "plebeians" indicated by the patrician witnesses would swiftly vanish if we walked the Fondamenta dei Vetrai, ducked into the back rooms of glassmakers' shops or the fields of the island's north, or strolled among the gawkers who stand waiting for the passage of power to begin. A multitude of categories, of hierarchies, of distinctions would spring forth, the very ones the commoner witnesses, implicitly, pointed out: the glassmakers, the fishermen, the market gardeners, the peasants, the artisans, the women, and the men, but also, more subtly, the masters and the apprentices, the bosses and the labour force, the heirs and the widows, the old and the young, the talented artisans and the needy workmen, the natives and the foreigners, the Bergamaschi and the Cypriots, the glassblowers and the fire-lighters, the rich furnace owners and the ragged beggars, the imbeciles and the rascals, the respectable wives and the wives of shaky virtue, the servants of solid families and those of more modest households. To speak of the *popolo* of Murano is thus not to talk about the poor, any more than a reference to the common folk conjures up those marginal or destitute. The diversity of professional activities and incomes signals internal hierarchies. In Italian towns and villages, the countless trades and professions, and the many social and legal standings shape a complex societal world, and the schema: rich/poor does its description little justice. True enough, nobles and bourgeois dominate European societies. For all that, the "people" is no homogenous group neatly and fully defined by its subjection to the elite. The hierarchies, distinctions, and power relations inside the people produce multiple, fluid categories that keep shifting in response to all interactions afoot.

In the lagoon of Venice, as elsewhere, in their everyday relations, at the shop or at home, in the street or inn, the inhabitants elaborate a discourse about the social order. They elaborate and choose the terms that let them designate and name one another. These words reflect a collective capacity to describe the professional, social and political hierarchies, and also to pass judgment on the world, to point out what is moral and immoral, good and bad, just and unjust. These categories reflect no pre-existent realities. They are not primordial social data, that men and women handily dip into when labelling society. The words that serve to name the groups and hierarchies, the trades and professional arts all emerge from the everyday action of the people involved. That is how a society becomes complexly dense; the inhabitants formulate criteria of distinction and designate the differences between one another. Because the elites seldom designate the inhabitants, save via general terms like "the people" or "the plebeians", negotiation over social categories falls first to the inhabitants and *popolani* themselves. The oft-unspoken collective labour that gives rise to categories is a thing to take seriously, as it is there that emerge the social realities that enable social change and evolution.

At Murano, the glass trade gives rise to a vocabulary based on rank and prestige (owner of a glassworks, master, *cittadino*), and on the industry's internal social hierarchy (master, worker, *serventino*, apprentice, *garzone*, domestic servant, foreigner, Bergamasco, Dalmatian); this nomenclature is also influenced by technical competence and *savoir faire* (master, glass blower, *conzador*, fire-lighter). The production of these categories, and their everyday use, permit Murano's society to build and organize itself in alignment with a multitude of nuances that give it shape. One can see this as a kind of political competence, or, at least, of collective savviness: the shared elaboration of a kind of "social knowledge" is what endows the societies of the Old Regime with their rich complexity. Behind the most visible hierarchies, laid out by the elites and deployed neatly in treatises on politics, lies the tangle of all those others, spun and knotted day by day, that organize the world of ordinary people.

## Chase off this dog that has ruined Muran!

Like the judges of the Avogaria di Comun, we first hear the tale of the Snowball Revolt from the ten inhabitants who are willing to testify. On 29 January 1511, the *avogadori di Comun* order the podestà to gather potential witnesses.[8] A few days later, they send one of their officials, Simone, to question them about what they saw and heard, about the identity of the guilty, and about the reasons for the hostility to Vitturi.[9]

Ten inhabitants are given a hearing; six of them belong to the glass industry: Nicolo de Blasio, *cittadino* of Murano, owner of a furnace and of the shop "At the Eagle"[10]; Domenico de Andrico, glassworker; Pietro Zorzi, alias Cortiner, master glassblower; Gasparo Furlan and Angelo Zeloxo d'Antonio, who work in the shop of Nicolo de Blasio; and finally Vincenzo da Murano, fire-lighter and glassmaker. Also testifying are Domenico Rizo, a physician[11] and Zuan Rizo, his son, Domenico Bertoluso da Murano and Tommaso Paliaga, a Venetian citizen who lives on the island. Among them, many have institutional functions: Domenico Bertoluso and Domenico Rizo are judges, Pietro Zorzi oversees the grain storage warehouse; Zuan Rizo is the chamberlain.

The ten witnesses tell how, several days before the ceremony, tension had already begun to mount. The times are hard and have been since the northeast of the Italian peninsula became the battlefield of the Italian Wars. Tommaso Paliaga explains how, the night before the ceremony, "the children here went chanting, to call the workers in the furnaces". Running the *fondamente* under cover of darkness, they shout out as long as they please, "Let Surian come and chase this dog!" The song fills the air in the shops, and surely the streets and quays resound too with wisecracks about this "dog of a Vitturi". The Muranesi unleash their rancour already, when the podestà is still preparing to depart.

Vitale Vitturi does not return till morning from Venice, where he spent the night. Debarking, he calls on the chancellor, with Zuan Rizo, later a witness, and then arrives at Campo Santi Maria e Donato. He waits near the palace of the podestà, looking out over the canal bank where his successor will debark. The electric atmosphere has everyone on guard. Crier Antonio Malcanton does his best to keep the peace among the children, while, already, they have started to heap snow in the palms of their hands and sing the notorious refrain. Some men slip through the door of the bell tower and climb the bad ladder up the fifty or so metres to the top. There were more than thirty, according to Nicolo de Blasio, but, given the tight spot at the top of the *campanile*, that number seems unlikely. They are carrying snow in their jackets. From on high, they tower over the whole *campo* and a goodly part of the island and so can keep an eye on the new podestà's arrival.

At last, there he is! Vitturi and the five magistrates of the *banco* leave the loggia and head toward the embankment where the *barcaruoli* are mooring the patrician's gondola. For a bit, the excitement certainly abates. Through the crowd gallops the rumour: the new podestà is here. On tip-toes, folk crane their necks to see him; there is shushing; one can hear the crier's words. "Many gentlemen and citizens of Murano" join the file that heads towards the church portal, careful lest they slip on paving stones covered by frozen snow.

The procession goes into Santi Maria e Donato. Before the altar, Vitturi consigns to Suriano the baton of command (*bacchetta*). The ritual unfolds with all the fussy precision that marks ceremonials of power. Once the new podestà has been installed, it falls to him to lead the procession out of the church, behind the crier, who clears the way. The ritual requires the new podestà to accompany the old one all the way to the craft that will spirit him back to Venice. Endowed with public authority, he can now preside solemnly over his predecessor's departure.

But at the moment that the two podestà leave the church and appear on the *campo*, a volley of snowballs hurtles onto them. From the campanile, the men can see their companions below, and the procession too. They take the bell and ring it. The noise grows deafening. Snow flies everywhere. Laughter, cries, songs, and wisecracks fill the air. "Surian, Surian, chase off this dog who has eaten our bread!"; "Chase away this Vitturi who has destroyed us"; and other "insulting words". The chant in its assorted versions plays with the rhymes: *Surian, Muran, can, pan* (Suriano, Murano, dog, bread) – in the nasal Venetian accent they go down well. The children are the first to amuse themselves with the verses, but "other persons" join the chorus. The cries are so loud, says Nicolo de Blasio, that "the persons who were there were dumbstruck". Then the attack redoubles. The air is saturated with snowballs "more than a hundred" if we are to believe Domenico de Andrico. The snow was "storming" or "raining", say other witnesses. The judicial official, Simone, then asks some of his witnesses, "Who were the people who *ballottavano* the snow that way?" He uses the verb *ballottare*, to "ball", a word ordinary applied to drawing political lots or voting, with little balls in the Venetian mode.

According to the witnesses, the men up the tower target deliberately Vitale Vitturi, who heads as fast as he can towards his boat, while a group of young men comes towards the bankside crying "Surian, chase this dog!" "Each doing his level best" the men atop the tower attack those down in the *campo*. Vitturi embarks, but the easy mark is just too tempting, so now it is the gondola's turn to be targeted. The podestà is constrained to put up the *felze*, a canopy that serves to shelter the crew from storms. Asked to specify at whom the snow was aimed, and if the podestà was hit, the witnesses hesitate. Angelo Zeloxo: "they were throwing snowballs at him, but I don't know if any touched him, even though it is true that I saw snow on his shoulder". Domenico Rizo knows nothing about it but says that he himself had been struck on the arm.

Domenico de Andrico refused to ride back with the podestà:

> And when Messer Vitale went on board to leave, many snowballs came toward him and towards his boat, from the bell tower. And I wanted to go aboard, to accompany him to Venice, as is the custom. But, afraid that it would capsize and sink, on account of the great tumult that was afoot, and on account of the snow coming from the bell tower . . . I stayed on the shore.

Domenico Rizo showed more courage. As judge, he was part of the crew, as was Domenico Bertoluso. "Two or three nephews" of Vitturi are also there. The canopy protects them from the snowballs: a number hit them, says the former, but, according to the latter, only a single ball lands on the *felze*. Pietro Zorzi is formal: "and I saw, on the cloak of Messire Vitale, when he left, a spot of snow".

It is with a meagre escort and even less glory that Vitale Vitturi quits Murano, an island where he probably never again sets foot. But he dodges an even harsher attack, to believe Pietro Zorzi: "And I also heard it said by the shop-lads [*garzoni*], but I don't know who they are, that if he had departed via the Rio dei Vetrai, there would have been a ruckus [*strido*]". A child would have needed only minutes to run from the *campo* where the snowball battle started and reach the Rio's shops to alert the master artisans, blocked by the furnaces, about what was afoot in front of Santi Maria e Donato. They would then have been able to gird themselves to receive Vitturi. By "choosing to leave by way of the Lagoon and the San Michele channel, the podestà avoids the Rio, and new harassment, via glassworkers" projectiles and jeers.

How to brand this event? What really happened on Campo Santi Maria e Donato that early afternoon of Monday 27 January 1511? Have the Muranesi fomented one of the rare revolts in the history of the Republic of Venice, or was podestà Vitturi just the unlucky victim of Muranese pugnacity?

The violence of the action remains limited, its message that accompanies it has short arms, the disorders that follow it are just sporadic. It is, for sure, a "little" event, in comparison with the more spectacular uprisings and bloody revolts that surface in the same epoch in Italy and in Europe. A month later, a hundred kilometres from Venice, there explodes a revolt of unheard of violence, the Cruel Mardi Gras (*Crudel Zobia grassa*). At Udine, in Friuli, on 27 February 1511, popular discontent and conflict among noble factions end in bloodbath, and then in turn the Republic of Venice decrees many death sentences to punish the guilty parties. In March, in the region, there ensues one of the most significant peasant revolts in the history of Renaissance Italy.[12] At the same time, Dalmatia, the eastern Adriatic zone of Venice's empire, is also the theatre of several popular revolts against local nobilities. The inhabitants take advantage of the temporary weakness of Venetian oversight to hamstring a political order that has lasted centuries.[13] This happens at Šibenik (Sibenico) in December 1510 and at Bar (Antivari) in 1512, in the Adriatic coast. In northern Italy too, the Wars feed all sorts of clashes, and the Snowball Revolt belongs in their ranks. It should lodge in this ensemble of demonstrations of hostility, and protests. Different in their forms and goals, these events have in common their origin in collective action and their reliance on a discourse of defiance that almost never targets the Venetian patriciate as a whole.

The *intrar* of 1511, in comparison with events of its time, is a dulcet, limited protest, in no way comparable with the brutality and violence elsewhere. But the act of the Muranesi, all the same, is a potential menace against Venetian power. The trial held over the next weeks is proof that the patricians are by no means indifferent. For they all know that the times are tough and that, in the tense international scene, it is wise to contain, among the Republic's citizens, any stab at sedition.

## Notes

1 ASVe, Formulari, reg. 7, 6v, 1425, quoted by Ermanno Orlando, *Altre Venezie. Il dogado veneziano nei secoli XIII e XIV (giurisdizione, territorio, giustizia e amministrazione)* (Venice: Istituto Veneto di Scienze Lettere ed Arti, 2008), 158.
2 Crouzet-Pavan, "Murano", 85–7.
3 ASVe, PM, 229, 2, Cassa fontico di Murano, book 1, fol. 19, for 15 October 1510; 7 May 1510. See also ASVe, PM, 229, 3, fol. 3v, 25 October 1509; 8 May 1509.
4 Marino Sanudo, *I Diarii*, vol. 38, col. 271, 8 May 1525.
5 Marino Sanudo, *I Diarii*, vol. 40, col. 671, 16 January 1525.
6 ASVe, Collegio, Formulari di commissioni, reg. 8, no date (end of the 1540s), fol. 123r-v.
7 ASVe, AC, MP, 142, no.17.
8 ASVe, Capi del consiglio de' Dieci, Lettere di rettori e di altre cariche, busta 78, no. 20, letter of Giacomo Suriano, 15 February 1511.
9 ASVe, AC, MP, 142, no. 17, fol. 1–6.
10 ASVe, PM, 43, Criminalium 4, 30 July 1509. Zecchin, *Vetro e vetrai di Murano*, vol. 2, 176–81.
11 Sometimes this person appears not as a physician but as a *chirurgus* or *aromatarius*: ASVe, PM, 44, 19 Criminalium 1, for 9 September 1509, against Sebastiano *famulo* of Domenico Rizo *aromatario*.
12 Edward Muir, *Mad blood stirring. Vendetta and factions in Friuli during the Renaissance* (Baltimore, MD and London: Johns Hopkins University Press, 1993), 111–88.
13 Angelo Ventura, *Nobiltà e popolo nella società veneta del Quattrocento e Cinquecento* (Bari: Laterza, 1964), 167ff.

# 4 The revolt in its time

The Passage of Power does not last long; it is a brief moment, saturated with deeds and words, during which the situation totters, as does the fate of many inhabitants of Murano. But the event's swift passage is ensconced in a longer time, that of the conjuncture of things happening – with the Italian Wars and Carnival, as well as the hard winter in Italy that year, and Vitale Vitturi's particular career. From the vagaries of the weather to the personality of the podestà, many external forces influence the course of events in their own way and clarify the ritual of 27 January 1511.

## Italy at war

Giacomo Suriano's entry into office takes place in a difficult period for Venice, the Wars of Italy, a train of conflicts and truces that bestrides the Italian peninsula. They begin in 1494, when the King of France stakes claims to the Duchy of Milan and the Kingdom of Naples. They roll on for some sixty years, while the hegemonic ambitions of European powers unleash, one after another, alliances and wars between the kingdoms of France, England, Aragon, and Naples, and the Holy Roman Empire, the Papal States, the Republic of Venice, the city states of Florence, Pisa, and Siena, and the Duchy of Milan.

From 1508, the Serenissima faces a new coalition, including the King of France Louis XII, the German Emperor Maximilian I, Ferdinand II of Aragon, plus Pope Julius II, bound together as the League of Cambrai, to attack Venice's possessions. On 14 May 1509, at Agnadello, near Milan, Venice suffers a resounding defeat that leaves its territorial positions in utter peril. After the retreat of the *condottieri* in the Republic's pay, a great part of its mainland falls under occupation. The territories of Verona, Vicenza and Padua pass under the control of Imperial and French armies, and the Lagoon comes under direct threat. An enemy at the gates of Venice: nothing of the sort has happened since the wars against Genoa in the 1380s. The occupation of the territories upsets the political equilibria of the Terra Ferma. Some local elites rally to the new occupiers, seeing a chance to shake off Venice's tutelage, but the majority of the Republic's subjects remain faithful to the Signoria, defying the nobles, who to their eyes stand for their political and social subjection.

From Summer 1509 on, military operations to retake the lost territories mobilize both the Republic's regime and its subjects, who are called up to serve in the Venetian army. Like most Italian city states, in normal times, Venice has recourse to *condottieri*, mercenaries fighting for hire at the head of their companies. In an emergency, the people are mobilized, atop the volunteer contingent. But the inhabitants of Venice and Murano are no soldiers; rather, according to the patrician Girolamo Priuli, "they were peaceful people who had grown up without war and without arms, very little suited to military action; men of trades, who worked and lived from the labour of their hands, and did not willingly abandon their craft".[1] This is the cause, he thinks, for their mediocre feats of arms.

In July 1509, just before Vitturi takes up his mandate, the Captain General of the Venetian army, the future doge Andrea Gritti, starts a reconquest of the Terra Ferma, with cavalry and infantry. For the occasion, Venice's government tries to set up a system of conscription, calling on the inhabitants of Venice and the Lagoon to serve the armed forces.[2] The podestà of Torcello and Murano are summoned to the Arsenale with all boats they can collect, each vessel with eight men aboard.[3] A month later, *provveditore* Pietro Marcello, in charge of military operations, finds himself at Treviso. He calls for reinforcements. The three podestà of Torcello, Murano, and Malamocco are sent to him with a thousand men, and such orders will recur many times.[4] Vitale Vitturi, like Pietro Morosini before him, has the delicate task of finding watercraft, mustering crews, and gathering the money needed to finance the war.

While Venice pays for the provisions and armament, it falls to the community to furnish the boats and men. The vessels arrive at the Terra Ferma, going up the valleys of the rivers Po, Brenta, and Sile. Venice wraps its commands in persuasive rhetoric, and Antonio Malcanton furnishes the voice. It falls to him to justify the mobilizations, and, on his rounds, he must not only publish the decisions of the Signoria, and of Vitturi, but also discuss them with the inhabitants, explain why they are necessary, and proffer a legitimating discourse to render them palatable. In January 1510, he announces publicly on the town's bridges that, "in execution of the letters of our most illustrious Signoria of Venice, we make known to every boat-owner of Murano and of its district, that he must come with his boat to the aforesaid podestà".[5] This call falls on all the men between twenty and fifty, who, if they refuse, incur heavy penalties: a fine of one hundred *lire*, two hoists on the *strappado* rope, and two months of prison. One year later, at the beginning of January 1511, just before the Snowball Revolt, all the men between eighteen and fifty, "glassworkers as well as fishermen, and the other inhabitants of this land of Murano, of whatever condition", must present themselves at the palace of the podestà at the sound of the bell, as must all the owners of boats.[6] At Sant'Erasmo, in September 1509, it is a list of horses, mares, and male and female mules, to be compiled at the request of the podestà.[7]

The boatmen are the first to be mobilized, but other inhabitants serve alongside. In May 1509, podestà Pietro Morosini has fifteen sailing ships fitted out, with a crew of almost ninety men – domestic servants, peasants, and labourers – and their names show the diversity of their trades and origins: Zorzi Caleger (shoe-maker), Vincenzo Griego (the Greek), Bernardin Torcellan (from Torcello), Battista Veronese (from Verona), Zuan Socha *verier* (glassmaker), Zorzi di Sibenico (from Šibenik).[8] In May 1510, Vitturi mobilizes twelve barks and more than seventy men, many of whom must be replaced at the last minute when they fail to show up for duty.[9] One finds the same cosmopolitan mix of names: Pietro da Santa Maria d'Antivari (from Bar), Simon Veronese, Francesco Padoan, Zuan Cremonese, Vincenzo Griego, Luca Schiavon (the Slavonian), Martin Saraxin, Francesco da Rovigo, Antonio da Castelfranco, and also many members of glassmaker families, including Zaneto Nason, Sebastiano Toso, Pietro Bigaia, and Andrea dall'Aqua. The final two are among the six Muranesi accused of having led the Snowball Revolt, and we shall return to them. Three days before the revolt, the *provveditori* of the fleet once more ask Vitturi to mobilize the ship-owners; he convokes seven: Pasqualin dall'Aqua, Donno Trevisan, Agostino dal Magazen, Bernardin Duro, Bartolomeo Gabano, Domenico da Caodistria, and Jacopo Griego.[10]

Of course, in this time of conflict, fiscal levies grow heavier. Normally, the Muranesi shunt toward Venice a part of the take from taxes and levies that fall on artisanal production and commercial transactions. Venice's fiscal system rests principally on indirect taxes; only the nobles and the very rich are subject to direct taxation and forced public loans. The *popolo*: artisans, workers, and domestic servants, on Murano as at Venice, pay no head tax, but fall under all sorts of other imposts. The merchandise that enters and leaves the Lagoon also pays duty, as commerce supports the state's budget. To finance the war, the Serenissima jacks up the levies and imposes on the population exceptional outlays, in the form of taxes or public loans that the state will pay back with interest, when at last peace comes.

In February 1510, Vitturi boasts to the Venetian magistrates of the efforts the Muranesi had shouldered to do their duty. "In reality, those who have not done so, I think it is impossible that they can satisfy the requirement, for some of them barely have anything to live on".[11] So, in May 1510, more than 150 inhabitants come before Vitturi. Among them are of course the owners of furnaces and members of the Thirty, including Nicolo and Angelo Barovier, Gasparo Capello, Vettor Blondo, Tommaso Dracan, Andrea Grasetto, Nicolo de Blasio and Jacopo Corona, but also Polo Forner, a fisherman, Alvise a miller, Marco a baker, Matteo a carpenter, Filippo a barber, Marco a dyer, Alesio a "maestro who works vineyards", the fruit and vegetable seller Zuan Rosso, and a woman called

Mantuana, a fruit-seller too (*fructaruola*), plus the innkeeper Pietro Amado, Maria Plavesana, and many members of the families Fuga, Bellencito, dall'Aqua and Bigaia, names we will find again in the trial after the Snowball Revolt.[12]

Still, the situation remains delicate. At the end of December 1510, little before the end of his mandate, Vitturi summons the Thirty to review the fiscal situation.[13] "It is manifest to everyone that the fiscal revenues of this excellent community of Murano are weak and insufficient for the the least part of its present poverty and needs." The citizens and residents have had to pay many taxes, not only to support

> the public needs of our most illustrious Signoria, as for the fitting out of ships and other necessary things, as well as the particular needs of this community ... And that has gone not without protest (*mormoratione*), and, presently, with infinite lamentation on the part of many poor folk, widows, children under guardianship and other suffering persons.

There follows a complex regulation that sets the rules for raising new taxes on the flour stored in the Fondego (warehouse), and setting out how the money is to be spent. The vote is very much split, a sign of discord, rather rare in the deliberations of the Thirty, a body generally prone to consensus.

On 27 January 1511, when anger rises against the man who has "ruined Murano" or "destroyed Murano's poverty", it is an indignant echo of the pressure recently inflicted on the inhabitants. Nevertheless, that does not suffice to explain what happens on that day, for the mobilizations and fiscal levies will continue to 1516 at least, without, it seems, stirring up new protests.[14] Vitturi is facing a complex situation, which the nearness of the enemy and the sharp danger render even more delicate.

## Noise of conflict

The War of the League of Cambrai is playing out in the Lagoon's immediate environs. Between 1509 and 1511, the countryside of Padua and the Veneto, a few kilometres from Venice and Murano, are the theatre of operations. Day after day, the conflict makes itself both heard and seen: from the thunder of artillery to the glare of fires, and from the numerous refugees to the actions of public officials. Murano lies in a forward position, as it is very close to the Terra Ferma, and it is quick and easy to go from there to Mestre, Campalto, and Tessera, the villages and ports that line the Lagoon's landward shore. Several months after Vitturi's departure, in October 1511, a peasant from the territory of Treviso, Antonio Vicentin, comes before the avodagori di Comun to lodge a formal complaint against the *cavalier* of Murano, its police officer.[15] Antonio explains that he had stored some sacks of wheat at Campalto, under the surveillance of his nephew Bastian, who fled at the approach of troops. Witnesses tell how, after the arrival of "enemies" and Frenchmen at Campalto and Tessera, "the whole world departed".[16] The cavalier of Murano and his officers take advantage of the fact to row all the way to Campalto to lay hands on the abandoned goods: a pig, a goose, and many sacks of grain. In contempt of their public mission, they try to take advantage of the fear and confusion provoked by the war.

Vitale Vitturi, Giacomo Suriano, and then Agostino Suriano keep watch on the comings and goings of the ships, to prevent smuggling and to keep an eye on the movements of soldiers and other outsiders in the Lagoon. Suspicious movements are supposed to be subject to a report to the Venetian authorities. In October 1511, two soldiers arrested by the podestà of Murano on Lio Maggiore, in the north-east of the Lagoon, Joachin dal Borgo and Hercules da Foligno, say that they have been part of the company of the *condottiere* Damian di Tarsia, and claim to have escaped the enemy's clutches.[17]

Soldiers are not the only ones to find their way into the Lagoon; many subjects of the Republic take refuge there to escape the fighting. Peasants flood in after the defeat of Agnadello, in May 1509, and continue to arrive for the entire succeeding decade. In August 1509, the chronicler Girolamo Priuli explains that "continually a great number of persons entered the city [Venice], that is to say, peasants from the territories round about, and that was because they were all fleeing the enemy's rage and violence, and feared dying, being robbed, and put to sack".[18] On September 11, Sanudo recounts that "all night long, peasants male and female (*villani et villane*), with children and their goods, arrived in Venice, fleeing the persecutions of the enemies, and they lodged in different places".[19] A month later, Benevenuta and Anzola come before Vitturi accompanied by their "poor family, burdened with children, who escaped on account of what is happening in the region of Treviso".[20] In the Lagoon, from 1510 to 1530, the temporary or permanent settlement of Terra Ferma residents fleeing the fighting shifts social equilibria and provokes tensions. New antagonisms surface, revealing the complexity of identities and of popular status arrangements in the Venetian state.

The affair of the German bakers of the Rio dei Vetrai, in October 1509, is a good example.[21] Several weeks into his term of office, the podestà receives the legal complaint of a glassmaker on the island, Bernardin da Mestre. He denounces Zane, the servant of maestro Nicolo, the German baker who keeps his shop near the Ponte de Mezo. The complaint also names Ambrosio and Maddalena, the baker's son and wife. Two peasants hailing from the region of Padua coming to Murano to deliver wood, Menego di Michele and Antonio Gebellato, have launched the complaint – as the former tells it:

We were leaning, on the bridge, in Rio, in front of the house of Nicolo the baker, where our boats were in the canal, with wood to sell. And so, on the bridge, we saw the servant (*fante*), whose name is Zane, who is in jail. With a knife, he was cutting, and peeling, above he door of the house of Mastro Nicolo, the image of Messer San Marco. [That is, an image of the saint, printed or drawn on a piece of paper]. And he was reprimanded by some people – I don't know who – and I went too, with my companion: so that he stopped. And he went into the house. So there I was in front of Mastro Nicolo's house, and I said to his wife, who was there, where they kept the bread: "Oh what a fine thing, that you let them peel off the figure of messer San Marco" And so this wife of Maestro Nicolo, mistress of the aforesaid Zane, began to say bad things at me: "Oaf, rascal, may you catch the plague!" And I said to her, "May you get cancer, and you will see – if I accuse you, some ill will befall you". And she answered me, "Beat it! Go denounce me, may you get the plague, boor, peasant". And I answered her, "German *manza sanza*, may you get cancer, you who cannot live except under the shadow of Saint Mark, and you dare do a thing like this!"

Menego and Antonio are two subjects of the Venetian territorial state, and they live in a zone then occupied by English soldiers. As for Nicolo and Maddalena, they have lived in the Lagoon for 22 years, first at Venice, and then at Murano for the past five years. Many Germans live in Venice – merchants, clerks, go-betweens, and translators at the Fondaco dei Tedeschi, bakers, printers, and bath-house keepers. Like many in the Lagoon, they are born elsewhere, but are immigrants to the cosmopolitan city, who swell worker and servant ranks. The very notion of foreigner, *forestier*, is a complex one; place of birth counts less than official residence in town. One can be born elsewhere but still take part in urban institutions, practice a trade, join a parish, pay taxes: all these are more telling measures than is foreign origin.

Amidst the Italian Wars, the bakers' German origin sparks hostility. After Agnadello, the troops of Maximilian I, the German Emperor, have occupied the Venetian Terra Ferma between May and July 1509. That is when, for Maddalena, the trouble began, so she tells the podestà. First, she apologizes:

I don't understand very well the Italian language (*lengua taliana*). If you ask me about my servant, I will tell you that, before the Signoria retook Padua [July 1509], they put a San Marco above the door of our house, to be mean, and we left it, saying "Let's leave it alone". Then last Wednesday, in the evening, they put another one, across from it. And in the morning, a fair number of children gathered, on a boat, and they were shouting and saying, "These rebels are selling San Marco". And when I went to buy water I heard the children's shouts. I don't

know if it was the servant or my son who said "Take down this San
Marco, that has been put there to show us scorn" . . . And then there
came some peasants, who began to say rude things, and they said to
me, with all due respect [i.e., forgive my language here], "fat-ass oaf",
"*manza sanza*"!

During the War of the League of Cambrai, the Venetian territories that
fell to the enemy or returned into the Venetian sphere saw the proliferation
of these images of Saint Mark in urban spaces, signs of resistance to the
occupation or of attachment to the Serenissima. As Marino Sanudo tells it,
in July 1509 "at Padua I saw many houses with Saint Mark banners on
their balconies, and paper San Marcos on the doors and stores".[22]
At Murano, the image serves to reproach the origin of these bakers, whom
the Muranesi frequent as ever, but still see as potential enemies. The son of
Nicolo and Maddalena, Ambrogio, also says that he has been the butt
of insults. Children laughed at him when they saw the images at his shop.
"The bakers don't sell bread; they sell Saint Mark"; "The rebels want to
sell Saint Mark!" they yelled at him. Another witness, the glassworker
Girolamo Pisani, reports that at first Maddalena was up for the sport, firing
back at the children: "A little Saint Mark is enough for me and I don't want
the big one, which was put up to scorn us, and we too are on Saint Mark's
side (*semo marcheschi anche nui*). I don't want more than one. . . ." That
is why she bade her servant take the other one down. The servant, who has
recently come from Germany, does not know "the Latin language", as the
trial papers spell it out, and before the judges of the Avogaria di Comun,
he is assisted by a translator. Perhaps he has failed to understand the
underlying stakes of what he did. But his master knows well what lies in
store for him once the events have ended. When his son comes back to the
shop after tearing down the image still up on the wall, the father tells him,
"In the devil's name, why didn't you leave this Saint Mark alone?" Their
doings avail them imprisonment and fines, "to set an example", but then
the podestà reduces the sentence.

This affair distils the social connections, belongings and identities in play
at a critical juncture. The two peasants from the Terra Ferma, like their
compatriots who fought to liberate the Paduan and Treviso countryside,
desire to flaunt their fidelity to the Signoria by pointing out bad apples
among the locals who fail to respect Saint Mark and Venice. Others
doubtless simply enjoy watching the comedy play out, or cash in on the
affair to settle old accounts or neighbourhood spats by accusing the bakers
of sullying the Republic's honour. Maddalena and Nicolo protest in self-
defence that they had never desired such a thing: "*semo marcheschi*" –
partisans of Venice, says the baker's wife. The saint's banner and his image
allow her to identify herself symbolically with Venice. Identities and
attachments are mobile, shifting with the situation, the context, and the
stakes. The Muranesi can oppose Venice when conditions warrant, but, all

the while, when enemy troops threaten the Lagoon they flaunt their loyalty to the Serenissima.

The war is not just an affair of *provveditori* and combatants; it is also a matter for the inhabitants, who must live with their fears and worries, and affirm their loyalty and stance. The subjects of the Venetian Terra Ferma, like those of the old original Duchy, whether peasants, glassworkers, or bakers, talk and fret about the war. All throughout the conflict, the Muranesi also paid in person, some heading off to serve the Republic, returning wounded, or, doubtless, even left dead, though the archives, in this matter, remain mute. Some glassworkers are accused of going off to find work elsewhere, a thing formally forbidden in the Statutes of the trade, which aim to keep privy the secrets of the art, everywhere except at Murano. Polo Ducato therefore has to explain, in Vitturi's presence in November 1510: "Me, I have not worked in the glass craft in any other place and any land, ever, at any moment, except at Murano. And in the days just past, I was on the field [of battle], in the service of the most illustrious Signoria, under the command of Messer Lasanrio [Lattanzio da Bergamo] and other *condottieri*".[23]

Moreover, with the conflict so close, it is far harder to keep a good eye on the Lagoon, and on the movements of unwelcome strangers, especially soldiers, who go armed.[24] On 21 June 1510, Antonio Malcanton proclaims at three places on the island Vitturi's decision on the matter; the day before, serious disorders had set the Rio dei Vetrai on edge.[25]

> Let it be known to any person, of whatever condition, whether from this land, or foreign born and outsider (*si teriera come alienigena et forestiera*), living in this place of Murano or passing through. Considering the troubles that have happened in this town on account of assorted persons of ill will (*maligna sorte*), who, without any respect for the orders, proclamations and laws, have carried arms and committed assorted crimes, damages, and harm to many persons, against the honour of our authority (*regimento*)

... the bearing of arms at Murano is henceforth forbidden. The penalties are to be severe: fines, prison, and the rope.

Indeed, just the day before, Vitturi has received, in court, many residents who testify to the chaos that very day at the end of the Rio, at The Angel, the shop of Zuan Ballarin.[26] The fifteen witnesses sketch out for us the shape of Rio social life: many glassworkers from assorted shops (among them Domenico Pisani, painter on glass in the shop of Zuan Ballarin, and Abraam, Zuan's *fattor*; Stefano Barovier, the furnace-owner, brother to Nicolo; Pietro Bresciano, fire-lighter with Angelo Barovier; Zuan Tamburlini, a worker at The Rooster). Also, Alvise da Venezia, who makes glasses (*iocularius*), Martin Saraxin, who loads wood, Salvator di Martin a fruit-seller on the Rio; Zuan d'antivari, a boatman from the Santo Stefano parish, who at the time in question was aboard his sailboat (*fisolera*), fishing in the Rio dei Vetrai in front of Ballarin's shop.

All witnesses lay the blame on five men stemming from Vicenza, friends and kinsmen who come to Murano for their pleasure: Vincenzo and Sebastiano di Bernardo da Seledo, "*cittadino* of Vicenza", who live at the Fondaco dei Tedeschi; Francesco and Battista dal Sal, who live near the Aseo bridge in Cannaregio, a northern quarter of Venice; Nicolo de Forno from Vicenza. Here is how their story goes. They stroll the Rialto; they hail Simon Padoan, *traghetto* gondolier, and ask him to row them to the glassmakers' island. Aboard the ferry is Zuan, a servant of Alvise Soranzo di Vittore, patrician, whom his master ordered to accompany the others. The men go to the wine-warehouse of Murano, where they drink glasses in fair number, eating bread and cakes bought from the island's baker and pastry-maker. They then make their way along the Fondamenta dei Vetrai, stopping first at Salvator, fruit and vegetable seller, to buy some shallots. Salvator's mother and wife are minding the shop, and the men cross assorted lines, asking if the younger woman is married and railing at her mother-in-law: "Give her to me!" In front of the shop of The Rooster, they insult the employee when he asks them, "Do you desire anything, sirs?" Then they buy oysters from a young seller on the quay, and sit on a nearby box to eat them. But they refuse to pay and when the lad insists they slap him. Still asking for his due, the youngster then bursts into tears.

This scene takes place in late afternoon, before the workshop called The Angel. Battista da Brescia, *conzador* (he mixes the chemicals for molten glass), sorties from the shop to insist the men pay "this poor child" as, "they are not his oysters, but his master's" and the youngster will be beaten if he comes back empty-handed. To the podestà, Battista explains his action: "and I, seeing that the little fellow was poor, felt compassion." According to many witnesses, the Vicentini then make for the shop, saying vile things and blaspheming, "Whore Virgin Mary!" Battista heads for shelter in the shop, but, knife in hand, they chase him, bellowing "Kill! Kill!" (*Amaza! Amaza!*) and "Flesh! Flesh!" (*Carne! Carne!*). Inside, the workers shout "Arms! Arms!" to rally resistance. Some defend themselves with tools, like Abraam, who brandishes the great fork he uses for grasping glasses in the furnace. The glassworker Domenico Pisani weighs in with his sword, hoping to drive off the Vicentini. But they manage to wound Battista on head and arm, and then attack the shutter of the shop next door, forcing the big window that, when swung open, serves as a counter. Inside, an old woman from Dalmatia tries to repulse them: "Off with you, dear sons!" But they break in, and, with their swords, "with a great crash" knock down all the glass pieces on the shelves, some of them decorated and painted. Witnesses later decry the countless broken bits and shards that still litter the shop floor.

The Muranesi all agree that these men were "dressed like soldiers or foreigners, and, it is said, they are Vicentini". That is the problem: they come from a district that, a few months earlier, went over to the other side when Imperial troops came close. One of them even lives at the Fondaco dei Tedeschi; two of the five accused confirm the fact, when they come to Murano four days later, not, as one would expect, to face charges, but to reclaim the goods that the podestà's officials confiscated from their gondola after they fled the scene. They each give their own version of the story, contradicting one another and offering implausible excuses. In their version, when the *conzador* Battista came out of the shop to tell them to pay the oyster-seller, he called them "rebels". This was the term blackening traitors who backed the Holy Roman Empire's plans, and the same word used against the German bakers. Well, say the two Vicentini, "we could not bear to hear such words", whence their violent reaction. They concede that they broke some things of glass, but no great matter, and they complain, above all, to have suffered at the hands of raging Muranesi. The locals have attacked and insulted them, throwing rocks from the embankment, and forced them to flee.

A witness recounts how the Vicentini tumbled into Simon's gondola: "Row off, whore – I am ashamed to say it! – Virgin-Mary, whore of God, cunt of the Virgin Mary, cunt of God, and other such very ugly expressions." The podestà's officers give chase on their own boat, shooting arrows. Near San Michele monastery, two hundred metres south of the Rio mouth, the Vicentini decide to abandon ship. They strip in haste, dive in, and swim to the monastery, where, first, they take refuge in the *sagrado*, the holy space before the church. But the officers keep on shooting, calling them "rebels", and force them to duck inside the monastery. If they are back at Murano a few days later, it is for those goods left behind in Simon's gondola, now impounded by the officers: three cloaks, two berets in the French mode (one scarlet, one black), a sword with its scabbard, a scabbard without its sword, a handkerchief with seventeen *marcello* coins inside, plus two *barcaruolo* shirts, quite threadbare.

Both the affair of the German bakers and the case of the Vicenza soldiers show how latent tensions readily spark quarrels and fights. The residents of Murano are deeply shaken by the war and by the political events taking shape at the frontiers of the Venetian state. During Vitturi's mandate, they experience the conflict and feel the effects, both direct and indirect, of the Italian Wars. The accumulated tension will burst back out with the Snowball Revolt.

## The great cold

Power's passage takes place in a season that, in unexpected ways, helps shape how things play out. As it occurs every sixteen months, the event slips around the calendar. Suriano replaces Vitturi at the end of January, a busy time for glassmakers. Although the furnaces work night and day, for part of the year they do stop. The *cavata*, the summer halt, allows maintenance, rest, and clear-out of inventory. The podestà's commission reminds him to respect the stoppage.[27] At the beginning of the sixteenth century, one works from mid-October to the end of July, although there is room to adapt to the times, as in September 1512, for example, when the guild observes that "this year the heat has been greater than in many years in the past", and therefore, seemingly, it curbs the flow of work.[28] Power's passage also takes place on a Monday, after the sabbath rest, when the inhabitants could have gathered and discussed the pending ritual.

So, winter is a season of intense activity. And, this this year, in Europe and in Italy, it is particularly bitter.[29] Since December 1510, again and again snow has fallen on the Lagoon and Terra Ferma, encumbering Venice's institutions. On 4 January, the Collegio draws few patricians, and the next morning, a blizzard bars the Maggior Consiglio from sitting. The wind and snow go on all night long, and on the following days, many sessions, each in turn, are postponed. The bad weather hobbles military operations on the Terra Ferma, just when Pope Julius II, an ally since July 1510, arrives to battle alongside the Venetians. Troops struggle to advance; artillery lumbers clumsily across snowy ground. On 18 January 1511, one no longer sends armed vessels into the Terra Ferma, as the Po and the lesser rivers are all frozen hard. At the end of January, the wind swings around, and a somewhat milder *scirocco* brings heavy, icy rains that help melt the rivers. But then, a few days later, back come the snows.[30]

The snow was a trigger, at once a mere contingency and a real clincher; without it the protest against Vitturi might never have arisen. So, was the snowball fight premeditated? That question is one of several at stake at the trial launched by the Avogaria di Comun; they posed it to witnesses and suspects. Did the accused decide ahead of time to attack Vitturi and carry snow to the top of the campanile, as ammunition? Not an easy question for the judges: even if the weather did incline to snow, nobody could have foreseen for sure a new snowfall in the night of 26 January.

The harsh weather has its impact on the Muranesi. They were already undermined by the Lagoon's outbreaks of plague at the beginning of the sixteenth century. Between 1499 and 1506, and again from 1509, the sickness has popped up here and there, at Murano or in one or another Venetian urban quarter.[31] Frequent proclamations have forbidden inhabitants to help the sick, or to aid the plague-stricken if they seek either to hide away or to flee the Lazaretto.[32] In December 1509, Vitturi has Malcanton proclaim a decision "to provide for the health of all and to keep this land intact, without the blot and presence of illness and of plague".[33] The inhabitants are granted three days to declare to their parish priests the sick among them, and, from then on, they will have to do this the very same day. The clerics must keep a sick-list, bringing it weekly to Vitturi. A register kept by the priest of Santo Stefano, from July 1510 to August 1513, seldom mentions plague but does list all sorts of other afflictions: smallpox, diarrhoea, "worms" (i.e. again diarrhoea), fever, pustules, sea-sickness, or simply remarks "does not feel well".[34] Children and the newborn are the most often afflicted; they often die of their illness. Some periods are more intense: July 1510 for instance, when some fifty sick persons are on the parish list, or October 1510, with some thirty cases.

When it is not the plague, syphilis is what most strikes fear. Of uncertain origin, perhaps coming from America, the infection spreads across Italy just when the early sixteenth-century wars break out. Always blaming foreigners, it is called "the Neapolitan disease", "the French disease", or "the Italian disease", depending on whom and where it hits. When the disease first shows up in Europe, the visible effects are hideous: swarms of pussy sores that consume the face and body. Dona Margarita Sclabona, who resides at the Santo Stefano hospital, in November 1509 writes of the recent death of one Cristofalo Targata, "rotted by French disease".[35]

A few weeks before the revolt, the podestà and the Thirty take steps against the "epidemic of plague that at this time is propagating in this place of Murano".[36] Three citizens are elected deputy to the board of health (Sanità), the two *giustizieri* Sebastiano Bellencito and Lazaro Maroza, and Domenico de Andrico, a future witness at the trial. Antonio Malcanton announces their election that very day, 6 December 1510, and reminds hearers that these men are under the protection of the podestà. So, let it not happen, as in the past, that "certain presumptuous person block them from doing their duty".[37] "Whosoever, of whatever condition or status, will be so bold as to hinder them, or to molest them in any way, to defame them, or block them" will be condemned to a fine and the rope. At the month's end, the podestà and Thirty again deplore the number of sick persons who have surfaced at this time of plague. "Worse still, once they are dead, they have not received those things necessary to the soul, confession, and other holy sacraments, a thing horrible to hear about and see."[38] In wartime, already difficult, it would be dangerous were epidemics to heighten the precariousness of the island's situation. Inhabitants suspected of the illness are sent to the Lazaretto, confined at home, or shut away in hospitals. In December 1511, the account books of the community mention outlays for the bread "given to the poor locked away at San Salvador as suspect of having plague".[39]

## *"Semel in anno licet insanire."* "Once a year it is permissible to get crazy."

Summer or winter, in peace or war, the passage of power is always and everywhere a moment when political tension spikes. It stands among those traditional rites of change, and passage from one power to another, and, in medieval times, it often uncaged a rumpus of discontent and grievances. A power vacuum, however brief, throws wide the doors to possibilities. At Venice, an interregnum sometimes let things boil over, as in 1595, when it took more than four weeks to elect Marino Grimani, who had the backing of the *popolo*.[40] But it was at Rome, most certainly, that the regime most feared those times, after a pope died, when sovereign power faded. At a time of conclave, the city and the remnants of the pope's regime kept an anxious eye on the populace, fearing mayhem.

At Murano, the ceremonies of power have long opened the door to a show of hostility. In 1347, a woman islander, Caterina Bellola, on the ritual's day, called the podestà a "grievous whore-chaser". In 1398, the solemn occasion is different; the Duke of Austria pays a visit to Murano, and the inhabitants vent their grudge against the podestà. But the Muranesi are not the only ones in the Lagoon to explode when power passes. In 1375, at the installation, on Torcello, of podestà Paolo Zulian, boatmen, over from Burano to see the ceremony, knife some Torcellani and throw rocks.[41] To avoid this kind of violence, in the fifteenth and sixteenth centuries the Lagoon's communities undertake to redraft their statutes. The Snowball Revolt stems from two conflicts: the lower folk flaunt their hostility toward their patrician rulers; and the inhabitants of a subject community defy their overlord.

For the members themselves of Murano's regime, power's passage can serve as a means to express their resistance against the rector. The Statutes ordain that they escort the new podestà. In particular, it falls to the two judges, who have to go fetch him in Venice and then come back with him to Murano, staying at his side until he receives the baton of command and settles in at the palace. They also must stay with him at any mass, and the chancellor must write down if they are absent. Five failures to attend and, in theory, they lose their position.[42] Domenico Bertoluso and Domenico Rizo, the judges who worked with Vitale Vitturi, are present for the ceremony of 27 January, as were they, in theory, for his whole mandate, for major festivals and high mass. In years to come, many podestà will complain that the usage has fallen away and that magistrates are often absent. In 1514, when Alessandro Michiel is podestà, there is express regret that Muranesi are too seldom at his side, "to honour this office that represents our most illustrious Signoria".[43] So, from then on, the rule insists, at high mass, besides the judges, the *giustizieri* and the *camerlengo*, there should be in present the overseer of the flour depository, and at least a fifth of the Thirty. So, going in and out of church, the podestà desires to be surrounded by a goodly number of inhabitants, and has the decision put down in the Statutes book. But this does not settle matters, and, in 1531, podestà Domenico Malipiero has another law voted in, where he reaffirms how much it matters that, whenever they enter or leave the palace of the podestà "our magnificent rectors, for the decorum of their office, should be accompanied at all times by persons of the *terra*, by the judges, *giustizieri*, deputies, *camerlengo*, overseer, *cancelliere*, *cavaliere*, and crier".[44]

Politics aside, power's passage on 27 January takes place right in the middle of Carnival. Oddly, no witness uses the word or refers to this season of release, fun, and pleasure. But, at Murano as at Venice, Carnival has started several days ago, shortly after the Feast of Kings (6 January), and it will run on until Fat Tuesday, the day before Ash Wednesday when Lent sets in. The people already have festivity on their minds.

As a time for codified excesses and for controlled reversal of social roles, classically, Carnival is thought to be a necessary moment of social appeasement, a sort of space laid aside for popular expression and protest. Masks and costumes hide identities. So, one can act without being recognized, and take on someone else's gender, age, or social station. Exactly one year before the revolt, to the day, citing the burdens of war, Vitturi reins the festivities in. On 27 January 1510 he

> made known to anyone, of whatever condition, from the *terra* or a foreigner, that he should not dare or presume to disguise himself, with a face-mask or a scarf, or any other fashion, without a permit from the magnificent podestà or a permission paper.[45]

The written authorization, furnished by the podestà, signifies his hold on the population, even during these traditional moments of amusement. The next year, in February 1511, in Venice, the heads of the Council of Ten have it proclaimed on Piazza San Marco and at the Rialto that no one "can wear a mask, or go in disguise around this land".[46] But the frequency of public cries aiming to curb such practices testifies as readily to the futility of such laws as to their success.

In 1510, at Murano, Vitturi also forbids dances, with the exception of the ball in his palace for Carnival Sunday, as custom insists.[47] The podestà and community leave the running of this ball to a resident, who receives a sum of money to organize "*la festa de comun*". A chapter in the Statutes lays out that the *festa* must cost no more than five ducats in gold, to be taken from the fines paid by inhabitants who lost a case in court.[48] In February 1509, Jeronimo di Zulian dala Farme and his companions receive 37 *lire* and 4 *soldi* (very close to five ducats) for the "Carnival *festa* of the bulls"; the next year, Zuan di Antonio, a linen-maker, receives 31 *lire*.[49] The prohibition on all private dances is repeated, but should they happen anyway, if is forbidden to make inhabitants pay to get in, "so that all can have entertainment, and dance without having to pay".[50] At the beginning of 1511, as the smell of fried dough and doughnuts fills the island's streets, all know that the celebrations of Fat Thursday and Mardi Gras are coming. The inhabitants catch the festive spirit, even if the wars pare away at their resources and their zest.

Carnival fun is not just for commoners; patricians plunge right in. They come to Murano for the dances, the banquets, and the shows in the *palazzi*. In these years, new kinds of theatre make their appearance; they play upon social distinctions, between citizens and peasants, nobles and commoners, or old-stock Venetians and foreigners. One year after the revolt, in February 1512, a *commedia* "with peasant costumes" is recited on the isle by a company of noblemen. They are called The Gardeners.[51] Twelve of Murano's "hidden women" (*scosagne*), seemingly prostitutes, are invited, "but dressed honourably, in silk". The master of ceremonies is the patrician Gasparo Contarini di Francesco Alvise, who is also Signore di Notte – Lord of the Night, a magistrate in charge of Venice's public safety and policing. Sanudo tells the story:

> There was a sumptuous dinner, and a meal where there were served sweet cakes (*spongade*), and then they put on a comic *mumaria* and danced with the women all night long, so that, when the party ended, it was daylight. And, as for me, I came back from it not having slept at all – it was a great affair, and, indeed, lovely to see.

To stay with Sanudo, in 1520, after mascarades in plenty in Venice, many balls take place at Murano, and Venetian men, and women in disguise, go there.[52] In 1529, some foreign merchants organize a party with "gorgeous prostitutes in disguise", a dinner, and a *buffonescha* – a kind of play then in fashion that makes ample use of buffoons.[53]

In 1550, Murano sets the backdrop for Giovanni Francesco Straparola, in his story collection, *Le Piacevole Notti* (*The Pleasant Nights*); the book was a great hit in sixteenth-century Europe. A precursor of the fairy tale collections that would become so popular from the next century on, the anthology borrows the model of Boccaccio's *Decameron*. The author strands a group of gentlemen and fine ladies on Murano, so that they may, day by day, each tell their tales. They arrive at the isle, "espying there a palace of marvellous beauty . . . with a spacious courtyard, a superb loggia, a lovely garden full of gay flowers and rich in varieties of fruit, and lush with green herbs".[54]

Most patrician socializing goes on out of commoner's sight, but the inhabitants do catch wind of the preparations. So, they see it when the rich, in noble or fine paid-female company, step from their their gondolas. In fancy dress the high-born arrive after dark and depart with the dawn. Deliveries of fancy foods and goods arrive before they do. No surviving document informs us how the Muranesi viewed these parties, in the setting up or the running. What happened when their respective amusements collided, what jealousies flared, what rivalries? We really have no idea. We do not know if patricians turned up at the ball at the palace of the podestà. Nor do we know if the elite invited some glassmakers and artisans to their own festivities. There may have been a space of encounter, but we have no notion of its features.[55]

All in all, as the island's events played out, as with all collective action there was a streak of chance and luck. Would confusion have exploded even with no snow that year? Would the locals have dared to lay hands on harder missiles to play out their grudge against Vitturi? Would the chant have caught on among the children had it lacked its nasal rhymes and alliterations? We will never know if the first hand to throw a snowball belongs to a child who has little inkling of what is afoot on the *campo* and just wants a little fun; if the first to chant "Surian, Surian" are the restless adolescents who, cut off from the stakes in power's passage, just want to vaunt the timbre of their voices; nor do we know if some old rivalry among the glassmaker families is stoking this battle.

Inside historical events there is always a dimension of uncertainty. No matter how convincing our explanations, they should not lead us to believe that collective actions always stick to rules, or that historical actors just fish their deeds and their behaviour up from a repertoire of actions, or conform to some grammar and ritual programme, however unconscious. In the events of 27 January 1511 there is a streak of indeterminacy. We do not know why some mobilizations take off, while others stall. The Murano protest arises from a complex alchemy, shaped by the accidents of the times, the bedlam of Carnival, the international political situation, and whatever dice the climate rolls. And to all this we have to add the personality of the outgoing podestà.

## Vitale Vitturi

From September 1509 to January 1511 – Vitale Vitturi's lot is not a happy one. His role in the mobilization of the ships, and his taxes, certainly make him unpopular. But his personality, and his political moves, also shape Muranesi opinions of the man.

Vitale is born in 1446, the son of Andrea Vitturi di Nicolo and of Manolessa Manolesso di Lorenzo, stemming from two minor families of the Venetian nobility. He is neither rich nor powerful, but he is of noble birth, and therefore has the right to sit in the Maggior Consiglio, which he enters in 1471, at age 25.[56] From that date on, he takes on assorted administrative and political tasks, for, like many impecunious patricians, he counts on a public career to earn a living. In 1475, he is elected *castellan* of Novigrad, in Istria (now Croatia), a posting in political and military administration much like the tasks he will take up, later, at Murano, although distance and the unfamiliar language do make it harder. Many a time he serves in minor judicial and fiscal magistracies, before, on 26 August 1509, he is elected podestà of Murano. On 20 September, he takes up his post.[57] So he is coming to the end of a political career of no great lustre. A few months after the end of his mandate, he is a candidate to serve in the defence of Padua and Treviso, but loses the election. He tries again in December 1513, perhaps attracted by the pay sometimes offered. This second try does no better.[58]

One does not know why Vitturi, already an old man, is chosen as podestà of Murano. The political and military situation of the summer of 1509 surely favours his election, for the wars call on the younger, competent patricians, to direct operations. At least, Vitturi has had no choice but to accept a task that looked unrewarding, for everyone knows that the mobilization of glassworkers and fishermen will be no easy thing. Especially so, as the financial problems of the Signoria make administrators' salaries uncertain.

Many years later, Vitturi has occasion to revert to his complicated months at Murano. In October 1529, he lays before the heads of the Council of Ten a request for grace, asking for release from his debts.[59] For several years, the law has pursued him, as he has not succeeded in clearing them away.[60] Vitturi is not the only patrician to encounter this kind of financial trouble, and, in the 1520s, many laws are promulgated to resolve the problem of impoverished nobles. In 1529, now past 80, poor and ill – to believe his words, Vitturi beseeches the kindness of the magistrates, "considering the calamity and misery of these poor and unfortunate gentlemen". So, it is that he comes to revisit the stages of his career.

> I, your nobleman, poor and your servant, Vitale Vitturi, son of Messer Andrea, I come before your magnificent and most illustrious Lordships, with, the present supplication telling and laying out how, during the times of the war, which was in 1510, and which was great in Lombardy, I was then podestà of Murano. It was decided and commanded that, in that said place, one had to fit out the greatest possible number of ships for the needs of our most illustrious Signoria, with all the costs of these ships at the expense of the men, and of the money of the said place of Murano. That was very difficult. Nevertheless, to satisfy the wish and desire if this most illustrious Lord (*domino*), I did everything, so that in a very brief time one fitted 25 ships in good order, without any expense for your most excellent Lordships. And I wanted to go with them to make sure they were well organized and governed, not sparing any risk of damage or danger to my own life, and in this undertaking I was forced to make all kinds of extravagant expenditures. And what is even worse, your poor servant became so ill that he nearly died, and on account of this illness his wife suffered such discomfort and anguish that she at once fell ill and died in little time. And this, my most illustrious Lordships, was the ruin of my house.

Vitale Vitturi refers here to the death of his first wife, the daughter of Tragnaco Contarini di Polazzo – perhaps descended from a Greek branch of the family, as her unusual first name, Manolessa, suggests – whom he married in 1488.[61] He continues his petition:

> On top of that, you decided not to cover more than half my expenses, and to take away from me the whole of the salary of my position (*regimento*), leaving me only 49 ducats for the 16 months, which is the half of my costs (*neto*). And that is why, most illustrious Lordships, your poor and unhappy servant had to keep up his boat and his

domestic servants at his own cost, an immense expenditure, without any reimbursement. And so, it is that I finished in great calamity and misery, and I had to arrange to sell the few goods that I had so as to be able to live from 1510 till now. And, barely was my mission (*regimento*) finished, I was at once sent as a debtor to the [Doge's] Palace for 30.40 percent of the 293 ducats, and on account of that debt I could not obtain any office to support my household.

Vitturi is evoking a decision taken by the Venetian authorities at the moment of the League of Cambrai. To limit public expenditure, they had suspended payment of a part of the salaries. Has he tried to compensate for this loss by laying certain of his expenses on the Muranesi? The Statutes of Murano regulate his expenditures but forbid him to have his officers and servants paid by the community.[62] At the time of the snowball trial, some witnesses summoned by the judges to give their view on Vitturi express their reservations. Domenico de Andrico explains: "Me, I cannot complain, but I have heard many things said about him. If they are true – me, I do not know!" And, according to Domenico Bertoluso, "Me, I know that he has comported himself well and that he has administered justice, but it is true that the crowd (*la briga*) complain that he has taken some 'carats', but he took them with justice [on his side]". We do not know if these "carats" refer to fines which Vitturi levied on the inhabitants, or to extra taxes that he raised to cover his expenses. As to the former, the podestà takes pains, at his mandate's end, to demand payment of all outstanding fines. By public proclamation, on 15 November and again on 30 December 1510, he informs the inhabitants that they have eight days to pay up, as he must balance his books before he leaves.[63] As for any supplementary contributions, the surviving records, uncertain and fragmentary, bar all firm conclusion.

Here is all that the community's account books mention in February and March 1511: "The expenditures made by the four deputies against Messer Vitale Vitturi as appear here below. For making him come before the Avogaria, 4 *soldi*. . . For the expenses of Messer Nicolo Baron, lawyer, 3 *lire*. . . ."[64] The total comes to 9 *lire* and 16 *soldi*. Sadly, the archives of Vitturi's successor in office have vanished, and do not let us to cast light on this mention, which could point to some affair parallel to the Snowball Revolt. Does it have to do with another trial, of which we have found no trace, the result of some communal demand have Vitturi cited to answer to alleged bad actions? The whole matter remains obscure.

As for Vitturi's request before the Ten, in October 1529, it ends as follows:

I find myself, at the end of my days – me a gentleman! – impoverished and unhappy, who cannot receive any benefit without the aid and grace of your most illustrious Lordships, and so, on bended knee, I your

supplicant beg you in all piety that you deign to suspend the said debt
for another two years, so that I might be able to hope, first, in God's
clemency, and that of your most excellent Lordships, to have a small
public office thanks to which I could bring to an end my calamitous life.

Eighty years and older! – the request is a bit of a jolt. But, clearly, he has
other debts he must settle, which go back to 1493.[65]

This is not Vitturi's first time in court. In January 1521, he is the subject
of an inquest and a trial for bigamy.[66] After his first wife dies at Murano,
Vitturi remarries in 1516, taking the daughter of the patrician Francesco
Minio. Then, in 1520, he marries Pitta, the daughter of a Venetian
*cittadino*, a *dotor* named Agostini. So Agostini is not noble, and Pitta
herself is the widow of another *cittadino*, Battista Bardi. Despite the laws,
which try to curb this kind of alliance, impoverished nobles often marry
daughters of rich and rising *cittadini*, who can thereby hope to see their
grandchildren join the Venetian nobility. In sixteenth-century Europe,
trading name for wealth is common practice. But Vitturi celebrates this
third wedding while still legally married to his second wife.

On 14 January 1521, the *avogadori di Comun* act on this as a bigamy
case and pass it to the Quarantia Criminale, who decide to strip Vitturi of
his right to take part in voting at the Maggior Consiglio, and to jail him
until they finish investigating. Ecclesiastical justice then takes interest in the
affair, which the patriarch refers outside the Venetian state, to the Bishop
of Cremona.[67] Thanks to jurisdictional conflict between civil and religious
powers the case drags on and on. In January 1523, Vitturi gets out of jail
and goes to a sitting of the Maggior Consiglio. It is his first time in two
years. But three days later, an *avogador* orders him back into line: true, he
is out of jail, but he is still on trial with the church, and so not authorized
to take part in voting. Vitturi contests this ruling.[68]

Sanudo finds this story entertaining, and reports in detail the hearing of
May 1523.

> Today, after the midday meal, at the court of the Judges of the
> *procurator*, was judged the affair of the old wife of Messer Vitale
> Vitturi; he wants to get her dowry back. There speak on her behalf
> Signor Constantin Zucuol, *dotor*; on his behalf, Jacomo Francho and
> Vitale Vitturi himself. A great lot of people came to hear the affair and
> the hall was full, for it was laughable, and almost a comedy, as the
> woman herself rebuts him, for, during the 26 months that Vitale Vitturi
> spent in prison, she fell in love with Messer Giovanni Donato, son of
> the late Messer Antonio, the lawyer of the said Vitturi, and his god-
> kinsman, who is still living in his house.[69]

One does not know how the affair ended, but when, in 1529, Vitale
Vitturi draws up his will, he leaves Lucia Bondi, "my very dear wife", the

whole of her dowry of 150 ducats.[70] Who is this woman? Is it some fourth wife who in her turn has offered the impecunious old noble a scattering of coin in exchange for his name? That might explain how the patrician, who calls himself a ruined man, is still in condition to leave sums of money to pious works, his family, his domestic servants, his bastard son Andrea, and his grand-daughter Marieta. He dies two years later, in 1531, 85 years old.[71]

Since the end of the thirteenth century, patricians elected to the post of Murano's podestà have trimmed the job to fit the circumstances, their experience, their aspirations, the expectations of the government in Venice and the relations they establish with Murano's own regime. After 1502, with the Statutes redrafted, the mission becomes more delicate. The jurisdictions of the Muranese magistrates are redefined, and the balance of forces shifts. Vitturi himself must make his peace with the institutions, but also with the inhabitants, dunned continually both for cash to fund the war and for military services. When they fail to respect the solemnity of the ceremony, the islanders affront the podestà's political position and his honour. To ridicule the event is to insult the sovereignty he embodies. Whatever one might say to gloss the event, its violence cushioned by the snow, there is indeed an assault on the podestà's authority, almost sacred because it is so public. So, in the trial set rolling a few days later, it is less the man than his public function that the Signoria struggles to defend.

## Notes

1 Girolamo Priuli, *I Diarii*, vol. IV, 214, 11 August 1509.
2 Girolamo Priuli, *I Diarii*, vol. IV, 170, July 1509.
3 Marino Sanudo, *I Diarii*, vol. 8, col. 518, 16 July 1509; Girolamo Priuli, *I Diarii*, vol. IV, 152, July 1509.
4 Marino Sanudo, *I Diarii*, vol. 9, col. 44, 10 August 1509; col. 154, 11 September 1509; vol. 10, col. 274, 6 May 1510.
5 ASVe, PM, 44, 1 Proclamatione, 29 January 1510.
6 ASVe, PM, 44, 12 Extraordinariorum 5, for 1 January 1511.
7 ASVe, PM, 44, 8 Extraordinariorum 1, for 15 September 1509.
8 ASVe, PM, 43, Extraordinariorum 1, for 31 May 1509.
9 ASVe, PM, 44, 10 Extraordinariorium 3, for 10 May 1510.
10 ASVe, PM, 212, documents 1509–19, 23 January 1511.
11 ASVe, PM, 44, 9 Extraordinariorum 2, for 25 February 1510.
12 ASVe, PM, 44, 10 Extraordinariorum 3, for 18 May 1510.
13 ASVe, PM, 44, 12 Extraordinariorum 5, for 31 December 1510.
14 See for example Marino Sanudo, *I Diarii*: vol. 13, col. 18–19, 4 October 1511; vol. 15, col. 22, 4 September 1512; col. 254, 22 October 1512; vol. 17, col. 95, 27 September 1513; col. 113, 1 October 1513; col. 378, 13 December 1513; vol. 18, col. 145, 19 April 1514; col. 216, 24 May 1514; vol. 20, col. 93, 2 April 1515; vol. 22, col. 432, 15 August 1516.
15 ASVe, PM, 45, Criminalium 1, for 7 October 1511.
16 ASVe, PM, 45, Criminalium 1, for 24 October 1511, testimony of Francesco detto Pezino.
17 Marino Sanudo, *I Diarii*, vol. 13, col. 61, 10 October 1511.

18  Girolamo Priuli, *I Diarii*, vol. IV, 219, 14 August 1509.
19  Marino Sanudo, *I Diarii*, vol. 9, col. 154, 11 September 1509.
20  ASVe, PM, 44, 8 Extraordinariorum 1, for 10 September 1509.
21  ASVe, PM 44, 26 Criminalium 8, for 11 October 1509. See also 8 Extraordinariorum 1, for 30 October 1509.
22  Marino Sanudo, *I Diarii*, vol. 8, col. 527, 17 July 1509.
23  ASVe, PM, 44, 25 Criminalium 7, for 7 November 1510.
24  Marino Sanudo, *I Diarii*, vol. 7, col. 588, 21 July 1508, ruling of the heads of the Council of Ten against carrying weapons.
25  ASVe, PM, 44, 1 Proclamatione, 21 June 1510.
26  ASVe, PM, 44, 22 Criminalium 4, for 20 June 1510.
27  BMC, Mariegola dei Fioleri, 26, fol. 14v-16r, 20v-21v; ASVe, PM, 200, *Commissio* of the doge Agostino Barbarigo to Francesco Barbarigo, podestà of Murano, 26 February 1493, ch. 35.
28  BMC, Mariegola dei Fioleri, 26, fol. 63v, 14 September 1512.
29  Cornelis Easton, *Les Hivers dans l'Europe occidentale. Étude statistique et historique sur leur température* (Leiden: Brill, 1928), 88.
30  Marino Sanudo, *I Diarii*, vol. 11, December 1510–February 1511, col. 673, 715–17, 720, 724–6, 731, 733, 750, 763, 781, 784.
31  See for example ASVe, PM, 44, 1 Proclamatione, 25 October 1509 or 2 April 1510. See also Lorenzo Del Panta *et al.*, *La popolazione italiana dal Medioevo a oggi* (Bari: Laterza, 1996), 53.
32  ASVe, PM, 44, 1 Proclamatione, 2 April 1510.
33  ASVe, PM, 44, 1 Proclamatione, 22 December 1509.
34  Archivio Parrocchiale San Pietro Martire di Murano, Registro degli ammalati (1510–13).
35  ASVe, PM, 44, 4 Testificationum, 7 November 1509.
36  ASVe, PM, 44, 12 Extraordinariorum 5, for 6 December 1510.
37  ASVe, PM, 44, 12 Extraordinariorum 5, for 6 December 1510.
38  ASVe, PM, 44, 12 Extraordinariorum 5, for 31 December 1510.
39  ASVe, PM, 229, 3, fol. 11, for 10 December 1511.
40  See Maartje van Gelder's ongoing research on this topic.
41  Orlando, *Altre Venezie*, 156–7, 286–7, 379.
42  "Statuto de Muran", book I, ch. 4, 241.
43  ASVe, PM, 236 bis, fol. 24, for 22 July 1514.
44  ASVe, PM, 236 bis, fol. 26, for 11 April 1531.
45  ASVe, PM, 44, 1 Proclamatione, 27 January 1510.
46  Marino Sanudo, *I Diarii*, vol. 11, col. 794, 2 February 1511.
47  ASVe, PM, 44, 1 Proclamatione, 2 and 9 February 1510.
48  "Statuto de Muran", book I, ch. 19, 255.
49  ASVe, PM, 229, 3, fol. 3v, 25 October 1509; 10 February 1509; ASVe, PM, 229, 2, Cassa fontico di Murano, book 1, fol. 26v, 8 January 1511; 12 February 1511.
50  ASVe, PM, 44, 1 Proclamatione, 9 February 1510.
51  Marino Sanudo, *I Diarii*, vol. 13, col. 483, 16 February 1512.
52  Marino Sanudo, *I Diarii*, vol. 28, col. 271, 21 February 1520.
53  Marino Sanudo, *I Diarii*, vol. 49, col. 430, 7 February 1529.
54  Giovanni Francesco Straparola, *Le piacevoli notti* (Venice, 1550), Libro primo.
55  Several hints let us suppose that there were encounters at this occasion. See for example ASVe, PM, 44, 22 Criminalium 4, for 6 May 1510, against Pietro Marcello's *famulus* (servant).
56  For the political career of Vitturi: ASVe, Segretario alle Voci. See also the online data base rulersofvenice.org.

57 ASVe, PM, 44, 1 Proclamatione, 20 September 1509. His first documented acts date from 23 September.
58 Marino Sanudo, *I Diarii*, vol. 12, col. 353, 10 August 1511; vol. 17, col. 394, 17 December 1513.
59 ASVe, Consiglio dei Dieci, Deliberazioni, Parti Communi, filza 10, no. 82, for 27 October 1529.
60 Marino Sanudo, *I Diarii*, vol. 28, col. 197, 21 January 1520.
61 ASVe, Miscellanea Codici, Storia Veneta, Genealogie Barbaro, vol. VII, busta 23, fol. 279.
62 "Statuto de Muran", book I, ch. 18, 255.
63 ASVe, PM, 44, 1 Proclamatione, 15 November 1510.
64 ASVe, PM, 229, 3, fol. 7v, for 17 March 1511.
65 ASVe, Consiglio dei Dieci, Deliberazioni, Parti Communi, filza 10, no. 82, for 27 October 1529.
66 Marino Sanudo, *I Diarii*, vol. 29, col. 545, 14 January 1521.
67 Marino Sanudo, *I Diarii*, vol. 29, col. 561, 19 January 1521.
68 Marino Sanudo, *I Diarii*, vol. 33, col. 576–7, 12 January 1523; col. 589, 25 January 1523; col. 594, 28 January 1523.
69 Marino Sanudo, *I Diarii*, vol. 34, col. 233, 29 May 1523.
70 ASVe, Notarile, Testamenti, 191, Girolamo Canal, no. 674, for 20 March 1529.
71 ASVe, Miscellanea Codici, Storia Veneta, Genealogie Barbaro, vol. VII, busta 23, fol. 279.

# 5    The sense of justice

Vitturi's humiliation cannot go unpunished, and justice takes the affair in hand. Murano has its own tribunal, but to have it officiate in a case like this is out of the question. The Republic is defending its representative; it reserves the right to rule on the case via the Avogaria di Comun, the institution that serves as court of appeal, and carries out the trials that oppose the Republic's representatives and its subjects. For the Muranesi, a trial is nothing exceptional; like the other inhabitants of Venice and subjects of the Serenissima, they have everyday relations with justice and its workings. All the time, they have recourse to the podestà, whose job it is to solve disputes and propose negotiated settlements. But this case is a matter for Venice's institutions, for they desire to affirm their authority and to take the situation back in hand.

## Justice

In Florence, and many other Italian cities, aspiration to liberty justifies rhetorically the actions of governments and the claims of the *popolo*. In Venice, things are different. There, it is justice and equality that legitimate political authority and motivate what the people demand. In the territories under Venetian domination, the representation of justice is omnipresent, in the form of statutes, bas reliefs and other images, handwritten or printed, and also in official texts and documents pertaining to the state, and in illuminations, engravings, and seals; these all represent this cardinal virtue as a long-haired woman with her pair of scales and sword.

Despite the standard image, the law is not universal, and each group has norms proper to its own status. Venice's subjects can approach specialized judicial bodies to work out their quarrels, arbitrate their disputes, and repair injustices. Criminal and civil affairs, conflicts concerning property, disputes about commerce, work, inheritances, or dowry matters, economic disagreements with foreigners: each such matter is the domain of a specific court overseen by a college of patricians. They, in the course of their careers, will sit on assorted magistracies, without necessarily having formal legal training. Rather, it is generally the secretaries and the notaries, chosen among *cittadini*, who are the law's professionals.

At Murano, the podestà defends the law and arbitrates the conflicts. As the first chapter of his mission statement commands: "You will give reason and justice to everyone according to the usage of the said place, and if the usage is lacking, you will do so according to the usage of your good conscience."[1] The inhabitants know that they can have recourse to his intervention. For example, at the end of September 1509, several days after Vitale Vitturi took office, one of the clergy of Santi Maria e Donato, Zuan Battista Rosso, is insulted by two local men.[2] Dining at home, he hears a ruckus in the street. Leaning out his window he sees Alvise and Andrea Moro, who call him "*bastardo*" and threaten to beat him. The priest's first reaction, once danger passes, is to register a complaint with the podestà. A few months later, in January 1510, a dispute flares up between Vicenzo, son of Dona Lazarina, and the miller Andrea del Piovan, about weighing a sack of grain. The former gives the latter a shove, berating him: "Out of here, by the blood of the Virgin Mary. If it weren't for Messer the podestà, I would show you a thing or two!"[3] In this instance, the magistrate represents the high court one could call on, to whose decisions one should defer.

Arbitration and peace-making both permit the regulation of ordinary conflicts, via a verbal agreement. Summary procedure avoids the business of a trial, and ends with a "sentence of arbitration", rendered by the three arbitrator-judges who assist the podestà in his judgments "by compromise".[4] In graver cases, the podestà presides over the tribunal, on Mondays and Thursdays, after the midday meal.[5] He sits with the two judges (who are part of the *banco*), who must be present whenever the inquiry decides to use the rope of torture (*dar corda*), even if in this matter they disagree with the podestà.[6] In the legal papers of Vitale Vitturi, kept from September 1509 to January 1511, eight of twenty-six notebooks are devoted to criminal trials (*criminalium*). In fifteen months, Vitturi takes on more than 130 criminal cases. That means, on average, two or three a week. Between January and February 1510, he sets in motion almost 30 trials; in July 1510, there are 26. By way of contrast, his predecessor has carried out only 90 or so trials between June 1508 and August 1509, and his inquests are generally much shorter, with a concentration of cases in the first months of his mandate (half of them between June and September 1508).[7] So Vitturi is particularly given to judicial activism.

The sentences combine the imperatives of Venetian law with the local regulations of the community. Book III of Murano's Statutes contains a litany of blasphemies, games of dice and cards, false witnessing, insults, and violent blows with sticks and stones, plus the rape of nuns or virgins, and adultery. They condemn those who gamble for cash or live off the avails of "fornication", and butchers who sell spoiled meat, not to mention bakers who make their dough with Lagoon water, and tavern-keepers who sell their wine watered, or market it at illegal hours, plus any inhabitants who dump garbage in the canals.[8] Those who steal bread, fish, wood and pigs, and burglars of the houses and the gardens are threatened with severe punishment. Thieves of all sorts swell Vitturi's registers: sixteen chickens and five geese stolen by night from the fruit and vegetable seller Zuan Rosso in October 1509; a box of textiles, including some shirts and a woman's black dress snatched from Ser Zuan di Muschi in July 1510; a small fishing boat moored at the shore and stolen from Ser Vettor Rizo a few days later.[9] In 1508, it was the turn of a cable lent by the Arsenale to hold up the Ponte Lungo while it was repaired; in the night, it vanished from the worksite.[10]

The Statutes also condemn crimes of speech, including insults proffered in the presence of the podestà.[11] Trials for abusive language, in this era, are far from rare. In August 1510, Isabetta, wife of Zuan Andrea Barovier, is accused of having called Zuana, sister to Angelo Zeloxo, a *putanaya vaca* (whore-cow). But Angelo's sister replies in court, she had just been answering back, tit for tat, an insult hurled at her: "*verola morta*" (smallpox-corpse).[12] *Bastardo*, *becco* (cuckold), *zoton* (lout), and *putana* (whore) all spice Muranese conversation, not to mention graver imprecations against God or the saints. Two chapters of the 1502 Statutes are devoted to blasphemies.[13] "Those who blaspheme God and the Virgin Mary" are condemned to a 50 *lire* fine and three months in prison. If they offend again, the penalty doubles. At the third offense, one cuts the tongue and banishes them for two years from Murano. Those who "blaspheme Messer San Marco and Saint John the Baptist" are also condemned, as the oath is akin to criticism of Venice and of Murano's government. In the wake of the efforts of the Counter Reformation, in 1537, Venice even founds a magistracy charged with prosecuting blasphemy (the *Esecutori contro la bestemmia*), and from this time on the control of words becomes a central mission of the podestà.[14] One must defend God and his saints, and ward off the spread of heretical talk, and statements against the Serenissima. Surveillance of language lies, in early modern times, at the heart of Venetian policy of state.

Whenever they come to blows, steal or curse, the Muranesi are subject to fines, which, in theory, can reach to 100 *lire*, or almost 15 ducats; that is serious money for a fisherman or apprentice, as it matches the year's pay of an unskilled labourer, or three times the annual rent of a small house. In reality, fines are most often just a few *soldi* (20 *soldi* make one *lira*), and they rarely go higher than 15 *lire* (a little over two ducats), as the podestà has the right to alleviate and forgive punishments.[15] Whenever the offenders cannot pay, their sentence is commuted into prison, at a conversion rate of one day per each ten *soldi*.[16] For graver crimes, the punishment combines prison, a fine, and the rope. In April 1510, for example, Vitturi rules that whoever concealed a smuggler named Lazaro Frapa, who is thought to have the plague, and who has fled with his goods in hand, would be condemned to a punishment of 100 *lire*, six months of prison, and two hoists of the cord.[17] Banishment from Murano and from the Lagoon, the gravest punishment, is rare, as, synonymous with disgrace and exclusion from the community, it brings on true social ruin.

In the daily lives of artisans and fisherman, justice is as often civil as it is penal. The two *giustizieri* preside over the regulation of economic matters – prices, wages, the quality of goods sold, and the honesty of weights and measures. Rigged scales, loaves baked from adulterated flour, rotted meat, sausages gone over-ripe and spoiled fruit are brought before the podestà, who, if the crime warrants, can have them burned. Scales and other measuring devices are checked once a year.[18] Shop-keepers and other vendors must present them to the *giustizieri* and the *cancelliere* eight days before the Christmas holidays, to receive an official certificate (*bollettino*), without which they cannot sell their merchandise. The jurisdiction of the *giustizieri* also extends to overseeing the sale and rent of real estate, evaluating the price of houses and lands – both at Murano and elsewhere in the podestà's district, assuring that debts are paid, and regulating inheritances and private business acts.[19] Vitturi's papers are full of registrations of debts and other credit matters: the Muranese economy relies in goodly part on credit and on the confidence the inhabitants grant one another.[20]

So, at the beginning of the sixteenth century, Murano is a very judicialized space, where the inhabitants regularly come face to face with justice. The tribunal is an essential element for the construction of social ties, as the affairs of the German bakers and of the Vicentino brawlers have both shown. At court, the inhabitants express themselves, defend their point of view and moral sense, and reveal their knowledge of the law. This familiarity with justice is symbolized by a marble statue, erected in the first half of the sixteenth century. It stands before the palace of the podestà, at the foot of the bridge of Santi Maria e Donato. It is the work of the sculptor Pietro da Salò, Jacopo Sansovino's pupil, who is still known in Venice for his statue of Gobbo (the Hunchback). Out in front of San Giacometto, the principal church at Rialto, this bow-backed man on bent knees supports the column on which public criers stand to make official announcements. Gobbo has survived down to today, but not Justice at Murano, who, sadly, has been destroyed.

The Tuscan Pietro Aretino, famous for his licentious writings and pornographic poems, despite that bent has left a lovely description of the Murano Justice, whose workmanship he lauds in a letter of 1548, to Pietro da Salò.[21]

> This image of justice holds in one hand the sword and in the other the scales, with a handsomely virile graciousness, and she seems more real than pretend. Very sweet is the gesture she is making; she moves with so much grace that one could swear that she is moving, taking a step, and not that she is standing still in her pose. Sweet and grave is the air of her expression, proud and benign seem the serenity of her brow,

lovely and soft is the form of her braid, in part wrapped around her head, and in part falling to her shoulders. Concerning the foot that she reveals, and the knee that she points beneath the light clothing that adorns her, made of folds both rare and well composed – one must praise her by remaining silent, as to speak of her would diminish her acclaim.

In the sixteenth century the statue has a dwelling in the mental world of the inhabitants, who lodge their expectations in this protective and reassuring feminine allegory.

Many other images of justice circulate at Murano. The *commissio* paper received by podestà Francesco Barbarigo in 1493 is adorned with a pretty initial-letter illumination showing a blond woman holding the sword and scales, seated on a throne decorated with feline heads, while the whole page lies under a golden winged lion resting a benevolent paw on the Gospel. A cup of the same period, by an anonymous Murano glassmaker, shows a feminine personage very like the former, on a chariot pulled by two felines: same blond curls and crimson garment, same sword and scales.[22] Surely, the inhabitants know other representations of justice, especially via the cheap prints that are beginning to circulate in the Lagoon, a few *soldi* the copy. Like that San Marco that the children, to amuse themselves, glue to the German baker's shop, many prints make the rounds at Venice, thanks to the Italian and German printers and the multiplying presses.

In their daily lives, the Muranesi are inured to this rhetoric of justice. As in any Christian society, the quest for salvation makes the Last Judgement a "horizon of expectation", a mental marker shared by all. On the day of the universal Resurrection, all will pass before this Final Judgement. The justice of God and that of men resonate with one another; eschatology makes judgments by one's peers the more acceptable. Justice's functionaries themselves make this connection, as does Vitturi in November 1510, where, in a public proclamation against Leonardo Caner, he identifies God's justice with that of the Signoria.[23] Caner, guilty of having knife-slashed the face of Vettor Rizo di Domenico, has been banished from Murano. But many witnesses report having seen him working and moving about on the island. Vitturi orders Malcanton to proclaim a new condemnation against "this Leonardo Caner, man of bad character (*sorte*), without fear of God and of justice, against the honour of our most illustrious Signoria and its laws, presumptuously scorning with many words our rulings and our commands".

Whether practiced equitably or not, whether it represents the unrighteous power of the masters or an ideal of impartiality, justice remains a shared value to which the people can take recourse. Out of necessity the Muranesi must agree over a shared conception of right, morality and justice, a common vision that the law guarantees. This mode of thinking lays down some rules on which to stand, in order to act, and to forge agreement; it reflects conventions the community needs.

# Law

Because it belongs to the Duchy, Murano is under the general *Statuto* of Venice, established in 1242 in the dogeship of Jacopo Tiepolo; this is a collection of fairly general regulations that serve as a foundation for Venetian law. Nevertheless, like other communities of the Lagoon, the island has maintained some of its customs (*consuetudines*). These were written down for the first time at the end of the thirteenth century. The first mentions of Statutes of Murano date from 1285.[24] Countless towns and communities, in Italy as in the rest of Europe, have produced or obtained, in the course of the Middle Ages, legal texts of this sort. Statute books are a great invention of the medieval cities, that, when they revive in the eleventh and twelfth centuries, have formidable zest for legislation. The new citizens take to drafting rules, to lay on their lords and princes the conditions of their autonomy. The statutes also stabilize the laws that guarantee civil peace and communal life in cities that are growing ever more densely settled. From the jobs and jurisdictions of the assorted urban councils to the quality of the drinking water, from the number of work-free days in the calendar to measures to assure garbage is collected, not omitting rules for the colour of prostitutes' clothing, for the good order of horse races, for the spaces for preaching, and for the processions that shame disgraced persons. Statutes also include the definition of the *popolo*, plus regulations for butchered meat and for dowries set aside for girls: everything falls subject to juridical codification, embracing the most diverse social practices and imposing on citizens a framework for life together.

At Murano, the first Statutes were drafted in an epoch when the island housed only a little community of fishermen, peasants, and artisans, where glasswork went on only sporadically. Two centuries later, these Statutes have lost pertinence; they do not let the community regulate new problems as they arise. That is why, at the beginning of the sixteenth century, the rulers of Venice and Murano agree to modify the text. In December 1502, a mere eight years before the Snowball Revolt, the inhabitants lodge a request in Venice:

> This *terra* of Murano finds that it has Statutes and ancient ordinances already hundreds of years old, made by the rectors and the good-men of that time. Which Statutes and ordinances, on account of changing times and the new fashion of living these days, no one obeys anymore.[25]

To renegotiate these new regulations and put them down in writing signals a major political initiative, in a time of crisis and of tensions between the Serenissima and the Duchy's inhabitants. The podestà Gabriele Venier, the *cancelliere*, and the members of the Council of Thirty, "the prudent and discreet citizens of Murano", perhaps assisted by a few Venetian legislators, are the drafters. Pietro Usnago di Alvise has for several months been the island's *cancelliere*, once having served as secretary to the Venetian court of Giudici dei Forestier.[26] The Statutes take shape from a first draft that we no longer have. But the new laws, like the old ones, are the fruit of discussions between the podestà and the island's inhabitants, and of adjustments between the written legal tradition, and the tacit rules and codified practices upon which the life of the community rests.

Agreements and disagreements, arrangements and accommodations have allowed the island to arrive at laws well adapted to the reality of occasionally scofflaw fishermen and of master glassmakers who have become some of Italy's best-reputed artisans. The heart of the text is a reflection of the everyday interactions of the inhabitants, who have been constrained to set up conventions so as to continue to live together. The drafters have not invented or created these laws, but rather collected and synthesized what the community and its citizens consider to be adequate, legitimate forms of behaviour. The law reflects principles as well as customs. Taking in hand this practice of formalizing what is admissible and what is not, the community functions as an active political body, endowed with collective competence and a capacity to spell out what is legal and what is moral.

Murano's Statutes have no counterpart at Venice, where it falls to jurisprudence to make good the gaps in the Statuto Generale of 1242.[27] Unlike the Venetians, the Muranesi can cite their text, single, and dense, which covers a wide variety of activities. The Statutes are divided into four books. Book I, "Of Orders" (*Deli ordeni*), contains twenty-seven chapters that define the institutional structures of Murano's government, and lay out the respective powers of the podestà and the magistrates. Book II, "On Civil Matters" (*Del civil*), is composed of twenty-nine chapters that lay down the rules of civil law that govern the administration of the island, in particular recommendations for the procedures of condemnation and legal notice. Book III, "On the Penal" (*Del criminal*), contains the thirty-eight chapters that bear on public order and justice. Book IV, "On the Confirmation of the Statutes" (*Dela confirmation deli statuti*), reviews in eight chapters how the negotiation of the Statutes played out, and how the Signoria recognized them. Meanwhile, for all cases not foreseen by the text, the "statutes, laws, decrees and customs" currently in vigour at Venice will dictate decisions.[28]

The whole text has been recopied in a mid-sized parchment register, some twenty folios with writing on both sides.[29] The cover, part-wood part-leather, closes with the help of iron buckles. Read in front of the Council of Thirty at the beginning of each podestà's mandate, and then frequently consulted, the book bears the marks of these many uses; the lower right-hand corner is especially dirty and floppy. In the years that follow, new regulations are added in the register, and they cover some hundred supplementary pages. The last act on the register dates from 12 March 1803, six years after the fall of the Republic of Venice.

These laws give shape and boundary to the everyday practices of the inhabitants and endow them with means for acting and intervening alongside the podestà. A symbol of the sovereignty of Murano, they find their visual expression in the widespread image of the island's coat of arms. The device surely surfaced in the podestaria's earliest days, as a crowned cock, with a silver body and red feet, on a blue ground. In the sixteenth century the image has grown more complex: the cock now holding in his beak a serpent and shouldering little gold fox.[30] Like the statutes, these heraldic images, sculpted in stone or marble and placed on the wells and the facades of houses, in their materiality incarnate the juridical autonomy of the island and the community.

The Statutes are conceded at the end of 1502, and they are accompanied by a fiscal arrangement that allows the inhabitants of Murano to reap a portion of the taxes on the glass trade, reserved to restore "the streets, the bridges, and the wells of this town of Murano, which has great need of it".[31] The definitive grant of the text occasions a great ritual, during the Christmas holidays of 1502. On 24 December, Doge Leonardo Loredan accords a ducal letter officially confirming the Statutes, now to be "published" – that is to say, presented to the collective inhabitants of the island.[32] Three days later,

> the general assembly (*publica contion*), convoked on the orders of the aforesaid magnificent podestà, at the sound of the bell, in the church of Santa Maria of Murano, by the aforesaid *cancelliere*, in the presence of the aforesaid magnificent Miser Podestà and all the people (*tuto el populo*), in living voice are published all the aforesaid Statutes, supplications, and graces.[33]

It is a solemn moment. The gathered inhabitants hear read out laws that no one from now on will ever be deemed not to know. Six years later, on 27 December 1508, the podestà once more convokes the *publica contion*, at the sound of the Santi Maria e Donato bell, and, in front of "all the *popolo*", publishes "the Statutes, supplications and graces signed" by the *cancelliere*.[34]

Most of Muranesi on the *campo* in January 1511 were present at these acts of publication. In the documents one cannot find explicit allusion to the memory of the event, but doubtless the inhabitants who hurry under the snow to come see Giacomo Suriano take up his job after the unloved Vitale Vitturi are marked by their participation in the negotiation of the recent new Statutes.

## Coercion

To see that the law is respected, the podestà, judges, and *giustizieri* are aided by the *cavalier*, the island's policeman.[35] In Vitturi's time, there serve first Ser Demetrio, and then Gasparo da Liesina (now Hvar, in Croatia) – also called Gasparo Barbier – at the post down to May 1510, and then Alvise Marascalco ("marshall"), and Ser Alessandro.[36] Mostly their origin is not given, but they are not from Murano. Perhaps they come from Venice, after the podestà nominates them.

The *cavalier* assures policing and security, especially at night.[37] In Venice, as in other medieval cities, it is forbidden to work at night, and a curfew is imposed, as there is no city light. Things are different at Murano, where the glasswork fires stay lit both day and night. Vitale Vitturi must pass judgment on many affairs involving workers on night shift or inhabitants who are taking advantage of the post-sunset cool to stay out on the streets and embankments.[38] Sometimes disputes break out with the Venetians who come to take their pleasure and to banquet, before quitting the island at the crack of dawn. Under the effect of alcohol, they are quick to goad Muranesi with their insults.

It falls to the *cavalier* to prevent fights, on an island where the locals enjoy a reputation for brawling. Giacomo Casanova, two centuries later, still says that he fears "the thieves of Muran, very dangerous cut-throats, determined assassins who enjoy and abuse many privileges, that government policy accords them thanks to the work they do in the glassworks with which the isle abounds".[39] In his term, Vitturi launches countless trials to punish these aggressions. In April 1510, Caterina, wife of the boatman Zuan Munega brings complaint against Zuan Maria di Andrea Moliner, who has insulted her. A witness retells the tale – how she has grabbed Zuan Maria by the hair, thrown him to the ground, and rained blows on him, while shouting, "this oaf has treated us like whores, me and my daughter".[40] Day after day the cases roll on: disputes, some violent, others less, insults traded, stones hurled from the shore at passing boats, collisions and boat-shoves on the canals, blows with iron tools in the workshops, races along the *fondamente*. The *cavalier* never has an idle moment, for he also has to keep an eye to on weapons, and on what people do with them.

"All the arms that are and will be forbidden at Venice are equally forbidden in this place of Murano", proclaim the Statutes, as well as "pole weapons of every kind, or bows with iron-tipped arrows".[41] Those who break the law are threatened with a prison sentence that the podestà can match to the weapon used.[42] In Vitale Vitturi's time, one may go armed so long as the weapon stays inside its sheath. In the documents, one comes across Muranesi armed with swords both long and short (*spada, mezzaspada*), with knives and daggers (*pistolese, cortella, pugnal*), with mailed gloves, pole weapons, bows and crossbows, not to mention harpoons for catching eels (*fossina*), and iron tools and glassblower's pipes.[43] In Vitturi's time no firearm is mentioned, but a few years later the Council of Ten recalls that it is forbidden to fire a long gun (*schioppo*) or arquebus from the windows and gardens of Venice and Murano. The only place at Murano where gunfire is authorized is the *versaglio publico*, the "public target" where one practices marksmanship, apparently to the east of the Rio, to judge by the modern place name – Bresagio.[44]

The *cavalier*, at the podestà's orders, goes out to arrest persons who break the law and lays hands on those who violate rules, as happens in August 1509, when he arrests a Venetian servant named Nonnulo, who has arrived in Murano with two women disguised as men.[45] He also keeps an eye on smuggling and on the activity of fishermen who do not belong to the community. So, in July 1510, he arrests some fishermen from Venice who have come to poach by night in Murano waters.[46] And it also falls to him, in November 1509, to denounce the glasswork masters who, despite the law, hire foreign workers.[47]

As a man with a public mission, the *cavalier* receives a salary, a fact judged to clinch his impartiality. He takes in a ducat a month, plus added income linked to certain specified actions. He is paid by the podestà, who takes from the community a sum that matches his salary and passes it on to the policeman. He also receives a house, across the way from the palace of the podestà, where inhabitants know they can find him, especially at night. In the summer of 1510, Vitturi lays out substantial money to have it repaired, at the same time as he takes on renovation of the *piazza* of Santi Maria e Donato and his own *palazzo*.[48]

Both to defend himself and to keep order, the *cavalier* himself carries a pole weapon (a lance with a wooden haft and a metal point atop it), and a bow and arrows to reach any malefactor who might try to escape him out on the water. He also has rope to tie up uncooperative suspects and carry out arrests. Despite his name, nothing suggests he patrolled on horseback (*a cavallo*). But he does have a boat, furnished by the community, with which to chase delinquents who try to slip off the island.

The *cavalier* is not alone. The documents attest to other officers, whose functions are not always clear. According to the Statutes of 1502, three of the four *caradori* (officers in charge of provisioning with wood), but not the public crier, "are obliged, at each request of the *cavalier*, when he has need of it, to go with him in his company".[49] The community also furnishes the *cavalier* funds to pay one or two companions to aid him, but does not itself directly hire them.[50] From September 1508, the officer's job stabilizes; the *caradori* no longer step in to do it. The officers' mission is "to block the evil intentions of bad persons and to guarantee obedience to this mission, and the security of persons", especially at night.[51] After discussion at the Council of Thirty about the chance of appointing two or three officers, it is decided that, for this mission, two will suffice. They will make four *lire* a month, funded from the fines inhabitants pay. The decision is far from unanimous: it scrapes by, fourteen in favour, ten opposed. In the 1530s, the *commissio* of the podestà still mentions four officers, "well armed and over twenty years of age" who serve alongside the podestà, one of whom must know how to write.[52] Unlike the cavalier, who comes from other places, the officers, it seems, are from Murano.

In the eyes of the inhabitants, the *cavalier* and his officers stand for those in power. They are sometimes targets for a hostility more readily vented at them than at the podestà and the ruling circle. On Saint John's Day (24 June) 1510, the parishioners of San Maffeo gather on the *campo* around a festive Saint John's fire.[53] Alvise Franzin, one of the officers, comes with his companions to pay court to a young woman of the town, Maria Offitiala. But a neighbour, Maria Facara, alias Rombola, starts to insult Maria, and, via her, the officers. "*Poltrona* whore, because of his love for you, nobody can stay on the *campo*." A few weeks later, the vice-*cavalier* Vincenzo denounces a noble youth, Ser Giovanni Donato, and his teacher (*eius pedagogum*).[54] He accuses them of having insulted him, and his officers too, when they walked by. There are many other cases lodged against inhabitants who resisted the *cavalier*; the podestà could cite a chapter in the Statutes that condemns all those who hinder the *cavalier* and his officers in the exercise of their duties.[55]

The power of the podestà could have no hold on the inhabitants without these agents, drawn from the lower orders, whose role is not simply to apply the law, but also to interpret it to put it to work. The use of force and arms is only one part of their capacity. It is also their ability to handle their interactions with the inhabitants, to justify their actions, to make themselves respected, that reveals their competence as public officers in the service of the podestà.

## Tribunal

The Statutes that dictate the law, the *cavalier* and his officers who oversee its application, the podestà and the magistrates who judge those who break it, all between them have not sufficed to deter the inhabitants from venting their animosity against Vitturi. So, it falls to Venetian justice to re-establish order and to impose a legitimate discourse on the illegitimate actions of 27 January. Pietro Contarini, Nicolo Dolfin, and Gasparo Malipiero, the magistrates of the Avogaria di Comun, take charge of the affair; it falls to them to run the inquest to establish guilt and assay the protest's causes.

The investigations of these judges begin on 4 February 1511, at Murano, by having their official (*fante*) hear the first ten witnesses. Then, on 26 and 27 February, they interrogate the accused. From 12 to 25 March, the judges collect the accounts of four Venetian patricians who were on hand at the passage of power, before, on 25 March, they return to interrogating the accused, this time using torture. A final witness is heard on 28 March. The *avogadori* then present the results of their inquiry and their sentence to the tribunal of the Council of Forty. That body is constrained to vote four times, from 29 March to 10 April, before it settles on the judgement, published at last on 10 April, in the *Raspe*, the penal roll of the Avogaria di Comun.

The whole procedure is then filed, in a document still extant in the State Archives of Venice, our principal source about this affair.[56] Nevertheless, it contains neither a request to proceed, nor a declaration by Vitale Vitturi, who, according to Sanudo, indeed did bring his complaint before the Avogaria. The document, drafted on shabby paper, has some twenty folios, or forty pages, no great thing if contrasted with the vast judicial dossiers courts produce from the later sixteenth century on, but, compared with Avogaria trials of the time, this dossier is fairly fat. The trial belongs to an archival series in fragmentary array, full of many dossiers that bear upon, among other things, cases that pitched Venetian rectors against communities subject to them.[57]

The trial document results from a labour of compilation and redrafting, using notes taken at the time of the inquest. One or several secretaries wrote down, as they happened, the hearings and interrogations, and then put them into good shape for the trial's final copy. The file is now in mediocre condition, with many pages damaged by damp and water, often the case with Venice. The Lagoon's humidity is clearly not the best environment for preserving papers or books; even so, Venice has managed to conserve one of Europe's richest archival collections.

Putting the event down in writing and composing an official version of the facts are one part of the business of taking back in hand and setting in good order a situation that had slipped the grasp of official power. The archive thus contributes to the construction of the affair all the while it conserves its memory. The inquest, the trial, and the sentence are discourses about reality that shape the people's memory of what happened. The verdict must circulate, and be proclaimed in Murano and Venice both, to remind hearers of law, order, and dominance by patricians and by Venice. The discourse in the trial has a performative function: the judges' sentence condemns the unjust, while also constructing the just and true.

Each stage in the trial hews to its own procedure. Every step reflects a particular interaction between the judges, on one side, and the witnesses and accused on the other; the conditions of the interrogation and the stakes for the men before the court shape what happens. The trial is built around successive versions of the tale, accounts of what happened that sometimes contradict each other. It falls to the judge to establish if certain witnesses and suspects are lying, or bending the truth. Our job, in contrast, is not to determine the truth or authenticity of the stories but to analyse the words employed, the justifications marshalled, the way in which the events are qualified, and the motives of the defence. What interests us most is the legitimate feel of the words pronounced in the precincts of the tribunal and of the expressions that the court writes down, for the juridical situation gives them acceptability, and the space in which the discourses unfold gives them their firm footing as truthful speech.

Certainly, the judges and their secretaries modify, in part, the words they hear. The mere operation of putting oral discourse down on paper occasions transformation: shorter, tighter versions of things said, translation of local expressions, refinement of words deemed too informal, simplification of scrambled formulations. Meanwhile, the magistrates impose on speakers tacit constraints, limiting their autonomy as they formulate their depositions. Down the seventeenth century, the speech of the popular classes is almost always mediated by elite pens – as that of women is filtered by the men – because the former rarely have access to writing. Their words pass through the magistrates' and secretaries' filters of reading and writing. The trial is no neutral document, but it is no less neutral than any other archival paper. There is no such thing in the archives as an impartial word, and no crystalline writing – with no intention lurking inside it. Sources, all of them, are conditioned by their function, and constrained by procedures, and by rules that stake out form.

Simone, the official of the *avogadori*, who writes down the first depositions on Tuesday 4 February, eight days after the events, influences the inquest's course. Like the town crier and the *cavalier* and the many secretaries, notaries, and officials who work for the Venetian chancery, Simone is an embodiment of the authority of the institution he represents. Even if the sources are silent concerning the part the secretaries played in how the inquest evolved and the sentence emerged, it is evident that their collaboration is decisive.

It is indeed Simone who embodies Venetian authority the day he debarks at Murano, notebooks under elbow and list of questions in his head. Dressed in a long black robe called a *romana*, and a head-cover that marks him out, perhaps accompanied by a second secretary, he has come to hear the witnesses, to translate into the vernacular a list of questions drafted in Latin and transmitted to him by the *avogadori*, and to hear and transcribe, one by one, the depositions.[58] He writes them down, summarizing things that run too long, and transcribes the witness' words, sometimes with great fidelity, sometimes lightly modified. The transcription itself, and then their copy in the official record, are essential steps in which the patricians have had no hand.

These interrogations are far from anodyne. Simone is looking for the guilty, and he encourages Nicolo de Blasio, Gasparo Furlan, Vincenzo da Murano and the seven other witnesses to denounce their fellow citizens, neighbours, and friends. The document does not reveal his modus operandi, but one can imagine how much the nature of the interaction counts for the outcome of the interrogations. His manner, in dealing with the inhabitants, the words he chooses, the force with which he repeats them, his smiles, his frowns, and his hesitations are all key to the interview, but the source, showing barely a trace of all such things, renders our reading cautious.

The trial of 1511 is taken down in the vernacular, the dialect spoken in the Lagoon. It is fairly close to Tuscan, which will with time become Italian. At the beginning of the sixteenth century, most official acts of the Venetian chancery are already in Venetian, no longer in Latin. The trials administered by Vitale Vitturi begin with a resumé of the charge, in Latin, which is then translated to the witnesses and suspects. The depositions are then taken down directly and retranscribed. To a reader's eye, the declarations of the Muranesi and the patricians reveal different linguistic competency, and a varied capacity to juggle the levels of the language and to master complex grammatical structures. In a Latin translation, such shadings would swiftly vanish. So, taking down testimonies in the vernacular permits greater fidelity to the spoken language of the inhabitants. But the document is no more transparent than the action of the judges, so it is necessary to keep these limitations in mind, to hear another version of the affair of the snowballs, that of the six inhabitants of Murano whom the *avogadori di Comun* arrested, and then interrogated, at the end of February 1511.

## Notes

1 ASVe, PM, 200, *Commissio* of the doge Agostino Barbarigo to Francesco Barbarigo, podestà di Murano, 26 February 1493, ch. 1.
2 ASVe, PM, 44, 19 Criminalium 1, for 26 September 1509, against Alvise and Andrea Moro.
3 ASVe, PM, 44, 20 Criminalium 2, for 9 January 1510.
4 "Statuto de Muran", book II, ch. 22–5, 266–7.
5 "Statuto de Muran", book II, ch. 1, 259.
6 "Statuto de Muran", book I, ch. 3, 240; ch. 20–1, 255.
7 ASVe, PM, 43, Criminalium.
8 "Statuto de Muran", book II, ch. 29, 268; book III, ch. 1–22, 269–76.
9 ASVe, PM, 44, 19 Criminalium 1, for 16 October 1509; 24 Criminalium 6, for 25 July 1510; 24 Criminalium 6, for 30 July 1510.
10 ASVe, PM, 43, Criminalium 2, for 22 September 1508, *Contro ignoto*.
11 "Statuto de Muran", book III, ch. 8, 271.
12 ASVe, PM, 44, 24 Criminalium 6, for 4 August 1510, Angelo Zeloxo against donna Isabetta.
13 "Statuto de Muran", book III, ch. 1–2, 269.
14 ASVe, Collegio, Formulari di commissioni, reg. 8, fol. 116, for 19 January 1538.
15 ASVe, PM, 229, 2, Cassa fontico di Murano, book 1, fol. 19v-23r, condamnations, November 1509. The Statutes restrain this practice: "Statuto de Muran", book I, ch. 22, 256.
16 "Statuto de Muran", book I, ch. 26, 257.
17 ASVe, PM, 44, 1 Proclamatione, 2 April 1510.
18 "Statuto de Muran", book III, ch. 33, 279.
19 "Statuto de Muran", book I, ch. 7, 242.
20 ASVe, PM, 44, 13 Pignorum.
21 Pietro Aretino, *Lettere* (Rome: Salerno Editrice, 2000), Tomo IV, Libro IV, letter 619, p. 380, Venice, May 1548, Al Salò.
22 *The triumph of Justice*, cup with enamel decorations, late-15th century, Florence, Museo nazionale del Bargello.
23 ASVe, PM, 44, 25 Criminalium 7, 28 November 1510, proclamation of Antonio Malcanton. See also "Statuto de Muran", 228.
24 "Statuto de Muran", Monica Pasqualetto, "Introduzione", 207–26, here 214.
25 "Statuto de Muran", book IV, ch. 3, 284.

26　ASVe, PM, 38, for 9 June 1502 and 21 October 1502. Eight other candidates are in the running but is is he who wins. In 1541 Pietro Usnago is still living at Murano. For his tax estimate and goods, see ASVe, Dieci Savi alle Decime, 1514, busta 82, no. 22.

27　"Gli statuti veneziani di Jacopo Tiepolo del 1242 e le loro glosse", ed. Roberto Cessi, *Memorie del Reale Istituto Veneto di scienze, lettere ed arti*, vol. XXX/2 (1938).

28　"Statuto de Muran", book I, Preamble, 237.

29　ASVe, PM, 236 bis, fol. 1–2v index; fol. 3–22 (fifty pages in the modern edition: "Statuto de Muran", 237–87).

30　Barizza and Ferrari, *L'archivio*, 32; Zanetti, *Guida di Murano*, 196.

31　"Statuto de Muran", book IV, ch. 5, 285–6.

32　ASVe, PM, 236 bis, fol. 22, for 27 December 1508.

33　"Statuto de Muran", book IV, ch. 8, 287.

34　ASVe, PM, 44: 8 Extraordinariorum 1, for 6 September 1509; 9 Extraordinariorum 2, for 14 February 1510; 10 Extraordinariorum 3, for 22 May 1510; ASVe, PM, 229, 2, Cassa fontico di Murano, book 1, fol. 19, for 15 October 1510.

35　"Statuto de Muran", book I, ch. 13, 250.

36　ASVe, PM, 44, 8: Extraordinariorum 1, for 6 September 1509; 9 Extraordinariorum 2, for 14 February 1510; 10 Extraordinariorum 3, for 22 May 1510; ASVe, PM, 229, 2, Cassa fontico di Murano, book 1, fol. 19, 15 October 1510.

37　BMC, Mariegola dei Fioleri, 26, fol. 10v, on working at night.

38　ASVe, PM, 44, 22 Criminalium 4, for 3 April 1510 against Jacopo da Brescia.

39　Giacomo Casanova, *Histoire de ma vie*, tome I, vol. 4, ch. VI, 777, our translation.

40　ASVe, PM, 44, 22 Criminalium 4, for 20 April 1510, against Zuan Maria son of Andrea Moliner.

41　"Statuto de Muran", book III, ch. 10, 272.

42　"Statuto de Muran", book III, ch. 11, 272–3.

43　Par example ASVe, PM, 44, 20 Criminalium 2, for 7 January 1510, against Master Zorzi barbier, mentioning a Bolognese dagger (*pugnal bollognese*).

44　ASVe, Consiglio dei Dieci, Proclami, filza 2, no. 319, for 11 May 1531.

45　ASVe, PM, 44, 25 Criminalium 7, for 23 August 1510.

46　ASVe, PM, 44, 25 Criminalium 7, for 23 August 1510.

47　ASVe, PM, 44, 20 Criminalium 2, for 20 November 1509.

48　ASVe, PM, 229, 2, Cassa fontico di Murano, book 1, fol. 19, for 15 October 1510.

49　"Statuto de Muran", book I, ch. 14, 252–3, "G".

50　"Statuto de Muran", book I, ch. 18, 255.

51　ASVe, PM, 43, Extraordinariorum 1, for 3 September 1508.

52　ASVe, Collegio, Formulari di commissioni, reg. 8, 1533, fol. 99.

53　ASVe, PM, 44, 23 Criminalium 5, for 24 June 1510, against Maria Facara.

54　ASVe, PM, 44, 25 Criminalium 7, for 23 August 1510.

55　"Statuto de Muran", book III, ch. 12, 273. See another example in ASVe, PM, 44, Criminal 2, for 24 August 1508.

56　ASVe, AC, MP, 142, no. 17.

57　The result is not statistical, but it is worth noting that of 70 identified trials carried out by the Avogaria di Comun between 1480 and 1580, seven concern Venice's official representatives, whether the victims of their subjects or the butt of their subjects' complaints.

58　Giovanni Grevembroch, *Gli abiti de Veneziani di quasi ogni età con diligenza raccolti e dipinti nel secolo XVIII* (Venice: Filippi editore, 1981), vol. 3, no. 18.

# 6  The accused

When Simone, *fante* of the Avogaria di Comun, arrives at Murano to interrogate the witnesses the podestà has chosen, his task is as much to establish the facts as it is to ferret out the guilty conspirators. He poses the same questions to the ten inhabitants who came to testify: Who threw the snowballs? Who chanted against "this dog Vitturi"? Who insulted the podestà? Thanks to the answers he garners, the magistrates establish a list of six accused, whom they cite at Rialto to appear in mid February. At that, a crier is sent to Murano to bid them to present themselves at the Signoria's prisons one week later.[1] At that point, there begins a new stage of the inquest. Interrogation of the suspects will allow the magistrates to compare their version of the facts with that of the witnesses, to put their defences to the test, to establish guilt and, in the end, to unmask premeditation.[2]

## Before the judges

Many names have emerged from the testimonies assembled by the Avogaria's official. All point out the public crier, Antonio Malcanton, and one Jacopo Cagnato as principal actors on the scene. Cagnato is a fisherman, say some witnesses, a market-gardener (*ortolan*), say others, and he was "the leader of this company". The witness Tommaso Paliaga also alludes to a Bisato and his brother, sons of a Jacopo dall'Aqua, Pietro Bigaia, and a fisherman named Daniele Bigaia. The *avogadori* amass and sift the testimony and verify the names so as to establish a list of accused. They finally decide to arrest six men: Antonio Malcanton, Jacopo Cagnato, Bernardin Bigaia, Pietro Bigaia, and the brothers Zuan and Andrea di Jacopo dall'Aqua.

In his *Diarii*, the chronicler Marino Sanudo mentions the event a second time. At the Council of Forty:

> One has brought those who made noise these days past against Messer Vitale Vitturi, who was podestà at Murano, when he conceded the governance to Ser Giacomo Suriano, saying "Welcome to Surian who has chased off this dog who has undone Murano" and threw stones at

him. And for that reason, it was decided to detain them and among those under examination there is the crier of the podestà of Murano. They have been brought by the *avogadori* to the Forty to be tried.[3]

Stones, not snow – perhaps it is the rumour going around at Venice, where a snowball seemed a bit too soft to pose a real danger, and made the whole affair look a little silly.

Locked in the Venetian jails, the six accused await their interrogation, which takes place on 26 and 27 February. They are heard one after the other by the three *avogadori*. One can only imagine the fear that the magistrates and the place inspire in these Muranesi. In the capital, in front of Venetian patricians clothed in the robes of power, surrounded by court officers and men at arms who tell them where to sit and when to answer the questions put to them, the Muranesi could not but be affected by these theatrics. The decorum of the tribunal and the procedure's solemnity reinforce Venetian order and patrician domination.

The town crier is the first to be interrogated. His name has assorted versions: Antonio dal Malcanton, Antonio Malcanton, or Antonio known as Malcanton, but also Antonio di Zuan, and sometimes Zuan Antonio. In the trial his identity takes different forms, as it does in Vitale Vitturi's official papers. In these times, names are rarely stable; often the same name has several spellings, not to mention the differences between its Latin and various Venetian forms. And many commoners lack a family name and are identified only by their given name and the first name of their father. Countless family names, even today, bear witness to this old practice (as with Martini in Italian, Martin in French, and Martin or Martins in English, all once for "son of Martin"). But the crier does have a family name, Malcanton, a Venetian toponym meaning either "bad corner" or "bad spot". The name designates either places where, at a narrow, bent embankment, one might fall into the water, or some isolated, empty spot where foe could pounce.[4] Antonio, his father, or their ancestors probably acquired this surname by living near some place so named.

Antonio Malcanton, in court, is prolix and eager to defend himself to the magistrates, who begin by asking him the reason for his imprisonment.

Me, I could not say, as I have not done wrong, and, on the contrary, I have even been a good servant of the magnificent Messer Vitale Vitturi; for he himself made me crier, may God forgive him for it.

*Why do you say that, that you have been a good servant of Messer Vitale?*
Because I served him as *barcaruol* and crier and I did all that he ordered me to do, and desired, and he cannot complain of me.

*Why can he not complain of you?*
Because I did nothing.

On the defensive from the very start, Antonio awakens the curiosity of his interrogators, who invite him to continue his account of the passing of power.

> That day, I stayed in the palace till midday with Messer Agostino Suriano, brother of the podestà who was doing the *intrar*, and the *cancelliere*, and others, with whom we were making ready the palace. Then the old podestà, Messer Vitale Vitturi, came from Venice and went to the *cancelliere*, Messer Pietro de Vielmo. When they were together one of his servants came to call the *cancelliere*, who was in the palace, to tell him that Messer Vitale had arrived, because, the night before, he had slept in Venice, and had gone to his house. The *cancelliere* set off, and I went with him, to go to his house, where they had set the table for the midday meal. When the podestà had finished eating, he went under the loggia to wait for his successor. Nobody threw snow then, except some children who, on the other side of the *campo* threw snow and said "Surian is coming" (*el vien Surian*). Then Messer Giacomo Suriano arrived – the new podestà. Messer Vitale Vitturi went from under the loggia, then they went to the church, together. And when they came out of the church, on the way back, everybody was throwing snow, playing together, and those on the bell tower were also throwing snow, here and there, while ringing the bell, as it had always been the custom to ring the bell when the podestà makes his official entry. And me, I could not cry out enough or reprimand them, and they kept on throwing snow, both from the bell tower and from the *campo*. Even the new podestà and everybody were hit.

It was indeed at his behest that certain inhabitants went to the top of the *campanile*, as he explains, for he had asked a young man to climb up before the ceremony began, so as to alert him when he saw Suriano's boat entering the San Michele canal. That way he could inform Vitturi, who could quit the loggia where he was keeping warm.

The judges are interested in the snow.

> *At whom were they throwing snow, those in the bell tower and the others on the campo?*
> At everybody.

> *Where did they get that snow?*
> I believe they took it from the bell tower.

> *And you: where were you when they were throwing snow?*
> Me, I was in front of the magnificent podestà, both going into the church and coming out, and I never left them.

The magistrates want to know the precise role Antonio played, and learn if he himself encouraged the actions of one or another person, and they ask him about the identity of persons present.

> It is true that, on the *campo*, there were little children who were no older than ten, and fishermen, and furnace-lighters, who were shouting, "Surian, chase off this dog who has ruined Murano", and I scolded them.

> *About whom were they speaking when they were saying "Chase off this dog who has ruined Murano"?*
> Me, I do not know who it was they were talking about, and I told them to shout just "Surian".

Malcanton's version is confirmed by the five other accused – Jacopo Cagnato, Bernardin Bigaia, Pietro Bigaia, Zuan and Andrea dall'Aqua. Jacopo Cagnato is a fisherman or a market gardener, or perhaps both. Bernardin Bigaia and Pietro Bigaia are fishermen. The two dall'Aqua brothers seem to be furnace-lighters at the glassworks. They are always called "Zuan dall'Aqua and Andrea his brother". The Bigaia and dall'Aqua are important Murano families, and some of their members are master glassmakers who, in recent years, obtained *cittadino* status. But not these four accused, who are not identified by the title of Ser or Messer, normally placed before the names of citizens.

Pietro Bigaia, who served in May 1510 on the armed boats, and who contributed to their fitting out, knows the justice system well.[5] He was the principal person accused in one of the last trials launched by Vitturi's predecessor, on 3 September 1509.[6] Bigaia with "his accomplices", armed, broke into the garden of the noble Alvise Marcello, in company with Andrea Bisato, the fisherman Vettor Forner di Polo, and Francesco Fuga, all three of whom were cited by some witnesses in the later trial of February 1511. And again, in March 1510, Pietro Bigaia and Vettor Forner came before the bench for a violent fight with the *cavalier* and his men, when the police were trying to arrest Andrea della Campana.[7] It all happened in the barbershop of Zorzi Rosso, at Ponte Lungo. Andrea was getting shaved when the officers showed up to arrest him. They bound him with ropes, gagged him, and pinned him to the floor with their knees. Vettor Forner, who was in the shop, swore at the police and grabbed hold of the *cavalier*, who to defend himself pulled a knife. A crowd gathered, more than fifty men and women said some witnesses. In the brawl, Pietro Bigaia took up his own weapons and, thanks to the crowd, the *cavalier* was forced to beat a retreat, losing his prisoner. Forner and Bigaia received heavy sentences, but asked Vitturi for clemency. He reduced the lower court's fine and annulled the banishment. So the Snowball Revolt is embedded in a context and a history of which we do not know all the details. Doubtless, lines of friendship and enmity help shape the affair, but the sources do not always let us untangle all these relationships.

The *avogadori* try to prove the existence of a plotter, but the accused deny acting on orders, planning their acts, or speaking or hearing "offensive expressions". Zuan dall'Aqua admits that the children were shouting "Surian Surian" but nothing more than that. And if, true, they threw snow, they were aiming at their peers (*pari*). In sum, they were taking part in a simple snowball fight, that, anyhow, went on after the podestà departed.

Venetian procedure allows the accused to argue that new witnesses be heard, to corroborate their version of the facts. Antonio Malcanton mentions a good number of them, including *cittadini* and Muranesi high officials: Bortolomio Dino, Sebastiano Bellencito, Santo Rivaben, one Marco, and a servant of Nicolo the fisherman, "who, I believe, is called Matteo," Donato di Simon and his brother Vincenzo, and "others too." Only one of these is indeed called in, the *cittadino* Sebastiano Bellencito, whose testimony turns out to be very important. On 28 March, he is the last witness, just before the *avogadori* propose a sentence.[8] Bellencito has been one of the two *giustizieri* during Vitale Vitturi's mandate. In the past sixteen months, he has regularly collaborated with the podestà. As an owner of fishponds around Murano's shores, he often has court summonses sent to fishermen whom he accuses of poaching in his waters, and, particularly, of stealing his oysters.[9] Even though he is a *giustiziere*, he himself is judged by the podestà for having, in his shop, sold oil for four *soldi* the pound despite the proclamation affixing the top price at three and a half.[10] In Carnival, demand goes up; raising prices is tempting. Bellencito is also accused of selling wine retail. Nevertheless, Vitturi acquits him, accepting his defence: when he was away all unwitting, his serving woman and his shop assistant sold wine and oil. At the end of his testimony before the *avogadori*, in March 1511, Bellencito recalls: "Messer Vitale condemned me to pay five ducats, but I do not consider myself offended by him and what I have said is the truth."

The morning of 27 January, Bellencito went for lunch at the *cancelliere*'s with Vitale Vitturi, Antonio Malcanton, the judges, and the second *giustiziere*. He tells how the *cancelliere* ordered the crier to go ready the loggia, and to put up the rack (*spaliera*) on which to plant the island's banners for the ceremony. Antonio then came back, reporting that "many children had come onto the *campo* and they were shouting 'Surian Surian chase off this dog who has undone Muran'". The *cancelliere* told him, "Go pull their ears" and Antonio went back towards the square.

Bellencito goes on:

> With the podestà, the judges and the *giustizieri*, we all went to the loggia to await the new podestà ... Antonio, the crier, was before Vitale. The children were shouting and Antonio answered them, "Be quiet, you rascals, or may you catch the bloody flux!" And as soon as

the children saw the podestà they went quiet and did not say a thing
... Antonio the crier stayed at the loggia the whole time, before Messer
Vitale, because now and again he ordered him to go see if the new
podestà was coming.

So, the first part of Bellencito's deposition confirms the version of the
six accused. But the *avogadori* are not easily convinced. To judge from
the questions they put to the crier, he remains their prime suspect.

## Antonio Malcanton, public crier

Malcanton is accused of having orchestrated the revolt. It is hard to
establish his purported role precisely, as he is, by definition, one of the
ritual's principal actors. It falls to him to organize the passage of power, to
ready the *campo* for the ceremony, to guide the procession into and out
from the church. His functions during the ritual are the high point of his
responsibilities. For the crier has major missions on the island, as is often
the case with this officer, in cities and communities around the medieval
West.

Criers are indeed essential figures in urban politics; their functions go
well beyond public proclamation. At times they participate in territorial
defence, the cleansing of the streets, and the opening and closing of city
gates. At Venice, there are some fifty public criers and every great institution
has an officer for promulgating its decisions.[11] At Murano, meanwhile,
Malcanton is the only "crier of the community".[12] Appointed for life, he is
charged with proclaiming the regulations put out by the island's podestà
and the government. In 1517, the *cavalier* describes the crier as a "public
and juridical" (*publica et juridica*) person.[13]

One of the crier's functions is to cite to appear inhabitants summoned by
the institutions (*comandar*), and another is to alert them to sentences that
concern them. "According to the duty of the oath, with good conscience,
without respect of persons, he must order anyone, according to what is
asked of him, and then to report it to the *cancelliere*" – so the Statutes tell
him, reminding him that he must eschew all favouritism. The crier is also
the organizer of the principal public rituals, such as the passage of power.
He also organizes the auctions in the palace of the podestà, putting up to
bidders' real estate, boats, and concessions, like the island's inn.[14] And,
finally, he rings the Raxon bell (the "reason" or justice bell), at the palace
of the podestà, to summon the Arengo, the Council of Thirty, or the
tribunal. With the bell, his voice, and his cries, he controls the soundspace
of Murano, in an epoch when the sphere of writing is finite and orality still
plays a crucial role in social relations and political communication.

In Vitale Vitturi's official papers, the first notebook records some twenty
proclamations by Antonio Malcanton during the sixteen months of the
patrician's mandate. That makes fewer than two per month.[15] But, beyond

that, there are many more specific circumstantial orders and injunctions. Most often cries take place on the Ponte Lungo and the Ponte di Mezo, and sometimes they happen as well on the Santi Maria e Donato bridge. Proclamations, true oratorical performances, must be done publicly in the presence of a goodly number of persons. When there is need to address a particular audience, the crier is sent to other Murano places. On 2 April 1510, he goes to the little *campo* where stands the San Bernardo convent, a few minutes westwards of Santi Maria e Donato, to proclaim that "whoever, of whatsoever condition, whether small or big, neither dare nor presume to play with a ball, be it small or big, on this *campiello*".[16] On the morning of Sunday October 6, it is inside the church of Santo Stefano that he makes an announcement about an inheritance, doing so at mass and in the presence of the priest Jacopo Ferante.[17]

As he reports in his testimony, Antonio Malcanton is also Vitturi's personal boatman (*barcaruol*). This mission is nowhere in the Statutes. The law forbids the podestà from asking the community to pay the expenses of his officials. He himself must pay his gondolier and his servants.[18] Has Vitturi gotten around this prohibition by asking Malcanton for his services or is it a custom of the island's podestà? We do not know, but it is clear that, in taking up this task, Malcanton became very close to the podestà. Like a chauffeur or coachman, he has followed his master's movements, observing his deeds and actions, and the smallest details of his work.

The crier's salary is fixed at a ducat per month. That is one third of the take of a crier in Venice in the service of the *provveditori* of Health, a half the income of workers at the Mint, and one tenth of what the Mint's secretary makes.[19] At the time, the average rent of a small house in the Rio dei Vetrai quarter is between five and eight ducats per year.[20] If the crier's salary is indeed limited, atop it, he receives a sum, set by sort, for each public document that he announces: a command to appear in civil court pays one *soldo*, a public proclamation eight *soldi*, and so on.[21] Moreover, he is one of the four *caradori* of wood, and he receives a part of the tax on that merchandise.

Antonio Malcanton also negotiates with the Muranese government to have a piece of communal land (*il luogo del comun*), on Campo Santi Maria e Donato, to build his house.[22] It involves replacing the old butcher's market, "there where earlier criers had their house". The empty lot lies beside the loggia and the little adjacent house of the *cavalier*, and near the San Marco flag, Malcanton obtains the right to build a wooden house for himself and his family, so long as he does not impinge on the street. But a few years later he returns before the Council for a permit to build in stone, "because it is much more useful to this comune, and also for me".[23]

At the beginning of his mandate, the crier receives a red beret, and an allowance of three *lire* is paid him every year on account of this hat.[24] This head-covering, singling him out, serves as his uniform. It symbolizes his power and gives him the look of public authority. The sign, the mark, the clothing, the colour, the uniform are figurations of his public mission. In some towns, for the most important cries, drums and flutes sometimes accompany the officer, but this seems not to have happened at Murano.

As the crier was appointed for life, his mission could last a long time. In the seventeenth century, Francesco Luna reports in his journal the death of the crier Tomaso di Mulineri, on Ascension Day, after fifty-five years and five months of service.[25] At the end of their career, criers are often old men, as was Malcanton's predecessor, Matteo da Brescia. Matteo has served a mere dozen years when Vitturi takes up his position and complains that Matteo cannot fulfill his mission, in particular, the job of boatman: "it has already been many days and months, on account of his age and infirmities, that he no longer exercises and cannot exercise his office as he should, and it is clear that in the future he will not be able to exercise it."[26] Antonio Malcanton, who started out as a fruit- and vegetable-seller (*fructaruol*), begins his career at the age of 27, as Matteo's assistant.[27] He is officially installed as vice-crier, by Vitturi, in September 1509.[28] Then, on 20 May 1510, the podestà makes him Matteo da Brescia's replacement. On 31 May, the Council of Thirty votes (24 for and 2 against) to confirm Vitturi's decision, and then the new crier takes his oath, at Council.[29] He is twenty-eight years old at the time, and already married, and the mention of his "family" when he receives the plot to build his house could mark him as a father.[30]

Vitturi, quick to praise Malcanton, justifies the nomination:

> Everyone knows the competence, the fidelity, and the goodness of Antonio di Zuan, who at present is exercising the office of crier in the place of Ser Matteo da Brescia, crier of this worthy community … The said community would easily have suffered if it had not had the hard labours of the said Antonio, who has shown no consideration for the comfort of this own person with the greatest satisfaction to the whole land, which surely would have suffered much. So, it is very proper to reward such labours. So, for the benefit of the land, the podestà, its judges, and the four deputies have decided to dismiss Ser Matteo the crier.[31]

For the moment, the new appointee will have to share the pay and the carat of wood with Matteo, down to his death, so that Matteo can conserve "the alimentation for sustenance in his last age, as is reasonable and just". So, Antonio will have to wait until his predecessor dies to receive the whole of the salary – this is a system that assures retired public officials their subsistence.

On account of the length of his tenure of office, the crier is the island's best-known official, but also one of its best informed. Appointed for life, he must know by heart the laws and successive deliberations, and he assures the community's memory. With time, Malcanton will learn to recognize the inhabitants, know where they live, with whom, and since when, and know their occupations, characters, reputations, and nicknames, plus their caprices, their networks, and their friends. But in January 1511 he is still too new and has lacked time to become used to his new mission. His testimony, like that of the other inhabitants, shows him busy on the *campo*, preparing the ceremony, without doubt intimidated by this first grand occasion. Would a different official longer on the job have handled better the mounting tension on the *campo*? Would he have known how to channel the children's growing excitement, the swelling racket, the collective exaltation? For, indeed, that is one of a public crier's necessary skills: to know how to act and react in the presence of the inhabitants. The job requires a sense of how interaction unfolds and a pragmatic capacity to adapt procedures to what comes up. One must learn to manage relations with one's fellow citizens, both by custom and by testing out what works, to single out moments of tension so as to master them lest they spin out of control, and to growl, shout, grimace or flee, as the turn of events requires. A good crier knows how to get out of a tight spot. Knowledge of places and of people is an essential resource, as is mastery of the dialect and its accents, and of habits and customs. It is necessary to foresee the inhabitants' reactions, to deal with them and to forestall conflict.

Like Simone, the *fante* who directs the taking of witness statements in February 1511, and like the *cavalier*, who serves as communal policeman, or the *cavacanali* who maintains the canals in Venice, Antonio Malcanton participates in the construction of a political order the patricians have devised. They are among the bureaucrats and under-officers who, at the end of the Middle Ages, play a central role in towns' governance. Even though they are commoners perforce excluded from institutions reserved for patricians only, they are charged with applying, and putting to effect, laws and decisions voted by the rulers. Without them, patrician deliberations would stay dead letter. They are patrician power's essential link.

Meanwhile, at power's passage in January 1511, Antonio Malcanton seems too inexperienced to know how to react. His task is hard, as he faces an unprecedented situation, a political interplay where each person's role is shifting. Who on the *campo*, at this moment, is in fact in charge? Does it really fall to Antonio to assure order, when he has at hand two podestà, many Venetian patricians, the judges, the *giustizieri*, and many or even all the Thirty? Besides, the *cavalier* is absent, we know not why. Has Vitturi's old policeman finished his job while Suriano's has not yet stepped in?

So, the 1511 ritual is ensconced in a moment of major transition: between two podestà, two criers and two *cavalieri*. Now the discontinuity of the structures of authority affords some opportunities. These moments when power lapses open the field of possibilities and offer space for the expression of new political intentions. In 1511, the inhabitants of Murano seize the day to express their hostility to the podestà, without, however – in so far as the trial papers reveal – asserting any other claims.

Malcanton has failed to keep the inhabitants in line, but for all that the judges do not manage to prove that he has incited them to rebel. The crier defends his actions and says that he has done his all to carry out his mission in accordance with the law's terms. But perhaps that is the problem, as is clear from a new element of the affair that he reveals to the judges.

## Scandal

When he testifies, the crier explains:

> After the *regimento* was handed over, at the moment when Messer Vitale went to embark to leave, Messer Father Zuan, parish priest (*pievan*) of San Donato, wanted me to ask the podestà to pay for his wife's burial. And me, I did not want to give him the order in the presence of the rector [Suriano], but Father Zuan said to me, "By the blood of the Virgin Mary, if you don't give the order, I will be the worst enemy you ever had". And I knew that my position obliged me to give orders to anyone, without consideration for who he is. I went slowly onto the boat and gave the order to Messer Vitale, and he told me that, by doing that, I had put him to shame.[32]

The priest puts Antonio in a double bind: he is caught between his job as an officer, and the role dictated by his place in the Lagoon's social and political hierarchy. The public mission of a crier expects him to "order anyone whomsoever". But he also must respect his master and defer to him. In the face of the priest's insistence, he must choose between these two contradictory obligations; Malcanton decides to privilege his public mission at the expense of the respect owed Vitturi. No witness heard at the beginning of the month mentions this episode. On the other hand, the four patricians interrogated in the middle of March stress it and tell how shocked they were. Sebastiano Bellencito himself lays these facts out; it was a thing, says he, that happened after the procession had left the church.[33]

> Then, when I was going with the new podestà towards the *palazzo*, Father Zuan Bellonato came up and grabbed by his jacket the crier, Antonio, who was there too, and he said to him, "Go order Messer Vitale, before he leaves, that I want him to pay me for the burial of his wife, as the chapter of San Donato orders him to do". And Antonio answered, "You want me to give him the order now that he is leaving! You will find him in Venice". And Father Zuan looked angry ... so Antonio went there. And then he came back and said to Father Zuan that he had given the order. To me, Antonio said, "It seems to me that I have insulted him, this gentleman, in giving him an order". And then he went to the palace of the podestà to carry out his task, as they were calling for him.

Father Zuan Bellonato knows the podestà well, having received him in his church for weekday and Sunday services, as well as for more solemn masses, during his sixteen months on the job. At the death of Vitturi's wife, daughter of Tragnaco Contarini di Polazzo, he had been in charge of the funeral. Unfortunately, we do not know the affair's details. In another trial, two years earlier, Father Zuan is called an "*assassino publico*", i.e. a well-known "killer" (that is, a bad character); the speaker is another priest on the opposing side in a law case.[34] But we know nothing more, as the *avogadori* do not take the time to ask him, and his testimony might have been essential.

The priest has taken advantage of this brief moment, with Vitturi no longer rector, but still present on the island, to reclaim his due. He leans on his ecclesiastical authority to defy patrician authority, by considering Vitturi subject to the community's ordinary laws, now that he has laid down his baton of command. But, in constraining the crier to give in public an order to make the patrician pay, the priest is debasing the podestà's power, doubly. He makes him an ordinary inhabitant like all the others, denying his power's exceptional character, and he also subjects a Venetian patrician to a law decreed both by and for the community of Murano.

So, Antonio Malcanton is accused as much of leading the rebel band during the snowball fight, as of acting scandalously vis-a-vis the podestà. Nevertheless, while the five other accused undergo a new interrogation on 26 March, this time under torture, Malcanton is set free early, before the trial's end. Podestà Giacomo Suriano, it turns out, mindful of how the crier's presence at Murano is essential, intercedes on his behalf. The archival dossier has a little note by Suriano, dated 24 February, shortly after the six arrests. The paper is in very bad shape; one cannot read the whole of it, but we can still make out the following: "I can certify that this community has only one public crier . . . appreciated by all the community for the goodness of his actions and his good condition." The podestà beseeches the *avogadori*, "on the part of your most faithful [inhabitants] of this land of Murano" to accept the guarantees laid out to liberate Antonio. We do not know if he refers here to a money-pledge in hand, but it seems that the community has mobilized collective support for the crier, via the podestà as spokesman. His intervention works, for Antonio manages to leave Venetian prisons and return to Murano, there to await the sentence of the *avogadori*.

The Snowball Revolt involves two violations of political order: on the one side, the shouts, the chants, the snow, and the protests against Vitturi; on the other, this disrespectful act of Antonio's towards the podestà, and the rupture in the ritual with his intrusion onto the gondola that is carrying Vitturi back to Venice. The first insubordination is done by the community, a plural body with its collective identity and capacity for political action. The second insubordination is the deed of the crier, who is a repository of part of public authority. Both these infractions connect to an intention, and to a complex of actions, that range beyond the single event of 27 January 1511. They reflect, in a deeper way, a specific political culture, a capacity for expressing critical opinions, and values.

## Notes

1 "Statuto de Muran", book II, ch. 4, 261.
2 ASVe, AC, MP, 142, no. 17, fol. 7–12.
3 Marino Sanudo, *I Diarii*, vol. 12, col. 99, 2 April 1511.
4 Tassini, *Curiosità veneziane*, 367.
5 ASVe, PM, 44, 10 Extraordinariorum 3, for 10 May 1510.
6 ASVe, PM, 44, 19 Criminalium 1, for 3 September 1509, against Pietro Bigaia. In November 1509, the book of the commune registers the amount of the fine that he must pay: ASVe, PM, 229, 2, Cassa fontico di Murano, book 1, fol. 20v, for 20 November 1509.
7 ASVe, PM, 44, 22 Criminalium 4, for 5 March 1510, against Vettor di Polo Forner.
8 ASVe, AC, MP, 142, no. 17, fol. 18v–19v.
9 ASVe, PM, 44, 24 Criminalium 6, for 25 July 1510; 25 Criminalium 7, for 25 August 1510.
10 ASVe, PM, 44, 20 Criminalium 2, for 7 January 1510, against Sebastiano Bellencito.
11 Cesare Vecellio's *Habiti Antichi et Moderni, The Clothing of the Renaissance World*, Margaret F. Rosenthal and Ann Rosalind Jones (London: Thames & Hudson, 2008 [Venice, 1590]), 169–70 in the modern edition.
12 "Statuto de Muran", book I, ch. 12, 249.
13 ASVe, AC, MP, 410, no. 14, fol. 6.
14 ASVe, PM, 44, 9 Extraordinariorum 2, for 18 February 1510, for the sale of a house on the Fondamenta dei Vetrai; ASVe, PM, 44, 13 Pignorum, 8 July 1510, sale of a *barca pedotina*.
15 ASVe, PM, 44, 1 Proclamatione.
16 ASVe, PM, 44, 1 Proclamatione, 2 April 1510.
17 ASVe, PM, 44, 1 Proclamatione, 6 October 1510.
18 "Statuto de Muran", book I, ch. 18, 255.
19 ASVe, Provveditore alla Sanità, reg. 726, fol. 22, for 29 November 1519; from this day forward, the monthly salary of the crier rises to three ducats.
20 ASVe, PM, 44, 9 Extraordinariorum 2, for 18 February 1510, for the example of a house rental. See also ASVe, Dieci Savi alle Decime, 1514, busta 82, Murano. Workshops and houses with shops in them are more expensive (from 15 to 50 ducats a year). For example, see declaration number 16, for a more comfortable house (*da stazio*) with a glassworks (*fornaxe*) and an empty lot rented for 50 ducats.
21 ASVe, PM, 236 bis, fol. 34–5, for 21 January 1588, where the tariffs are revised.
22 ASVe, PM, 45, Extraordinariorum 2, for 9 May 1512.
23 ASVe, PM, 45, Extraordinariorum 2, for 23 May 1512.
24 ASVe, PM, 229, 3, fol. 12, for 31 December 1511.
25 *Diario di Murano di Francesco Luna* 68, May 1630.
26 ASVe, PM, 44, 10 Extraordinariorum 3, for 20 May 1510.
27 Archivio Parrocchiale San Pietro Martire di Murano, Scuola di San Giovanni Battista dei Battuti, Registro dei confratelli, fol. 2, for 16 September 1544, for a mention of the death of Antonio at the age of 62.

28  ASVe, PM, 44, 8 Extraordinariorum 1, for 20 September 1509. The statutes foresee the replacement of the crier if he falls ill: "Statuto de Muran", book I, ch. 12, 249.
29  ASVe, PM, 44, 10 Extraordinariorum 3, for 20 May and 31 May 1510.
30  ASVe, PM, 229, 3, fol. 7v, for 17 March 1511.
31  ASVe, PM, 44, 10 Extraordinariorum 3, for 20 May 1510.
32  ASVe, AC, MP, 142, no. 17, fol. 8.
33  ASVe, AC, MP, 142, no. 17, fol. 19r-v.
34  Archivio Parrocchiale Santi Maria e Donato, Fabbriceria, Atti generali, Prima serie, busta 6, processo no. 18 (Avogaria di Comun), fol. 13v, Angelo Angelo.

# 7 Political actions, political intentions

Neither the ten witnesses heard by Simone, nor the six suspects interrogated by the tribunal, nor the three magistrates of the Avogaria di Comun use the words "revolt" or "tumult". They speak about Suriano's *intrar*, the ceremony, with the inhabitants assembled, before it degenerated. Still, the protest, the actions, and the chants against Vitturi, the nature of the facts, the intentionality of the actors – all these things invite us to venture a political reading of the snowball fight, rather than deem it some mere disorderly charivari. The words and actions of the inhabitants are lofted by intention and enabled by a capacity for mobilization, whose roots lie well beyond the bourn of what transpired on 27 January. From a reading in the archives of the podestà, and in documents produced by glassmakers and *traghetto* boatmen, there emerges the image of a political society both complex and active. The show of hostility against Vitturi should be placed in a much wider ensemble of practices, usually less spectacular but just as politically significant. By placing the Snowball Revolt in its context of action one can better understand its meaning.

## The appropriation of ritual

Rules and codes lay down the proceedings of the passage of power, but on 27 January 1511 the inhabitants pay them little heed and appropriate the *intrar* to reroute its meaning. A ritual rests on repetition, regularity, and tradition. Venetian order is all the more readily imposed because it passes for a secular rhetoric, with political implications that the inhabitants understand. But, that day, they amuse themselves, taking advantage of the circumstances and the actions intended to guarantee the moment's dignity.

The sanctity of the place is no more respected than is protocol. The inhabitants take over Campo Santi Maria e Donato, the place of civil and church power, to turn it into the battlefield for snowballs. Gathering before Suriano arrives, they establish their presence, settle in, and fill the air with their talk and laughter; in so doing, they establish ever greater control of the island's central space. The *campo*, the *platea communis* (square of the community), is the public place *par excellence*; it delimits power's legitimate space. The palace of the podestà and the prison, the statue of Justice, the houses of the *cavalier*, *cancelliere* and crier, the banner of San Marco, the principal church, the *campanile* and the house of the parish priest of Santi Maria e Donato define, between them, a political and sacred geography repeatedly reworked by civic and religious rituals. The *traghetto* gondoliers go there on holidays to receive the podestà and accompany him to Venice in a floating procession.[1] Actions and events that happen there, in their essence, have a public, political dimension.

More than any other building, the palace of the podestà grants the place its symbolic value. Built in the first half of the fourteenth century, down to its destruction at the beginning of the nineteenth it incarnates Venetian presence. The covered gallery at ground level, the loggia, echoes the one that girds the Doge's Palace at San Marco. It marks the meeting of two spaces: closed palace and open square. A hybrid space, belonging at once to the *palazzo* and the town, to podestà and *popolo*, the loggia is considered "public space". What one does there is seen and known by all.[2] At the time of Vitturi and Suriano, the community lays out substantial sums to renovate the palace of the podestà, financing both materials and pay for artisans, masons, and blacksmiths. In 1510 and 1511, it orders glass for the windows, wood and locks for the principal door, and a walnut high seat for the audience hall. Benches are installed under the loggia, and balconies of Istrian stone, and then they renovate the kitchens. In the same years, the house of the *cancelliere*, a communal property, also sees renovation, while the crier builds his home nearby. After that it is the San Donato bridge's turn for refurbishing, and then the prison's, where they change both locks and chains.[3]

On 27 January 1511, the public space of the *campo* becomes the prize, in play between the ritual's actors. While the Venetian patricians and the Muranese *cittadini* carry out power's liturgy, the island's inhabitants install there another form of action, shifting its use and function. To the order that the two podestà are trying to represent, they oppose the disorder of battle. Had the fight happened elsewhere on the island, if Vitturi had been attacked along the Rio dei Vetrai, or while shipping off Lagoon-wards, the deed would have lacked its special impact, nor would the inhabitants and patricians have read it as they did. The Campo Santi Maria e Donato grants the battle a political dimension.

When they climb the *campanile*, the Muranesi add yet more to their action's import. As often, in Venice and all Italy, the bell tower is detached from the church. In Murano, it stands a few metres to the south, halfway between Santi Maria e Donato and the palace of the podestà. The bell calls parishioners to mass, but also rings out a summons to those solemn occasions that gather all the island's inhabitants. On Saturday evening, and on the eve of holidays, the bell announces the start of a day of rest.[4] The Muranesi can tell the difference between its sound and that of the island's other bells, the parish churches and the Raxon bell atop the palace of the podestà. It falls to clergy to ring the church bells, while to the crier goes the Raxon.

The capture of the *campanile* is the telling symbol that good order is tottering. By laying hands on power's sound and redirecting it, as revolts traditionally did, the inhabitants make their protest ten-fold stronger. The intrusion of the sound of bells, and of collective racket, in the ritual's well-ordered sound-space reinforces the critique. Of course, the ceremony foresees that the inhabitants cheer and applaud the two podestà, crying out enthusiasm and approval. Instead, they utter their scorn for Vitturi, lambasting him and adding to their boos a disordered clangor of bells. Does the racket make its way into the church? In the trial there is no mention, but surely one must have heard the bell, beating on the fly, and the noise, chants, and laughter, all swelling on the *campo*.

As they leave the church, the ruckus is so great that many witnesses link its loudness with the violence of the actions. Domenico de Andrico had expected to board Vitturi's gondola, but "I was afraid that it would turn over belly-up on account of the great racket (*stridor*)". Likewise, according to what Pietro Zorzi says, it was indeed because of the "clamour" that Vitturi chose not to use the Rio dei Vetrai to leave the island. At Murano, this association between sound and action is common. At the time of a trial launched by Vitturi a few months earlier, a plaintiff denounces insults and the blows he suffered, evoking "a great tumult of words".[5] In giving the revolt its character, the words are as important as the actions. The booing eggs the snowball fight on and makes the interaction all the more jarring, especially as there is that chant that all sing in chorus.

### The performance of the revolt

The accused, like some of the witnesses, deny having heard anything beyond the collective clamour that names the new podestà: "Surian! Surian!" But many witnesses insist on it, and Marino Sanudo tells it too: the inhabitants entertain themselves with a chant, in verse, and rhyming, and, when testifying, they offer various versions to the *avogadori*. So, from one and another deposition:

> Surian! Chase off this dog who is eating our bread!
> Surian! Surian! Chase off this Vitturi, who has destroyed and consumed us!
> Surian! Surian! Chase off this dog who has eaten the poverty of Muran!
> Surian! Chase this dog who has undone Muran!
> Let Surian come, chase off this dog!
> Come quickly Surian and chase this villain who has undone the poor of Muran![6]

The witnesses have retained different versions, or, perhaps, have partially reconstructed or invented them. But, despite slight nuances, all make Vitturi into a "dog", picking up a classical medieval insult, perhaps inspired by biblical metaphors that associate the animal with impurity and evil.[7] Infidels and heretics are dogs, as, more generally, are enemies of the state and traitors. Vitturi is not characterized as a cuckold (*becco fotuto*), a good-for-nothing (*furfante*) or scoundrel (*zoton* or *gioton*), some of the Lagoon's commonest insults of the time, but as a dog, disqualifying both his person and his actions.[8] The name of his successor, Suriano, invites this rhyme with *can* (dog), as also happens with many other Venetian family names – Grimani, Loredan, Pisani, or Trevisan, for example – when they are pronounced in Venetian, which often drops the final vowel. In 1499, after Antonio Grimani's fleet loses to the Ottomans, children roam Venice chanting, "Antonio Grimani, ruin of the *cristiani*, may you be eaten by the *cani*, and the *cagnolli*, you and your sons [*fiulli*]!"[9] The family names evoke also the rhyme with *pan* (bread), which stands for the inhabitants' main food, their economic resources, and their survival chances, especially in times of famine, which from the start of the 1520s are frequent.[10]

The Muranesi also pick up a second rhetoric, current at the time, to point out corrupt rectors. In June 1509, the chronicler Girolamo Priuli criticizes sharply some Venetian administrators on Terra Ferma, whose scandalous behaviour, he maintains, explains why the inhabitants, at the time of the League of Cambrai, rallied to the enemy. He evokes the poor citizens, eaten (*mangiati*) by these bad magistrates, who "were eating, and scattering the goods of the poor subjects" (*mangiavanno et disipavanno li poveri subdicti*).[11] *Magnar/Mangiare* means "to eat" but also to abuse one's power, and the term *manzador* is used to describe administrators and rulers who take advantage of their authority to impose unfair rules and levies.

The longest version of the chant ("Come quickly Surian and chase off this lowly-rustic [*vilan*] dog who has undone the poor of Murano") is given by one of the four patrician witnesses, Paolo Contarini di Bortolo. He is the only one to use the adjective *vilan*, which, as we have seen in the affair of the German bakers, stigmatizes peasants and residents of the Terra Ferma. Whether Contarini made this expression up, or did hear it, it only underlines the violence of the words against the podestà.

So Vitturi is all these things together: a dog, an unjust rector, a rustic, and a bad administrator. The clash is cobbled out of words borne by the children, workers, and fishermen, who enjoy the rhymes and play with the tune, frolicking in this turnabout where the supreme magistrate is insulted in shared song. Nevertheless, the chant against Vitturi does not range past him to denounce the whole government or the Venetian patricians, targeting Venetian domination.

Chants, by both definition and nature ephemeral expressions, are hard to reconstruct. Collections and transcriptions of chants do exist, but they rarely let us date their moment of production or give the place and occasion of their performance. Nineteenth-century collections do gather songs, sometimes very old, but we lack the information to pin down their medieval origins or their sixteenth-century diffusion. Here and there, with luck, witnesses and sources offer furtive mentions of chants, which, at Murano, surely were not rare. In September 1509, the master barber Zorzi Rosso recounts how he ran across three companions strolling the *fondamente*: the porter Zaneto, Pompeio di Matteo Pelizza, and Bernardin (or perhaps Benedetto) di Andrea Boier. The three pass him singing, until Matteo di Nicolo Caverlino, a fisherman sleeping on his boat, threatens to beat them if they don't leave.[12] The glass workshops were also a place where one sang, to believe more recent accounts by masters.[13] Down to the 1950s, before the transistor radio arrived, men hummed to give the work its cadence or to mark the length of some procedures. At the bakers, refrains matched the timing of the kneading of the loaves, and among the glassmakers counted couplets measured out the second roasting of glass vials. Back then, when instruments to measure time's passage were rare, song helped gauge its length. These oral practices have left few traces in the sources, but the song against Vitturi, all evidence suggests, fits well in this tradition of everyday activity.

Songs also stabilize knowledge and memory. In early modern Murano many lack ready access to writing. Some do know how to read, numbers at least, and fewer can write. But when they can write, often, their documents are not kept. The patricians and ruling classes, meanwhile, dispose of written supports to stabilize their opinions, discourse, and thoughts. Elite politics is constructed in texts, thanks to the conservation, generation after generation, of power's words. Reflections on the meaning of the State, political theory, laws, and deliberations pile up like sediment. Writing lets ideas spread and helps shape debates.

For the *popolani*, who lack the same written resources, the production of political knowledge passes through orality and memory. So, knowledge and opinion become stable by way of rhymes, chants, and poems. We know neither how the ditty against Vitturi was created, nor if it follows a well-known tune, nor if other podestà before him have been called "dog". But works by historians and anthropologists, on other places – nineteenth-century France or the USA during the Vietnam war – show that song is an efficacious means of political expression as well as a tool for memorializing intentions and convictions. When they work out their anti-Vitturi discourse, via song, the inhabitants enable both the creation and diffusion of a collective critique.

Atop the word, there are the deeds. The Muranesi united on the *campo* know that they are obliged to participate in performance of the ritual. The *intrar* involves actions that symbolize the power of the rulers and the submission of their subjects. In ostentatious, sometimes extravagant fashion, princes and lords make their functions visible as they move about and use telling gestures, moving head and hands as the ceremony requires. In turn, the inhabitants show their allegiance by applauding, shouting, and moving, or stay calm and silent. In certain medieval rituals one cries tears, and, at some mystic performances, people faint. On 27 January, however, the inhabitants turn out not to the ordered, expected repertoire of gestures and emotions, but rather to chaos and a snowball fight.

The conflict emerges from the gap between the solemnity of the moment and the snow's triviality. Snow is an ambiguous weapon: it does not wound like a stone or dagger blade. Now, in law, what defines violence is bloodshed. Trials of the period often contain the deposition of the barber-surgeon who describes the wound and measures out the slashed flesh, information necessary for determining a crime's gravity. But the snow leaves no mark on Vitturi's body. Nor does it defile like spit or sully like rotten fruit. For a few seconds it leaves a spot on the podestà's vestments and then melts and vanishes. To the patricians, none of that makes it the less shocking, as they are alert to the gesture's nature; it scorns as well as stings. The chronicler Marino Sanudo speaks of stones, perhaps in light of Venetian rumour, but also perhaps because news of a Venetian representative departing under a snowball barrage makes the Serenissima seem feeble and silly.

The battle also upsets the social and political hierarchy that the ritual means to stage: the dominance of the patricians over the folk of the *popolo*; of the Muranesi *cittadini* over the other inhabitants; of the master glassmakers over their workers; of adults over children. The fine layering of hierarchies is the basis for the island's structures of domination, and it is against them all that the cries, snowballs, and disorder flare up, making the clash and critique all the livelier. But, still, no other claim consorts with the action of the Muranesi, who restrict themselves to rejecting the actions and policies of Vitturi. There is no higher aspiration, or denunciation of a political or economic injustice. Shaped by and for the moment, the Snowball Revolt does not stray beyond protest against Vitturi.

And, finally, the ritual presupposes absorption in a regime of emotions that goes beyond the actors' rationality. Emotion is the necessary ingredient to power ceremonies, but it depends on a risky alchemy. The presence of the crowd gives intensity to the collective performance and magnifies the expected sentiments. But there is always the risk that the enthusiasm will get out of hand. At Murano, the excitement and racket contribute to the general effervescence. Set free, aggression gives rise to the snowball fight, which becomes subversive.

The protagonists, for all that, are not acting under the influence, merely, of unleashed irrationality, of accumulated frustration and the pull of the crowd. The chant is not invented on the fly by adolescents gathered in some corner of the *campo*, nor does the denunciation of Vitturi's injustices emerge from the moment's exaltation. The inhabitants' actions are not just carnivalesque rituality. It is tempting to see, in this event as in any other charivari and popular protest, another form of ritual. Historians, classically, have interpreted both carnival and many popular demonstrations as laying out the repertoires of action and regular features of the crowd. That is especially true for carnival, which allows the people to invert social roles and hierarchies.

As convincing as this approach might seem, it rigidifies collective behaviour, whose course does not always hew to rules or fit snugly into unconscious structures. The sources give the impression of regularity, just as medieval chroniclers tend to tell tales of revolts by using codified narratives and by inserting their stories into a pre-established rhetorical framework. This is a very effective filter, so we should try to side-step it: the seeming rituality of the revolt comes as much from the narrative choices of medieval authors as it does from the facts they record. Now, in reducing the people's political action to forms of ritual violence, one risks depoliticizing their strategic intentions. Although anthropological analysis may be useful for understanding the modes of action, it does not suffice. The revolt, and the ritual forms of action, are far from the whole story: they do not exhaust the list of modes by which the people expressed their critique of power.

In 1511, at Murano, doubtless, before the events there was debate, of which the documents conserve no trace. It is only in the seventeenth century, with the appearance of institutions of popular surveillance, that police reports and spy depositions inform us as to the everyday drift of public opinion. For earlier times, one must track systematically the possible links between a people's political culture, and the language and action employed in their everyday lives. Meanwhile, the events of 27 January can be put in perspective by examining other forms of intervention in the public sphere, less violent and less destructive, whose existence, nevertheless, preconditioned the denunciation of Vitturi's policies.

## Making politics

The inhabitants' indignation, and their accusations, reflect a norm by which they judge the podestà. This capacity to appraise his action is built elsewhere, in bodies like the devotional confraternities and professional associations – the *scuole* and the *arti* – to which many inhabitants belong. To understand how the protest took hold, one must investigate these organizations' culture and political resources, to ask how these traits take form within these institutions. The confraternities and guilds build strong connections; they are spaces of sociability, where inhabitants of various conditions mingle. There, by collaborating, they learn to act in the name of common good and collective entity. Places of negotiation, action, and initiation, these institutions teach members a rhetoric and set of practices that allow them to develop opinions, intentions, and ideas that, in turn, shape the social and political order.

At the beginning of the sixteenth century, there are several confraternities at Murano: those of San Giovanni Battista and Santo Stefano, founded in the fourteenth century, and of San Vincenzo Ferrer, at San Pietro Martire, created in 1469, as well as the very recent Confraternità del Santissimo Sacramento at Santo Stefano.[14] Founded on 29 November 1506 by thirteen inhabitants, this "*scuola, compagnia et fraternita*" gathers men as well as women who seem to desire to distinguish themselves from the confraternity of San Giovanni Battista, then the most important. Neighbours' squabbles and tensions between assorted interest groups may have led to this foundation, which contains the glass-furnace owners Domenico Angelo di Francesco (At the Cock), Vettor Blondo di Bortolo, Angelo Barovier di Alvise and Gasparo Capello di Bortolo (At the Hat), the glassmaker Domenico Pisani di Jacopo, the physician Zuan Rizo di Domenico, and the binder Zuan Todesco.[15] In 1510, judge Domenico Bertoluso, furnace owner Jacopo Corona, and spice merchant Zuan Rosso also belong.[16] The creation of this new institution requires organizing, and coming to agreement over norms and common practices, on the model of other institutions of the time.

This new confraternity cannot, however, compete with San Giovanni Battista, which appeared as a flagellant brotherhood amidst the Great Plague of 1348.[17] Housed near the Rio dei Vetrai, it gathers members from the entire island, and at the beginning of the sixteenth century, among its members are Domenico de Andrico, the glassmakers Baldissera Capello and Nicolo Barovier, the crier Antonio Malcanton, the priest Pietro Alvise Baffo, the gondoliers Martin Saraxin and Matteo Follega da Zadar, Alvise Usnago the *cancelliere's* father, the judge Domenico Rizo di Zuan (who in 1508 is its chief, the *guardian grande*), Angelo Zeloxo and members of the families Fuga, Bigaia, and Ballarin.[18]

Beyond its missions of devotion and solidarity, the confraternity is a powerful device for social regulation. When, as its Statutes announce, the Scuola of San Giovanni Battista sets rules for the relations among its members, it condemns violence and insists on compromise.[19] So the *scuola* serves as a tribunal, at which the members and *guardian* arbitrate quarrels, proscribe peace oaths, and sort out conflicts. At the start of 1509, the *guardian*, in the presence of the confraternity brothers, convokes Jacopo Fuga and Bernardin Torcellan, "commanding them to make peace and set aside all hate and rancour".[20] "Because our brotherhood should be in harmony as much via love as via justice", in December 1511 the guardian summons the fisherman Polo di Donato Forner, as he has battered with oars his confraternal brother Zuan Maria Chaulin.[21] He is condemned to a one-ducat fine, and, to remain a member of the *scuola*, he must choose to pay it. Much like the podestà with his justice, the confraternity controls the inhabitants' violence, in deeds as well as words. In July 1512, Angelo Zeloxo is reprimanded for having insulted the gravedigger Monte Padoan in the church of Santi Maria e Donato, at the moment when the San

Giovanni procession was lining up, "without respect for the place, nor for the custom of the company". The next morning Monte rails at the *guardian* who comes to reprimand him, "without respect for either his person or our ruling, with vile words that, out of decency, one does not utter here".[22]

Alongside the institutions of the police and justice, the confraternities participate in the construction of social order – an emanation of collective will. When the brothers neglect to take up their reciprocal obligations, they are called to justify themselves, while the rest of the *scuola* weighs their arguments. In December 1509, Bernardin and Marco Bigaia fail to take part in the funeral for their fraternal brother, the late Franco da Zara. The *guardian* asks them the reasons for their absence.[23]

> Making their excuses, they say that they bought fish for some sixty *lire* with an eye to selling it at Treviso, and the fish was far from fresh and aging, and they thought that, if they went to the burial, they were running the risk of losing the fish.

"Which excuse is not accepted by the congregation", the assembly concludes, condemning them to a one-ducat fine. These judgments and sentences are collective, and are based on conventions expressed, decided, and admitted by all.

Things are just the same in the professional associations, made up of men and women who practice the same activity and collectively defend their trade. So, the gondoliers of the *traghetto* show up regularly as the Muranese authorities' interlocutors. In spite of their precarious economic position and legal status, they make their guild a place for action and for the protection of their interests. A few days before Vitale Vitturi arrives at Murano, on 31 August 1509, the guild holds a meeting of the twelve Venetian gondoliers and the twelve Muranesi of their governing council, so as to elect representatives.[24] After a complex procedure combining drawing lots and voting, Matteo Follega da Zadar is chosen *gastaldo*; Alessandro Facchin and Andrea Grassela are *massari* and will thus preside over the administration.

A month later, Matteo is summoned by Vitturi, who asks him to justify the absence of many gondoliers from his own *intrar*, just a little time ago.[25] It fell to them to escort him at his arrival, and to celebrate with pomp his recent election. Matteo defends his colleagues, assuring the hearing that "all those whom one commanded to come did come". Three of them had been hired in Venice by customers. The others were old and could no longer do the work.

> Many others are not there because they are at Padua, some in one place, some in another, the times being as they are. And also because one did not know the intentions of his Magnificence until Sunday at the hour of tierce, while usage expects that one give notice at least one day ahead of time.

Matteo thus is justifying his companions against Vitturi's accusations. The guild legitimates its intervention and authorizes a simple Muranese gondolier to hold his own against a Venetian magistrate.

In February 1524, the guild members complain to the Signoria about the patrician Leonardo Gritti, who owns some warehouses near the embarcadero by San Canciano, in Venice, at the *sottoportego* (covered passage) along the Rio di Santi Apostoli, still visible today.[26] Gritti has blocked it off with wooden planks. In answer to the gondoliers' request, the authorities order him to re-open the entry as fast as possible. In 1508, they had already brought complaint about the difficulty of moving around near the *embarcadero*, and about conflicts that had set them against the Gritti.[27] The *scuola*, clearly, is an instrument of pressure, as well as a place for defining a trade and negotiating with the podestà.

One problem the guild must confront concerns its members' number: the more *barcaruoli* offer services, the lower are individual profits. In 1509, they decide that they cannot exceed sixty.[28] But in 1519, the podestà Filippo Barbarigo imposes the right of each future rector to add a new boatman to the guild, and thus to enlarge its number.[29] In 1530, the *barcaruoli* number 67, and is necessary to return to 60.[30] Between the guild members and the podestà, disagreements continue.[31] A new stage in this trial of strength arrives in 1557–8. At this point, the podestà Marco Antonio Querini proposes that the *barcaruol* named by the podestà be entered at once into the guild, for fifteen years, and if he dies sooner his heirs can stand in for him for the stint remaining. The *barcaruoli* denounce the move:

> If we do not provide, this thing can serve as an example, and all the other gentlemen who will step into this office of podestà will desire, for sure, the same thing, expanding perhaps to 15, 20, 30, 40 or 50 years the concession, and turning the right to this poor *traghetto* into a permanent legacy (*fideo commisso*). That means the total ruin of so many poor *barcaruoli* to whom will be denied all hope that their poor sons will ever be able to enter in their place.[32]

The Senato acts in their favour and suspends the power of the podestà to nominate a gondolier, reserving the right to members of the *scuola*. Their number is then limited to fifty.[33]

The gondoliers perceive the risk of seeing membership in the *scuola* opened to outsiders and turned into a *fideicommissio*, an inalienable inheritance. Family transmission excludes the other members of the *scuola, de facto*, from the process of accepting a candidate. Turning public charges and functions into family property is a classic sixteenth-century phenomenon, especially among the Venetian patricians and *cittadini* who occupy the public offices, and, more widely, in all of Europe. The *barcaruoli* set themselves against this custom, as they must control membership in their guild if they want it to remain an economic and political counterweight, to defend their corporate rights. The arguments they raise against the podestà's proposal spring from an articulate, and efficacious guild discourse

That is why governments try to control institutionalized groups, for they know that they can foster collective criticism. The statutes of the glassmaker guild ordain, for example, that

> no one of this craft should dare or presume to make any sort of arrangement, company, community, or conspiracy, by oath or giving faith, or by any promise, against the honour of Messer the Doge and the commune of Venice, or against any other person, under pain of banishment. And everyone of the guild is held by oath to denounce, as soon as he can, to Messer the Doge and his council, or to the lords *giustizieri*, all those he knows to be guilty of that misdeed.[34]

A few decades earlier, the statutes of the confraternity of San Giovanni Battista also tried to control potential seditious intentions of its participants, reasserting that each member must

> make an oath, on the statutes, that during his entire life, he will not go against the Signoria of Venice and our orders. If he learns that someone intends to go against, he should tell the Signoria as promptly as possible or Messer Guardian, under pain of being perpetually removed from this Scuola.[35]

Such regulations show that the inhabitants did not wait for 27 January 1511 to show political intention and collective action. If the law provides for the prohibition of conspiracies, it is not they that threaten to gnaw away at Venetian power. And to declare them illegal does not suffice. In 1534, the heads of the Council of Ten of Venice write the podestà,

> having heard that at Murano one commits very great inconveniences against the quiet life of this place, and in particular of the action of the glassmakers, when the *cavalier* of the magnificent podestà comes to take some step, all of them together, men and women, come out of the shops and do him violence with great tumults, so that he cannot carry out what was commanded. We order the magnificent podestà of Murano to see to this as will seem best to his prudence, so that the *cavalier* and his deputies (*ministri*) can do their job and what the magnificent podestà commands them to do.[36]

The injunction is proclaimed "in the habitual places" of the island.

## Political acknowledgement and juridical status

The guilds are spaces of negotiation with power, and here the glassworkers' guild is beyond doubt the most powerful, for they exploit their economic clout and reputation to try to impose their claims. From the end of the fifteenth century, the chapter of the glassmakers' guild is composed of its own internal podestà, the *gastaldo*, and some "companions", as well as of some furnace owners.[37] Meetings are held in the palace of the podestà, and are dominated by the owners of the workshops, who are often also members of the Thirty.

At Venice, in the fourteenth century the practice of international trade became the condition for the status of nobles, who, all agreed, should never do manual labour. On Murano, in like fashion, but only in the fifteenth century, the glassmaking art was the condition for access to institutions and for citizen status. In effect, the glassmakers' capacity for organization has led to the negotiation of the status "*cittadino* di Murano". Appearing at the end of the fifteenth century in various different documents, the title becomes the object of spirited debate for the entire century to follow. The Statutes of 1502 make frequent reference to the "good *cittadini* of the *terra*", without, however, spelling out the legal conditions for belonging. In the beginning, the *cittadini* seem to be those who enjoy enough renown to be known as such by others. But the state of affairs cannot last amidst demographic growth. By mid sixteenth-century, it is necessary not only to ensconce the statutes in a legal framework but also to lay out the group's boundaries. In 1546, by law, the Thirty becomes a Forty. Thenceforth, each family of "good *cittadini*" is held to take part in the election of the council's quota. At that point, the definition of *cittadino* status is set precisely: "it is declared that the good *cittadini* are the sons of natives of Murano [that is to say of a father born at Murano or in the Duchy], and likewise those who own buildings (*stabili*) in the *terra*".[38]

These dispositions are still not satisfactory, and in March 1554, the podestà must convoke a general assembly to

> put an end to so many, and infinite controversies that have taken place down to now in this land, concerning the governance of this body and of its Council, on account of which there have sprung up great hatreds and enmities, sects, leagues, and cabals (*odii et inimicitie, sette, maone e conventicule*) among the citizens of this place.

The decision is taken to enlarge the Council to "all the citizens of this town, that is to say one per house, among those older than age 25". Fifty members, at least, must meet if the deliberations are to be considered valid. The definition of *cittadino* status remains the same, with one additional condition: to be *cittadini*, sons must issue from a legitimate marriage. The Venetian Senate ratifies the decision on 14 April 1554, laying out that this Council (labelled *generale* or *maggiore*) will have at least one hundred members, and will vote to elect the officers and magistrates, as well as a Minor Council of twenty-five members, charged with governing with the podestà. Property owners at Murano obtain *cittadino* status only after five years of residence "in this *terra*, place, and hearth".

The decision swells the number of *cittadini* considerably, as is clear from the list in the Golden Book (*Libro d'oro*) established at the beginning of the seventeenth century. Taking as its model the Venetian Golden Book, which, for a century, has recorded noble births, Murano's book results from a new modification of the citizenship law, formulated in February 1602 to remedy the bad effects of the two laws of 1546 and 1554. The change they brought

> has not engendered a good effect, but, to the contrary has brought a terrible corruption (*pessima corruttella*), as the number of families has grown so much that as many as five hundred persons come to a meeting of the Assembly, who bring on great confusion and scandals.

To avoid further problems, the heredity of the status is established, restricted from now on to the "sons of those presently legitimate *cittadini*, and their sons and grandsons and others who will succeed them, issued from legitimate marriages". As for those who have acquired citizenship after having bought properties on the island, their successors will maintain status even if they lose the properties in question.

On 9 April 1603, the Golden Book is inaugurated, and it remains open for two years, during which many inhabitants try to have themselves registered.[39] In 1605, the definitive copy comes out. More than 640 inhabitants are in the register, members of some fifty families, among them many lineages of glassworkers who have been in the craft since the fourteenth century. From 1605 on, the glass-making craft is reserved to *cittadini*, and citizenship is tightly bound to the industry. Casanova, more than a century later, denounces these privileges: "to prevent their emigration, the government accords all these people the right of citizen of Venice".[40]

The process has been slow, but it works, and in the space of one century, Murano has seen the emergence of a new juridical status, negotiated by the inhabitants and recognized by Venice. Among the *popolo* themselves, henceforth a distinction separates the more modest inhabitants from the wealthy artisans. Workmen without high skills, labourers, and domestic servants are barred from citizenship, as they are from guilds. Those bodies are reserved to those *popolani* who enjoy professional and geographic stability and have sufficient economic resources to pay their admission fees and to buy their tools of trade (boats, raw materials). The poor workers, those who suffer structural instability, often change job and residence. They sell their arms for a daily wage, shifting place at the beck of contracts and openings. They are harder to spot, as their interactions are less often caught by documents. For all that, they are no less members of the community, and, as the judicial records testify, they too are spurred to debate with colleagues, neighbours and friends. Just like the glassworkers and the fishermen, they could puzzle over the legitimacy of Vitturi's decisions, and discuss the actions carried out by those who dominate them, from the petty artisan who employs them in his shop all the way to the members of the Thirty who govern the island at the beginning of the sixteenth century. Because they are members of the community, and in particular of the community of Christians, and because the church integrates them into the parish, they too belong, and participate in society.

## To vote and elect

One of the clearest signs of commoner familiarity with political speech and practice appears in the customs around elections. A trial that arises after the election of the priest at Santi Maria e Donato, in the spring of 1508, reveals the details of a complex electoral procedure, in use at Murano as it is at Venice, where the priests are chosen by their parishioners.[41] The priest of Santi Maria e Donato is chosen by a broad community, not only because of the importance of the church, thought in common usage Murano's cathedral, but also because the parish is made up mostly of fishermen and market gardeners, who do not suffice to choose their priest. So, the participants in the vote are the parish's inhabitants and property-owners, and, more generally, the entirety of Murano natives. In March 1508, before the end of his term of office, podestà Giovanni Alvise Pisani must organize a replacement for the priest, who has just died. Assorted clerics are candidates, and it is Angelo Angelo who is elected, a member of an influential glassmaker family, the Angelo dal Gallo, at the Cock. His brothers, Andrea and Domenico, own a workshop and participate in the island's institutions.[42] But the other candidates contest the election's result and in the days that follow carry their complaint before the Avogaria di Comun, denouncing how the vote played out. The Venetian magistrates take up the inquest and interrogate many witnesses, both Venetian patricians and Murano inhabitants, and their testimony reveals this election's sense and procedures.[43]

As custom requires, the voting was announced at Venice and Murano a few days ahead of time. On 6 March, the Venetian crier Stefano di Polo has proclaimed in public, at Rialto, that,

> the following Friday, after the midday meal – and if there is a meeting of the Senate on that day, rather on the day after – one will choose the priest of Murano, to replace the one who died. So, all the *signori*, all the gentlemen, and the *cittadini* who have a house at Murano should go to Murano on that day.

The candidates must declare themselves to the *cancelliere*. The same call is proclaimed on Murano's bridges. Next Saturday, election day, the rumour runs at Rialto that the Bishop of Torcello has had it annulled, and many patricians decide not to make the trip, as one witness, Gabriele Venier, later reports. That day too a strong wind is blowing across the Lagoon, and the trip might be risky. At Murano, too, Father Zuan Vio has heard it said that the bishop threatens those who vote with excommunication.

As it turns out, at Santi Maria e Donato, when, after the midday meal, the nobles come from Venice and the inhabitants of Murano first assemble, the bishop's chancellor tries to take the chair to announce a decision by his master. But the public shout him down, "Off with you! For your own sake!" The chancellor gives way and lets the procedure take its course. With the podestà slow in coming, more than 250 men assemble in the building. The patricians, shocked by the meeting's disarray, insist on having the podestà, who finally arrives and establishes a little order. "It was necessary to vet those who were supposed to vote, because there was a great confusion, many kinsmen and friends of the candidates", explains the patrician Andrea Pasquaglio. At the podestà's request, the crier then proclaims that all who lack the right to vote must quit the premises, and then the rector orders the two judges (Dominico Bertoluso and Domenico Angelo dal Gallo, the brother of the priest finally elected), the two Procurators of the Churches (Alvise Trevisan and Zuan di Zorzi di Pietro), and the *cavalier* to circulate in the assembly to find out who is there and to expel any who lack a reason to be present. According to the podestà, "There were a great number of persons of low condition whom I did not know. Those from Venice – I knew who they were". Some are sent off, such as the two sons of Domenico Bertoluso, who leave the church at his behest, but the magistrates do not always agree on who has the right to vote and ask the podestà to arbitrate. Not to drag the election out further, the podestà orders the church doors shut, to signal in legal mode the procedure's start: thereafter it is forbidden to enter or leave, and the voting can begin.

The podestà places himself at the altar, behind a table set there, surrounded by the two judges, the two procurators, and the two patricians installed to preside – chosen because oldest in the parish: Pietro Duodo di Nicolo and Agostino Donato. The next step is to set up a list of electors, but the procedure drags on and on, and night begins to fall. As Andrea Pasqualigo tells it, the patricians invoke a law of the Council of Ten of Venice that forbids assemblies that keep their doors closed after dusk or after the *Ave Maria*. They want the podestà consulted on the point, asking him to defer the election, given that many Venetians have not come, whether heedful of the storm or ignorant of the election. According to Pietro Duodo, "as it was late and the weather was bad, many gentlemen began to protest, and others wanted to leave, saying that the thing would be long".

To make the operation swifter, Giovanni Alvise Pisani decides to enrol the electors as they vote. So, he has two candles brought, to brighten the table. But, Andrea Pasqualigo recounts, "all the rest of the church was in the dark, without torches or big lights, and one saw badly what was going on there". It is even necessary to tell the voters where is the urn for placing their vote. Each in turn, the candidates for the priest's job are called to the chair to declare their position, and then they must return to the sacristy at balloting time. After each presentation, all the electors are called to the urn. One by one, they approach the table, give the chancellor their name, and then go fetch the little ball for voting, which they then place in the urn compartment matching their choice: yes or no. The procedure is slow, and it must be repeated for each candidate. But, above all, it is the irregularities that arise that awaken protests by unfortunate candidates, who later denounce to the *avogadori di Comun* many actions on which successive witnesses are then invited to pronounce.

For one thing, many persons have taken part in the election when they should not. Several members of Angelo Angelo's family were present, a thing forbidden by the law. Indeed, all the witnesses have seen Andrea and Domenico, the priest's brothers, plus his cousins and his nephews. Angelo himself recounts the presence of "my kinsmen, two brothers, twenty-one cousins and nephews", but, he parries: none of them have voted for him. Many children also participated, some "twelve or thirteen years old, sons of some poor women, and also of furnace-lighters . . . and it was shameful", according to the glassmaker Angelo Barovier. Others are aged from twelve to fourteen, or from eighteen to nineteen, testifies Father Zuan Battista Rosso:

> sons of Dalmatians and people from other places, like Vincenzo son of Jacopo de la Campana, who comes from the Treviso region, and a son of Bernardin Sopiazo, whose father is a slave, and a son of Bortolomio Gomiato, who is a peasant . . . and a son of Zuan Alvise, who was born at the Giudecca.

But priest Angelo has arguments in his own defence:

> If there were sons of households, it is because it is the custom in this place, and it is the same thing at Venice itself, where it is common in an election like this that sons vote for their father . . . especially among your gentlemen, whose fathers, especially at this time are busy in greater matters, and it is the same for other men of worth.

Indeed, before the *avogadori*, the podestà admits that "other times, I have voted on behalf of my mother in the election of the priest of Santa Maria Formosa", revealing with his words that women too can vote in such a hustings, even if none is mentioned for this day at Santi Maria e Donato. Another patrician, Michele Priuli di Constantino, explains,

> it is true that I voted many times in my father's name in such an election, and, according to me, that is the custom, if one recalls that when one made the election of the other priest now dead, I voted in the name of my father, there at Murano.

Angelo Angelo justifies the Muranesi customs, comparing them with those of Venice, and of the patricians. He hints that, amidst the war, many of them are away from the capital and must arrange to be represented. The argument is effective, as Angelo produces a ducal privilege dated 12 September 1495, accorded to the island's inhabitants, that spells out the list of persons authorized to vote at such a time, "one per house". In referring to the law's terms, and bringing proof of what it says, he uses the legitimacy both of things in writing and of juridical tradition to justify himself before the *avogadori*.

The ducal privilege spells out that owners of real estate on the island and natives of Murano can take part in the election. Now all the witnesses have seen voters who were neither one nor the other. So, the Angelo family and its allies seem to have mobilized many people to assure themselves a win, and, beyond their illegitimacy as voters, there is also a problem in how they have been drafted. Angelo and his brothers are charged with "simony", a term labelling commerce in spiritual or sacred goods. Alvise Trevisan and Father Zuan Bellonato (the very man who in turn will a few years later become priest and who will have dealings with podestà Vitturi) tell how they heard it said that the brothers had bought electors' votes, promising cash, flour and wine. According to Angelo Barovier, Domenico Angelo had arranged with many workmen make good the half-day's work that they would lose by coming to the church. The fire-lighter Francesco Varoter di Antonio recounts,

> Ser Bortolomio Maroza, who works the glass at the place of the priest-elect Angelo dal Gallo, told me that day, "Francesco, give your vote to Father Angelo, and Andrea will pay you . . . Come with me; I will have you given money". But I did not want to go there and be given money and I wanted to vote in accordance with my conscience, for the person I wanted and who pleased me.

And finally, one last problem: once the vote for Angelo Angelo is over, many members of the assembly refuse to participate in the votes that come after, although the *cavalier* insists that they stay. The podestà threatens to keep everybody shut in till morning if they do not come to the urn to put in their *ballotta*. According to Father Zuan Bellonato, a third of the crowd (*briga*) gets up and makes a great noise, refusing to vote for the candidate from Burano. A rumour goes around that just when they are going to vote for another candidate, somebody dumps the urn's contents on the floor. And, finally, a number of balls are missing, proof that not everybody has voted. At the end of the proceedings, reports Father Zuan Vio, the candidate Pietro Alvise Baffo goes to the podestà to launch a complaint, but it is too late: "You should have protested sooner. So, go to the Avogaria" is his answer.

The Avogaria inquest is an occasion for the patricians to parade their indignation in the face of such methods. "Never have I seen an election more confused" complains Gabriele Venier di Domenico. "And they said that the kinfolk of the candidates were voting, and there reigned an immense confusion, that I have ever seen, and behind me they were saying that somebody had voted three or four times", says Andrea Pasqualigo. For Pietro Duodo di Nicolo, there was "a great multitude of persons, more than 250, and above all persons of beastly ways, ignorant, without judgment, riled up, that it is not possible to control", all a critique that fits easily the stereotyped discourses and prejudices about Muranesi that, many a time, we have seen circulating among Venetians.

From his position, Angelo Angelo elaborates a systematic defence, producing arguments and justifications to parry the accusations launched against him. The family of Angelo dal Gallo – have they bought votes? Impossible! Because they "are not men of that sort, but well known, both at Venice and at Murano, and held to be men of worth, discreet, prudent, and good", using here the usual adjectives for describing Venetian citizens. The reputation and public place they enjoy in the Lagoon warrant their honourability. The priest also, as we have seen, takes refuge in juridical texts: a copy of the ducal privilege of 1495, another of the public decree made at Rialto a few days back. He benefits, beyond doubt, from the help of patrician members of government. Angelo also insists on the legitimacy of the procedure that validates his election: the podestà presided at the session, as did the two honourable presidents, who verified the steps taken, and protected "reason [*raxon*] and justice". Moreover, the election has been made public, "the bells have been rung in the usual way, the cries have been made on the Rialto stairs and the bridges of Murano", as warranty of the procedure's regular unfolding.

Finally, he justifies his election by lodging it in his family history and in tradition.

> For this church, my family has spent much money, in particular the late venerable Father Zuan Angelo who was my uncle, who was priest of this church and all that goes with it, and who administered it as everyone knows to the great contentment and satisfaction of the whole *popolo* of Murano, and mindful of that, the electors have wished to elect me . . . and I do not want to imitate those who started quarrels, persons of bad tongue and little good spirit, who speak ill and say false things of those complained of, as they do (if falsely) against me. For I say that at this parish the *popolo* of Murano and the magnificent gentlemen, and those who have houses at Murano, have considered me capable and apt for the governance of this church.

He is particularly scornful of Father Zuan Bellonato. "He is not only a man of bad reputation, but also a widely known killer, and he neither can nor should be allowed to bear witness." As for the witnesses, he thinks no better: Francesco Varoter, "as his looks and face indicate, is a man of bad reputation and a person of no account, and of such social condition that for a sardine or drop of wine, he will say what one tells him to".

The Muranesi are familiar with electoral practices: citizens participate in the election of the Thirty and of government officials; the fishermen, gondoliers, and glassworkers vote for their representatives, their *gastaldi* or *massari*; parishioners choose their priests. In spite of the disorders of 1508's procedures, which reveal that the practice remains the fruit of constant adjustment and arrangement, the inhabitants are accustomed to expressing their choice. The elections follow the current usage in Venice, which combine lottery with voting; by that device, on assorted occasions they permit many inhabitants to express their counsel and opinion.

Political action takes varied forms, and it shows up among the folk of the *popolo* more often than one might think. From participating in the machinery of election, to chanting at a demonstration, there is a great gamut of ways of intervening, and it is best not so see them with an eye only to the short resources and social fragility of those who carry them out. The inhabitants of Murano collaborate according to the many modes offered by the island's complex political space. They deliberate, debate, and take action alongside patrician power, within or beyond official policy, and sometimes they do take part in policy itself. Their action, however, has no specific form, nor does it fit snugly into configurations belonging to the common people. Rather, they take collegial decisions that apply to everyone, defend common interests, make collective claims, as do patrician governments in other public arenas. The inhabitants also contribute to the construction of order, to the production of laws and rules, and to the defence of political choices, be they of either particular or general interest. The hostility that Vitturi provokes makes visible an exceptional mobilization, which however probably trails a critique more latent and insidious. The two types of action need one another: political culture, slowly elaborated, is what generates moments of acceleration; short, rapid attempts are nourished by resources, accumulated over the long haul, that permit the inhabitants to take action.

## Notes

1  Crouzet-Pavan, "Murano à la fin du Moyen Age", 56.
2  ASVe, AC, MP, 410, no. 14.
3  ASVe, PM, 229, 2, Cassa fontico di Murano, book 1, fol. 19, for 15 October 1510; ASVe, PM, 229, 3, fol. 8, 8 April et 29 April 1511; 8v, 22 June 1511; 9v, for 8 August 1511.
4  Zecchin, *Vetro e vetrai di Murano*, vol. 1, 6 (1279).
5  ASVe, PM, 44, 19 Criminalium 1, for 26 September 1509, against Alvise and Andrea Moro (*gran tumulto de parlar*).
6  ASVe, AC, MP, 142, no. 17, passim.

*Surian! Caza fuora questo can, che se manza el nostro pan!*
*Surian! Surian! Caza via questo Vitturi, che ne ha distruto et consumando!*
*Surian! Surian! Caza via questo can che ha manzado la poverta de Muran!*
*Surian! Caza sto can che ha disfato Muran!*
*Vegna Surian, caza via sto can!*
*Vien presto Surian et caza via questo vilan can che a desfato li poveri de Muran!*

7  Stuart B. Schwartz, *All Can Be Saved. Religious Tolerance and Salvation in the Iberian Atlantic World* (New Haven, CT and London: Yale University Press, 2008), 48–9; Kenneth Stow, *Jewish Dogs: An Image and its Interpreters: Continuity in the Catholic–Jewish Encounter* (Stanford, CA: Stanford University Press, 2006).

8  Elizabeth Horodowich, *Language and Statecraft in Early Modern* Venice (Cambridge: Cambridge University Press, 2008), 125, lists the most common insults in sixteenth-century Venice. *Gioton* is not on her list but at the time it is one of the most frequent insults at Murano.

9  Marino Sanudo, *I Diarii*, vol. 3, col. 1, 1 October 1499 (*Antonio Grimani, Ruina de' cristiani, Rebello de' venitiani, Puòstu esser manzà da' canni, Da' canni, da' cagnolli, Ti e toi fiulli*).

10 In 1595, the election of doge Marino Grimani occasions many popular demonstrations, where the dwellers of the poorer quarters chant in the streets and squares "Marin Grimani will make fat big loaves of bread" (*Marin Grimani farà grossi e grandi pani!*). See ch. 4, n. 40.

11 Girolamo Priuli, *I Diarii*, vol. IV, 31, June 1509.

12 ASVe, PM, 44, 19 Criminalium 1, for 13 September 1509, against Zaneto *fachin* and his friends.

13 *La memoria del vetro*, 170.

14 BMC, Mariegole, IV L 7 Scuola di Santo Stefano in Santo Stefano di Murano; IV L 8 Scuola di San Vincenzo Ferrer in San Pietro Martire; BMC, Mariegole, IV L 10, Confraternita del Santissimo Sacramento in Santo Stefano di Murano; BMC, Mariegole, IV L 17, Scuola di San Giovanni Battista dei Battuti.

15 BMC, Mariegole, IV L 10, fol. 2r-v. Although the statutes announce the presence of women, none is ever mentioned by name.

16 BMC, Mariegole, IV L 10, fol. 8.

17 BMC, Mariegole, IV L 17. For other copies of the Statutes: BMC, Mariegole, B 26/227 and B/228; British Library, Manuscripts, Add MS 17046.

18 BMC, Mariegole, IV L 17, fol. 16–18.

19 BMC, Mariegole, IV L 17, fol. 5v-6r, ch. 13.

20 Archivio Parrocchiale San Pietro Martire di Murano, Scuola di San Giovanni Battista dei Battuti, Parti e sentenze, March 1509.

21 Archivio Parrocchiale San Pietro Martire di Murano, Scuola di San Giovanni Battista dei Battuti, Parti e sentenze, 27 December 1511.

22 Archivio Parrocchiale San Pietro Martire di Murano, Scuola di San Giovanni Battista dei Battuti, Parti e sentenze, 25 July 1512.

23 Archivio Parrocchiale San Pietro Martire di Murano, Scuola di San Giovanni Battista dei Battuti, Parti e sentenze, 9 December 1509.

24 ASVe, PM, 44, 8 Extraordinariorum 1, for 31 August 1509.

25 ASVe, PM, 44, 4 Testificationum, 1 October 1509.

26 Marino Sanudo, *I Diarii*, vol. 35, col. 419, 13 February 1524.

27 ASVe, PM, 43, Extraordinariorum 1, for 8 September 1508.

28 ASVe, PM, 44, 8 Extraordinariorum 1, for 22 September 1509.

29 ASVe, Milizia da Mar, 219, Traghetto de Muran, fol. 2r-v, for 29 December 1519.

30  ASVe, Milizia da Mar, 219, Traghetto de Muran, fol. 5r-v, for December 1530, in Collegio Cinque Savi.
31  ASVe, Milizia da Mar, 219, Traghetto de Muran, fol 7v-13r.
32  ASVe, Milizia da Mar, 219, Traghetto de Muran, fol. 9v-10r.
33  ASVe, Milizia da Mar, 219, Traghetto de Muran, fol. 11, for 16 September 1559, in Senato.
34  BMC, Mariegola dei Fioleri, 26, fol. 8.
35  British Library, Manuscripts, Add MS 17046.
36  ASVe, PM, 187, Lettere al podestà, letter of the heads of the Council of Ten, 27 June 1534.
37  Zecchin, *Vetro e vetrai di Murano*, vol. 2, 186–7, law of 15 March 1483.
38  Zecchin, *Vetro e vetrai di Murano*, vol. 1, 217–18, for the whole discussion of negotiations around citizenship and membership in the Golden Book.
39  Zecchin, *Vetro e vetrai di Murano*, vol. 1, p. 218; *Il Libro d'Oro di Murano*, ed. Vincenzo Zanetti (Venice: Stab. M. Fontana, 1883).
40  Giacomo Casanova, *Histoire de ma vie*, tome I, vol. 4, ch. VI, 776–7, our own translation.
41  Archivio Parrocchiale Santi Maria e Donato, Fabbriceria, Atti generali, Prima serie, busta 6, processo no. 18 (Avogaria di Comun). See also, for a discussion of how to elect the members of the Council of Thirty and the chancellor: "Statuto de Muran", book I, ch. 2, 239; ch. 10, 245.
42  Andrea and Domenico Angelo, the brothers of the man elected priest, are two glassmakers of the Rio who have their patronym, Dal Gallo (of the Rooster), added to their sign. One year earlier they received a 20-year privilege for making "mirrors from crystal glass, a thing which is valuable and singular". See Zecchin, *Vetro e vetrai di Murano*, vol. 1, 187.
43  Archivio Parrocchiale Santi Maria e Donato, Fabbriceria, Atti generali, Prima serie, busta 6, processo no. 18 (Avogaria di Comun). All the quotations that follow are extracted from this trial: fol. 1–2, 15 March 1508, the complaint; 2r, 15 March, Francesco Contarini di Pandolfo; 2v, 16 March, Gabriele Venier di Domenico; 3r, 18 March, Andrea Pasqualigo di Pietro; 4r, 21 March, Ser Angelo Barovier di Alvise; 5r, Ser Zuan Ballarin; 5r, Pietro Duodo di Nicolo; 6r, 21 March, Father Zuan Vio di Burano; 7r, Father Zuan Battista Rosso; 7v, 23 March, Father Zuan Michiel; 8v, 27 March, Father Zuan Bellonato; 9r, Francesco Varoter di Antonio, fire-kindler at the Hat; 9v, 3 May, Ser Andrea di Matteo dell'Urso; 10r, 4 May, Father Domenico Focher; 11r, 8 April, Defense by Angelo Angelo; 14v, 17 April, Giovanni Alvise Pisani; 15v, 17 April, Pietro de Usnago; 16v, 18 April, Carlo de Bici; 17r, 18 April, Filippo Vinacese; Stefano di Pietro; 18r, Agostino Garzoni di Garzon; 18v, Ser Domenico Bertoluso; 19r, Luca Donato di Leonardo; 20r, 27 April, Filippo Basadonna di Alvise; 20v, 6 May, Angelo Angelo; 21r, Ser Nicolo Bonacosa; 21v, Battista di Luchino; 22r, 9 May, Ser Alvise Trevisan; 23r, Angelo Angelo; 23v, 6 May, Filippo Vinacese; 24r, 8 May, Michele Priuli di Constantino; 25r, copies of the ducal privilege of 1495, 25v, copy of the proclamation.

# 8 The trial
## A test of truth and persons

With Vitturi now gone, tension eases ever more on the *campo* and the island. The chants fade, the excitement wanes, the snowballs cease flying, and the inhabitants go back home. Giacomo Suriano, still at hand, in the company of some patricians and Murano *cittadini* settles in the palace of the podestà, where talk flows fast till evening. Now comes the time to forget, and to remember. So, begins the event's second life – of recounting and memory. The revolt's brief time, marked by spontaneity and the swift press of actions, yields to history's long time, lodged in temporal stretch and story. Memory sets in motion its work of selection and reconstitution. This process is a new stage in the Snowball Revolt, where the affair is untangled and settled. Whatever the real motives of the Muranesi gathered on Campo Santi Maria e Donato, and the true nature of their actions and intentions, the event's interpretation falls mainly to those persons summoned to testify and, in the end, to the *avogadori di Comun*.

### Reconstructing the truths

On the evening of 27 January, the inhabitants doubtless already begin to tell themselves what was it that happened on the *campo*. From here on, the Snowball Revolt exists only in these memories continually in recon-struction. Divergent versions surface, as the accounts later deposed at court make clear; narratives, complementary and sometimes contradictory, are proffered by those who saw the facts or peddled by persons never present. Selective memories, partial and partisan visions, and particular sensibilities fashion revolt's account. One repeats over and over some anecdote or some variation on the chant, changing it, inventing amusing details or expanding on things for the pleasure of the telling. The patricians too, once back at Venice, surely report their versions of the facts – in the great halls of houses and the corridors of the Doge's Palace, on Saint Mark's Square, and at Rialto's markets. And now, patrician power must exact the control of memory, and one of the trial's jobs is to impose an admissible account of what just happened. The judges have the duty to take good hold of the discourses about Suriano's *intrar*, to contain and shape them. After the revolt's disorder comes the firm order of justice.

With its start in February's first days, the inquest will last eight weeks and more. The judicial procedure, and the document it produces – both of them called the *processo*, the trial – reveal the tension between the protagonists.[1] The Snowball Revolt rolls on, by morphing into an affair of words, interpretation, and commentary. Each witness offers up his reading of the facts; he qualifies, judges, denounces, or justifies them, while trying to impose his own categories to describe the doing and shouting, the violence and festivity, the engagement and the excitement. The witness and the accused have finite autonomy in how they choose their words to recount the event and its background. Clearly, they are first hemmed in by the procedure and by the judges' power. Then their declarations must slip the filter of secretaries' and scribes' writing. But witnesses and suspects still have some leeway. The magistrates do not yet know for sure what words they will hear and put on paper. Beyond the trial's sentence, the real stake is crafting an official, consensual version of the facts. Of course, it is still necessary to pass judgment on the accused, to decide their guilt, and to make the punishment fit the crime. But the judges must also choose the story that the archive will lodge on file. The trial permits those who have power in hand to legitimate or delegitimate the account of one and another speaker; they dispense the final voice that fashions their institution's memory. Sovereignty, both Venetian and patrician, holds sway thanks also to this mastery of language about society and social order.

Justice functions as an occasion for reconciliation, where the order temporarily unsettled by the events manages to regain its composure. Justice, as institution, is one of the most powerful, and most apt for giving shape to shapelessness, but it is surely among the greatest chatterboxes too. In all of Europe, judicial organs – the offices of summary justice, the tribunals and the high appeal courts – have generated millions of documents that conserve the statements and opinions of millions of persons who otherwise left few traces in the archives. In 1511, by giving the inhabitants the floor, justice offers them the chance to speak.

The actors caught up in the trial take advantage of their hearing to justify or criticize the snowball battle, aware of the risks they run and of their own stake. Borrowing a device from the recent French "sociology of critique" (*sociologie de la critique* or *pragmatique*), let us follow these justifications from close up, to understand how they are assembled and deployed within the enclosure of the tribunal.

## Denunciations

The act of denunciation sits at medieval justice's foundations. Down to the end of the twelfth century, to start the work of justice accusation sufficed. Then appeared inquisitorial procedure, and the inquest, which strove to reconstitute events and to verify them by words of witnesses. From then on, denunciation does not vanish from the judicial system, but thenceforth it summons up the business of verification. Venice, to bolster the course of justice, prods its inhabitants to denounce their peers. At several places in the city, from the fifteenth century on, there are orifices that allow one to submit written denunciations. These "lion mouths" (*bocche di leone*) take the shape of human figures, or monsters, with an open mouth to swallow small papers. Only in the seventeenth century will this system become the norm, thanks particularly to the spread of writing and growing literacy, but at the time of the Snowball Revolt, the inhabitants are already familiar with it. At Murano, the Statutes protect "denouncers", whose identity must remain secret.[2] Meanwhile, a severe penalty awaits any who make false denunciations.[3] As for those who give false witness in court, they are threatened with a tongue cut out and three years' banishment from the island.[4]

The first ten witnesses heard by the official of the Avogaria di Comun come forward voluntarily. Giacomo Suriano has it on the docket to round them up, but they likely present themselves spontaneously. Five are overtly hostile to their fellow citizens and, in particular, to the crier: the furnace-owner Nicolo de Blasio and his workers Gasparo Furlan and Angelo Zeloxo, plus Pietro Zorzi and Tommaso Paliaga. They express their disapproval and undermine the actions of (as Pietro Zorzi calls them) the rabble (*canaglia*) or the crowd, or "brigade" (*brigata*) (Tommaso Paliaga).

In part the witnesses' motivations escape us; once more, they seem to originate outside the affair's confines. One knows, for example, that Nicolo de Blasio is close to Vitturi. In trials putting him at odds with assorted inhabitants, the podestà has made some rulings in his favour.[5] In August 1510, he also grants him the privilege of keeping the furnace open during the annual closure.[6] But the glassmaker guild's *gastaldo* asks Venice's Council of Ten to annul this permission, and, in September, they do so rule. The Venetian magistrates hold that Nicolo should abide by the regulations of the craft and, like the other artisans, quench his ovens. If Vitale Vitturi and Nicolo de Blasio do have shared economic interests, no contract or financial agreement to prove the fact has so far turned up in the archives.

As for Angelo Zeloxo, who works in Nicolo de Blasio's shop, it seems that he is using the trial to settle old quarrels that set his boss against his rivals. In his deposition, Angelo denounces many inhabitants, one of them Gasparo Capello. Now six months earlier, on 21 August 1510, Nicolo de Blasio brought a complaint before the podestà, accusing Gasparo's brother, Baldissera Capello, of insulting him and beating him up.[7] One week later, the two Capello brothers themselves lodged a complaint against Nicolo, for curses and threats.[8] As one witness then heard by Vitturi puts it, "they are enemies and all day long they say vile things, and insult one another".[9] Is Angelo Zeloxo exploiting the trial to settle old accounts with the Capello, accusing them of taking part in the Snowball Revolt?

Whatever their motives, these five inhabitants tell stories that undercut the accused, especially Antonio Malcanton and Jacopo Cagnato, whom they single out as organizers of the crowd, who incited all and sundry to pick up snow and to climb the campanile. The witnesses likewise flay the disorder and the cries. For Nicolo de Blasio, "the ruckus was so great that persons present were thunderstruck". The chant was particularly shocking, and the snow compounded the confusion. According to Angelo Zeloxo, there was so much of it "that it seemed that it was raining". Pietro Zorzi saw some on Vitturi's gondola; Zeloxo spotted some on the podestà's shoulder.

All the while they denounce their fellow citizens, they laud Vitturi's actions. "I do not believe that anybody could complain, because he did a great deal of good, and he has had compassion for our poverty", attests Nicolo de Blasio, while Gasparo, his worker, explains, "it seems to me that Messer Vitale conducted himself well, even though he sentenced me for fighting, because it is an honest thing that justice take place". According to Pietro Zorzi, "it seems to me that he has acted worthily, and with justice, and it is possible that there will come one worse than him. He willingly listened to everyone, with great familiarity".

The four patricians who testify, between 12 and 24 March, express hostility, fed by prejudice against the islanders, and against commoners in general. Paolo Contarini di Pietro and Alvise Contarini di Francesco of Santa Trinità, heard by the Avogaria on 12 and 15 March, are Vitturi's nephews (the first via his father, the brother of Vitale's wife; the second "on my father's side, but I know not to what degree"). It is in that capacity that they came to see the passing of power. The third witness, Paolo Contarini di Bortolo, accompanied Giacomo Suriano "because he was like a son to me". Finally, the last patrician, Domenico Contarini di Matteo, gives a rather confused deposition, in a declaration dated 25 March but transcribed by his daughter Maria. The declarations of the four patricians fill out and confirm those of the first witnesses. They evoke the "great quantity of snowballs", "a fury of balls" tossed both from the campanile and from the *campo* and the *fondamente*, as well as the shouts and deafening chants. Pietro Contarini di Bortolo evokes the insults and "the great noise of all those who were shouting". Alvise Contarini and Paolo Contarini di Pietro say that, as for them, they did not hear the famous chant, but they learned later that it had made the rounds.

Unlike the inhabitants of Murano, who did not mention the gondola episode, for the patricians it is the thing that most stands out. On board themselves, or not far off, they saw "Antonio, Murano's crier, jump with great force on the gunwales of the boat" and almost flip it over, before turning to Vitturi "without any reverence". Alvise Contarini specifies

> I know that because I was present on the boat with Messer Vitale and, as soon as we could, we went back with the boat. And we left by way

of the outside because an Angelo Zeloxo told us that if we went with the boat via the interior of Murano, they intended to throw rocks and stones at us, and to chant a certain song that said "Surian Surian, chase that dog who has undone the whole of Muran".

Two of the four patricians who stayed on Murano after Vitturi left report conversations that took place then, and the criticism that swelled à propos of the battle, concerning which "all had had displeasure". Paolo Contarini di Bortolo recounts that the new podestà and the "men of good standing" at the palace of the podestà complained of "these plebeians" (*plebei*), "these Muranesi, that is to say of the children and the youths, these vulgar persons (*persone vulgar*)", who for three or four nights had already gone around Murano chanting against Vitturi.

Paolo Contarini di Pietro denounces the offense to Vitturi and to the collective patriciate.

> I went a few days later to Murano, and, speaking with the podestà, I said that that thing yesterday had been an ugly deed, with little decorum for our State, and that His Magnificence could judge that, given their great ignorance, they were in the wrong ... and that that could easily happen to anyone if one let it go unpunished. The podestà answered me that he was very distressed by this affair, telling me that if he had not been there it would have been a good deal worse ... And I told him that it was a universal thing, not a particular one, and that is was not only the person of Messer Vitale who had been affronted, but the whole land.

At stake was the honour of the Venetian state and of the patriciate. So, the four patricians graft the facts in a broader interpretive framework. The cries, the chaos, and the snow are thus a manifestation of violence against the nobles, as a group, and Vitturi's humiliation is the Republic's own. Such a reading is not risk-free, for it gives the event a strong political complexion. But that, in fact, is what the judges seem to try to dodge, as do the accused, who, rather than give the snowball fight deep meaning, try to strip the action of its garb of resistance.

## "*Io sum per neve.*" "I am there for the snow." On justification

Among the Muranese witnesses, not all speak against their fellow citizens. On the contrary, some want to keep them out of trouble and prove they did no wrong. They simply celebrated Suriano's *intrar* by joining in the festivities; the accused themselves would take up this argument. This is the justificatory voice adopted by Domenico di Andrea, the two judges Domenico Rizo and Domenico Bertoluso, and by the chamberlain Zuan

Rizo. If one adds the *giustiziere* Sebastiano Bellencito, testifying a few weeks later, it is clear that the representatives of Murano's institutions side with the accused. Their testimonies are allusive and vague, their accounts tending to attenuate the protest's violence. They do concede the presence of Antonio Malcanton and of Jacopo Cagnato, but, as to the identity of the other participants, they stay vague, claiming they could not recognize or see them. They are content to evoke a "big crowd" and "a great number of persons". Domenico Rizo puts it this way: "Me, I don't know whom it was about because I take no interest in these matters." And further, "I don't know if the snow came from the *campanile* or from elsewhere because I did not look up". Now clearly, this is impossible. The witnesses must have known, given both their presence at the event and the rumours afterwards that swamped the island.

The whole testimony of Domenico Bertoluso is a stab at defence: "I don't know who was in the *campanile*, nor who was throwing snow." Somewhat maliciously, he singles out his companion Domenico Rizo, who testifies just before he does. Besides, both are named by Antonio Malcanton as having been hit by snow, for he knows that he can count on their testimony. Bertoluso denies having heard any chant at all and belittles the Muranesi actions. "I believe that it is the custom to play with snow, and it had snowed the night before." The inhabitants targeted one another, in no way the podestà. And likewise, if they rang the bell, it was because "it was the custom to do it for the festivity". For Zuan Rizo, they had thrown snow "more out of ignorance than from ill will". Vincenzo da Murano, moreover, tells that after Vitturi's departure, the fisherman Bernardin Bigaia descended the campanile and went to the palace of the podestà to ask "the brother of Giacomo Suriano to give him a gift of appreciation because, with his six companions, he had rung the bell". Was this bravado towards the new podestà or a mark of ingenuousness? For the witness, in any case, it was a mark of his own good faith.

The final witness heard at the end of March, the *giustiziere* Sebastiano Bellencito, also produces a tale altogether favourable to all the accused, and especially to Malcanton. Interrogated about the crier's words, Bellencinto explains: "I never heard him say anything, and *if he had said it* [these words are crossed out on the paper], rather, as I have said, he never moved far from me." Is this a scribal error here, or is it a hesitation by Bellencito, who heard Malcanton proffer some insult? Nothing here is certain, but clearly the witness wants to keep the crier out of trouble.

The accused, on their part, must do their best to prove their innocence and avoid condemnation, which would at best entail a fine, and more likely imprisonment, or corporal punishment, or even banishment from the island. Their justifications, each with its own timbre, reveal their ability to divine seemingly acceptable motives and courses of action.

Antonio Malcanton is in a tough spot: he cannot deny that he staged the ceremony but insists that he never orchestrated the revolt. If indeed he spoke to some persons throwing snow, or asked others to climb to the bell tower's top, it was just the better to do his job. The judges attempt to make the other accused confess that the crier was the ringleader who fomented the revolt and rallied his accomplices. By branding Malcanton as the main guilty party, from whom the protest came, they make collective mobilization seem the fruit of one man's choice. But the five accused give no satisfaction, never once signalling the crier's role in organizing the revolt, which, in fact, was never premeditated.

Like some witnesses heard before them, the accused do their best to dodge the questions about who was present on the *campo*, as they clearly have no wish for further company in the Signoria's jails. They use vague, generic categories to evoke the "crowd", a "considerable number of persons". "I believe that all Murano was present", says Antonio Malcanton, "in any case more or less 300 persons". "We were very many young men of Murano", says Andrea dall'Aqua, and the snow was thrown at "a good group of persons". See, the top of the campanile was too high, one could not recognize anybody. According to Zuan dall'Aqua, "There were many youths and children but I don't know who they were".

By dint of insisting, and repeating their question, the *avogadori* succeed in extracting a few names. Bernardin Bigaia cites, "we who are in prison, Vettor Forner, Francesco Fuga, Vicenzo son of Dona Lena, Zuan Maria Zuminian, Vettor Forner who is another, the son of Ser Rado Chaniega and others". Zuan dall'Aqua speaks of "two Forner who are called Vettor and a son of Brasco and one Rosseto and a good many others". But none of those named are arrested, perhaps because the new podestà protects them, or the judges think it unnecessary to pursue the inquest further. Better not to multiply arrests if one wishes the affair not to grow.

The accused, like the witness before them, stress the role played by children, linking the disorder to their youth. The violence and impulsiveness of young folk are feared in the Middle Ages and in early modern times. Many a ritual, rite of passage, festivity and association helps hedge adolescent ardours, the better to control them. Jousts in the saddle and rock fights are devices that give youths a vent in rough behaviour, but that box in just how they do it. On the Campo Santi Maria e Donato, the young are the ones – the children (*puti*), youths (*zoveni*), the youngsters (*fantolin*), the "little children not more than ten years old" – who started the fight and made the racket. Their tender age allows the accused and the magistrates to minimize the impact of what happened. Irrationality, ignorance, and aggression carry the day, at the expense of intention and critical opinion.

A crucial argument for the defence is the snow. "I am there for the snow" (*io sum per neve*) says Zuan dall'Aqua, as the judges write it down with a touch of notarial Latin. Never saying "tumult" or "revolt", and merely stressing the snowball fight, the accused tame the interpretation of their actions. So, they denounce the weather: it was the wind and storm that set snow swirling on the *campo* and off the bell tower. "The storm carried the snow this way and that" and "the wind blew the snow everywhere", say Pietro Bigaia and Jacopo Cagnato. "The cold wind carried the snow this way and that", explains Andrea dall'Aqua.

If all the accused admit having thrown a ball or two, they deny targeting the podestà. They were aiming for the children, their peers (*nostri pari*), "at nobody except our buddies". Social equivalence – *pari* or *compari* (literally fellow-godparents, but by usage just "pals") and the pelting of all and sundry both diminish the activity's meaning. "Even the new podestà" took a hit, explains Antonio Malcanton, who hopes that way to prove that Vitturi was no sole target. As for Andrea dall'Aqua, he explains that, huddled in the loggia, Vitale could never have been hit.

As the interrogations go on, there emerges the tale of an affair sharing little with revolt. The snowball fight is linked into a longer chain of events, beginning before the ceremony's start and stretching past Vitturi's departure. According to Zuan dall'Aqua, the battle began "two long hours before the podestà made his entry". Andrea dall'Aqua and Jacopo Cagnato confirm this. Pietro Bigaia speaks of twenty-five persons all around the square who were playing before the podestà appeared there. And Andrea dall'Aqua recounts that, after Vitturi left, the battle went on "more than an hour". Moreover, according to Bernardin Bigaia, the fight spilled well beyond the *campo*: the people "were playing with the snow all along the Fondamenta of San Donato and in the whole of Murano".

To justify the acts, the accused insist on the event's festive and joyous ambience: "one feted our podestà", "to celebrate our new podestà", for "the happiness of our podestà", "and we did not think we were offending anybody". And Antonio Malcanton, in self-justification: "I could not tell them anything much." In the festivity there mingled "play", "pleasure", and "laughter". "Everybody was throwing snow and playing together." For that was "tradition" and the "custom" on such an occasion. According to Bernardin Bigaia, "we went to the *campanile* to ring the bell as the custom when the podestà come in".

And, finally, the suspects attenuate greatly the import of the chants. Malcanton recounts that the children were crying, "Surian, chase off this dog who has ruined Murano". "How did you answer them?" ask the judges. "To shout just 'Surian'"; this is a version that Domenico Contarini confirms a few weeks later. "Me, I did not hear anybody say anything whatsoever, nor have heard that anything of any sort was said." So, says Bernardin Bigaia in self-defence, in a tone like that of Andrea dall'Aqua. His brother Zuan admits that the children shouted, but nothing more than "Surian, Surian". Anyway, he was up the *campanile*, too high to make out the shouts. Jacopo Cagnato, asked about the song that made the rounds, answers, "Me, I don't know. Me, I go fishing".

A ruckus that spills well beyond the ritual, and which is not exclusively linked to Vitturi's departure, the pleasure of the festival, and the play, plus the influence of tradition – these are the descriptions offered by the accused.

Belittling the value and consequences of their actions, they scupper all chance at political interpretation. Their deployment of these justifications testifies to their understanding of the stakes. Their capacity to set in motion a political action is expressed not only in their original protest against Vitturi, but also in their self-justification when on trial. The production of a narrative and of acceptable categories for describing the event bears witness to strategy. The *avogadori di Comun* end up encouraging the suspects to deny any critical intentions whatsoever, suggesting themselves the themes of fete and play. They edge the riot towards well-known forms of collective expression: carnival, charivari, and tradition. In that way, they write the event back into pre-existent, well recognized interpretive registers.

At the time of the trial, the objectives of the accused and judges converge: the former understand that they must make their actions look banal so as to dodge a heavy sentence, while the latter do their best to obliterate the event's aspect of defiance. That way the Muranesi can hope to avoid condemnation, but they cannot extract themselves from under the high hand of the patricians who constrain their discourse. Justice shapes both story and memory.

The three magistrates seem to fail to agree on an interpretation of the events, or on a sentence, for they decide to proceed to a second inter-rogatory, this time with torture. This procedure is employed by Venetian criminal justice to make recalcitrant suspects confess. On 26 March, the magistrates use it against the five residents of Murano (by this date, the crier has been freed at the request of Giacomo Suriano), perhaps to punish them a first time, rather than because they really hope to extract new information. The accused are brought into the torture chamber (*camera tormenti*), to be subjected to the ordeal of the *corda*. With their hands tied behind their backs, hitched to a stout rope, they are hoisted slowly upwards. At each new question, a turn of the pulley-wheel inches them higher, and they are soon in an unbearable posture. The procedure is dangerous; it often produces wounds and bleeding. Accused often end up confessing just anything whatever to end their agony.

Zuan dell'Aqua, who is sick, begs the magistrates, "I pray your lordships not to hurt me because I have had the fever, and I don't know anything but what I said". But they all end up hanging from the rope. The interrogation then follows a new logic. The questions, shorter, come swiftly, and evoke brief answers. The *avogadori* begin by putting the accused under warning: "Tell the truth, my poor fellow. Do you really want to let yourself be wrecked?" They then unfurl their litany of questions, the same ones as at the first interrogation. "I have already said it", answer the accused. "Said what?", the judges then ask, in a dialogue in which their side never seems to flag. Several aspects of the event attract their attention: the words pronounced at the bell tower's top, the shouts of the children on the *campo*, the chants against the podestà around Murano on the days before, whom the snow targeted, the early orders that might have gone heeded, and the presence of the crier at the *campanile*'s peak. The speed of the interrogation invites simple answers already contained in the questions' wording.

This new hearing, however, brings no new information and the accused stick to their first declarations. Bernardin Bigaia repeats with resignation, hanging from the cord, "Your Lordships can do with me what you want, and even if I were quartered, I would not know anything different". The *avogadori* must face the facts: nobody is willing to confess to having fomented the Snowball Revolt.

When on trial, the accused must deploy several registers of justification to minimize the meaning of the event and to avoid a heavy sentence. This banalization of their actions, in the end, seems to serve the judges' goals. The accused and the court use complementary terms and explanations, making the snowball fight slide from the regime of political protest to that of carnivalesque disorder. The singularization of the action keeps the critique from rising to the level of the general, so that a protest against the podestà does not become one against Venetian rule. Justice's task is to empty the event of its political meaning, to interpret it as a momentary breakdown tied to excitement over the ceremony and the snow. The trial participates in the return to order, where the possibilities once offered by the chaos on the *campo* before the judges then shrink drastically.

The choices made by Venetian power are not banal. In the same period, other states condemn demonstrations and popular protests with great severity, not hesitating to read far too much into the sense of actions, at the risk of finding there a subversive meaning that perhaps they never had. By making certain noisy festivities into "political" protests, those in power justify the severity and pedantic ferocity of their sentences. They judge the actions as crimes of *lèse majesté*, flaunting their unbending hostility to some forms of popular expression.

At Venice, the patricians' choice is instead to hem and silence political interpretation. What we call the notable absence of revolts in the Lagoon, from the first years of the Commune down to the Fall of the Republic in 1797, may thus be the result of an efficacious strategy that avoided calling "revolt" any popular demonstration that partook of the nature. The rulers avoid the term; they prefer to speak of muffled protests (*mormoration*), of assemblies, leagues, and cabals (*maone, conventicule*), of gatherings of inhabitants on the steps of the Doges' Palace. That is how they evoke, for example, the demonstrations by oarsmen of the merchant galleys in October 1498. The Senators remark then that one cannot "in any way tolerate the complaints and exclamations that they make every day before the steps of our Palazzo [Doge's Palace], the poor oarsmen and crew members".[10] A few months later, in 1499, it is those who served in the army who demand their pay, "every day at the steps of the Palazzo".[11] These protests before the Doge's Palace, like the disorders that in January 1511 accompany power's passage, reveal that in the Lagoon collective criticism is possible. It remains to consider how it features, and the diversity of its forms.

## Return to Murano

Pietro Contarini, Nicolo Dolfin, and Gasparo Malipiero, the *avogadori di Comun*, finish their inquest at the end of March 1511. It is time to propose a judgment to the members of the Quarantia Criminale, the Venetian assembly charged with voting on the sentence.[12] The *avogadori* suggests accepting the accusations against the five inhabitants of Murano and thereby putting their guilt up for voting. The Council of Forty proceed to a first vote on 29 March. Of the thirty-three patricians present at the Quarantia on that day, twelve declare the accused guilty, fourteen innocent, while seven abstain. After discussion, a second vote takes place, with no greater success: fifteen for guilty, twelve against, and six abstentions. No majority takes shape. The assembly is divided more or less evenly between those who want the accusation to go forward and those who favour letting the accused off. On 31 March, the assembly meets a second time and holds three votes, but no decision carries the day.

On 1 April, a third session is organized. It begins once more with discussions of the affair. The vote is without result: fourteen for, fourteen against, five abstentions. The *avogadori* then propose that the assembly pronounce only on the case of Antonio Malcanton. The archival document, in very bad condition, suggests that the crier's reprieve does invite more consensus: twenty-six vote for, seven against, and nobody abstains. But it is necessary to decide the fate of the five other accused so, for a solution, the committee is enlarged. On 2 April, a fourth assembly is convoked, this time the two Quarantia, the Civil and the Criminal, with sixty-eight members.[13] A majority emerges at last: nineteen vote for prosecution, forty against, and nine abstain. The five Muranesi are thus acquitted, escaping both prison and a fine.

The official decision is recorded by the Avogaria di Comun the 10 April 1511.[14] The crier does not appear in the sentence, which applies only to Jacopo Cagnato, Bernardin Bigaia, Zuan dall'Aqua son of Jacopo, Andrea his brother, and Pietro Bigaia, tried for having climbed the *campanile* "with so much rashness and overweeningness", for having thrown at podestà Vitturi and his company many snowballs, for having used "bad, shameful, and injurious words against Vitale Vitturi, to the detriment of our most illustrious Signoria, and to the personal dishonour of our representative".

The Venetian patricians did not come to the decision easily. The many debates, successive meetings, and repeated votes prove that they had a hard time agreeing as to the sense to give the affair. In proclaiming acquittal, the Venetian judges made the snowballs, cries, chants, and bells into a demonstration that needs no punishment. Condemnation of the Muranesi would have meant recognition of the element of protest in their action and would have turned the event into a public affair. The members of the Council of Forty do not want to risk letting the inhabitants of Murano seize on a decision that could crystallize new claims. Doubtless the tensions and fears the trial stirred up quickly faded, but the unfortunate loss of Giacomo Suriano's official papers bars knowing more about what happened. Most of the archives produced on the island from February to October 1511 have vanished. Moreover, it is quite likely, in any case, that they never picked up any trace of the reactions and discussions that followed the trial and release of the accused.

Antonio Malcanton resumes his functions as public crier in March 1511, to go on to a long career. For the next thirty-three years, down to 1544, he serves one podestà after another, and also the community. Then a new crier takes his place: Vincenzo Malcanton. We have no firm proof but assume that this is either a son or nephew. When, in 1512, Antonio negotiates the permit to build a stone house on Campo Santi Maria e Donato, a clause foresees that it would go half to the new crier and half to Antonio's heirs. Keeping the succession in the bosom of his family, he guarantees that they keep possession of the house. In 1542, under podestà Marco Manolesso, Vincenzo Malcanton begins to assist Antonio, by then sixty, taking over some public proclamations.[15] The next year he assumes the whole job alone. Antonio has become too old and perhaps sickly as had, before him, Matteo da Brescia. Antonio dies in 1544, aged sixty-two.[16]

## After the revolt

Down to the fall of the Republic, the island remains under the domination of Venice and its podestà, living to the rhythm of its glass production and other economic activities. After the 1797 occupation by Napoleon's French soldiers ends, Venice becomes a province of the Austrian empire and Murano, always seen as a satellite of the capital, also finds itself under foreign domination. A census at the beginning of the nineteenth century estimates the island's population at 3,800 inhabitants, far fewer than three centuries earlier.[17] Among them figure nine employees working for the communal authorities; forty-three merchants of crystal, wood, fish, oysters, or wine; two physicians and one surgeon; three boat builders, eight boatmen, seven furniture-makers, six smiths, four cobblers, a tailor. On the island there are seventeen glassworks, one boat for commercial purposes, four barges for hauling freight, thirty gondolas for the *traghetto* and eighty-five boats of assorted sizes for carrying wood, vegetables and fruit. The composition of Murano society has changed little. In 1866, the community, still under control of Venice but retaining its own institutions, is attached to the new Kingdom of Italy.

At the beginning of the twentieth century, the Fascist regime imposes far-reaching administrative reforms and decrees Murano's political attachment to the commune of Venice. On 21 November 1923 the communal council votes unanimously against this merger.[18] But a few days later the council is dissolved and the community is placed under the direction of a royal commissioner, Libero Vitali. Acts of vandalism flare up, tricolour flags are placed in windows, and at assorted meetings the inhabitants, glassworkers especially, make a great show of disagreement.[19] On 4 December, a women's demonstration ends up in front of the campanile of Santi Maria e Donato, and the women take possession of the tower. Then the inhabitants manage to break into the tower of San Pietro Martire. Bells of protest toll across Murano. In the days that follow, on the bridges and *fondamente*, clashes set inhabitants against *carabinieri*. The demonstrators shout, whistle, and chant in the island's streets; several times, the towers are occupied and bells ring across the Murano night. On 6 December, the prefect of Venice issues a decree:

> In light of the fact that at Murano, for several days, there has continued, and intensified, an agitation, with political meetings (*comizi*) and repeated demonstrations of hostility against persons, with an abuse of bell-ringing and attempts at work-stoppage in the industrial establish-ments . . . there are forbidden, at Murano and its environs, meetings and assemblies of more than five persons, and all sounds of bells that do not depend on regular religious practice. It is also forbidden to anyone to carry arms in public or in a public place, whether licit or illicit.[20]

At the end of December, as snow starts falling across Italy and on Venice, the clashes recommence. A few days later, Muranesi autonomists adorn walls with the image of the rooster, symbol of island autonomy.[21] On the evening of 10 January 1924, *carabinieri* are posted in front of the *campanile*, but the 600 workers gathered on Campo Santi Maria e Donato overwhelm them easily and the bells resume their racket. Reinforcements are awaited, to come by the commuter *vaporetto*. The Muranesi, armed with sticks, take over the floating landings, where they have removed the lights that let boats steer by night. At the arrival of the forces of order, they shout, "We won't let anybody off the boat except Muranesi, not the forces". Clashes follow, with wounded on both sides, and more than twenty inhabitants are arrested, among them one Vettor Fuga, aged fourteen. The youngest are sent back home to their parents; the others are carried to the jail on the Giudecca, an island lying just south of Venice. On the Campo Santi Maria e Donato, inhabitants protest the police presence, throwing rocks and clods.

The next morning, the workers, returning to their shops after the midday meal, gather on the Fondamenta dei Vetrai and then parade to cries of "Viva Free Murano! Viva autonomy!"[22] Workers issue from the workshops brandishing their blowpipes, with incandescent glass still attached. The Patriarch of Venice, Cardinal La Fontaine, launches an appeal to calm. "Let me, Father of your souls, address you a word of love. I am distraught at these tumults, especially when they happen among good folk, workers as you are. You will understand that in making a tumult, one cannot please God."[23] Despite it all, attachment in the end is made official, and, notwithstanding sporadic protests in the weeks that follow, on the island calm gradually returns.

Even though, today still, the Muranesi conserve a certain reputation as brawlers, the island seems nicely calm. With some 5,000 residents – when Venice numbers no more than 60,000 – Murano seems stunned by the changed market for glass, which suddenly went dry thanks to underhanded competition. For the tourists, the Fondamenta and the Rio dei Vetrai remain the main draw. On the island, a few talented masters still offer their customers work both precious and refined. On the other side of Ponte Lungo, the streets, the little *campi*, the gardens, Campo Santi Maria e Donato, and the *fondamente* have kept all but intact the decor of the revolt's day. Many palaces built at the end of the Middle Ages still line the quays. Children freed from school gather on Campo San Bernardo to play ball, in spite of the podestà's old prohibitions. The church of Santi Maria e Donato still has the precious mosaic pavement on which Vitturi and Suriano followed Malcanton to the choir, and it preserves the gilded vault that, for centuries, sheltered power's passage. Boats jam the canals. The gardens still blossom. To the north of Murano, a vast expanse of empty terrain, buffeted by winds and aswarm with rabbits, does its level best to digest the tons of scrap dumped for decades by the glassworks. Amidst the weeds, coloured shards, green, blue, red, polished by the rains and the salt spray mingle with the Lagoon's loam.

## Notes

1   ASVe, AC, MP, 142, no. 17.
2   "Statuto de Muran", book III, ch. 6, 271.
3   "Statuto de Muran", book III, ch. 6, 271.
4   "Statuto de Muran", book III, ch. 7, 271.
5   ASVe, PM, 44, 7 Sententiarum 2, for 15 July and 12 August 1510.
6   BMC, Mariegola dei Fioleri, 26, fol. 62, for 15 September 1510.
7   ASVe, PM, 212, documents 1509–19, for 21 August 1510.
8   ASVe, PM, 44, 25 Criminalium 7, for 28 August 1510, against Ser Nicolo de Blasio.
9   ASVe, PM, 44, 25 Criminalium 7, for 18 September 1510, Ser Stefano di Pietro.
10  ASVe, Senato Mar, reg. 14, fol. 165, for 19 October 1498. See also Girolamo Priuli, *I Diarii*, vol. I, 291, April 1500.
11  Marino Sanudo, *I Diarii*, vol. 2, col. 718, 14 May 1499.
12  ASVe, AC, MP, 142, no.17, fol. 20–2.
13  Marino Sanudo, *I Diarii*, vol. 12, col. 99, 2 April 1511.
14  ASVe, AC, Raspe, 3661, fol. 12r-v.
15  ASV, PM, 57.
16  Archivio Parrocchiale San Pietro Martire di Murano, Scuola di San Giovanni Battista dei Battuti, Registro dei confratelli, fol. 2, for 16 September 1544.
17  Barizza and Ferrari, *L'archivio*, 22–3.
18  Barizza and Ferrari, *L'archivio*, 24.
19  *Il Gazzettino*, 30 November 1923, 4–6 December 1923; *Gazzetta di Venezia*, 5 and 7 December 1923.

20  *Gazzetta di Venezia*, 7 December 1923.
21  *Il Gazzettino*, 29 December 1923, 1 January 1924; *Gazzetta di Venezia*, 1 January 1924.
22  *Gazzetta di Venezia*, 12 January 1924.
23  *Il Gazzettino*, 15 January 1924; *Gazzetta di Venezia* 16 January 1924.

# Conclusion

Was the Snowball Revolt really a revolt? Not to the eyes of the patricians, who decide to acquit the accused and whose sentence serves to defuse the event's impact as opposition. In declaring the Muranesi not guilty, justice absolves their action and denies its critical dimension. At power's passage, the inhabitants expressed in a visible, public, legible manner their shared political competence, at once inherited and built by them, but the patricians choose to disqualify the sense of their demonstration. Unlike the rulers of many Italian and European cities, they prefer to read these acts and intentions as singular and banal, and to register them in a regime of action that has nothing to do with politics. Collective action and public speaking exist in Venice, but their violence remains contained, and how the patricians apprehend them diminishes their impact all the further. It is also because there is no discourse about revolt that there is, at Venice, no revolt.

Power's passage on 27 January 1511 is a petty event, and, the sentence helps shrink it smaller. In comparison with other revolts of the same epoch, it seemed easily dismissed. Everywhere in Europe, in the fifteenth and sixteenth centuries, urban and peasant seditions, battles over faith, and popular protests had results far bloodier. What happened at Murano is not their like, neither in the protagonists' aspirations, nor in the means employed, nor in its violence, nor in the authorities' chosen reaction. Nevertheless, in a space where such demonstrations are always rare, the Snowball Revolt cannot be considered harmless. Agreed, it was not pre-meditated. But the chant against "that dog Vitturi", the collective indignation, the protesting, the denunciations amassed by secretary Simone and the justifications heard by the *avogadori di Comun* reflect the islanders' capacity to express, in certain situations, their criticism and judgment.

The absence of revolt does not mean that people do not express their intentions, or that they are excluded from the process of constructing politics. Murano's example shows how many and how variegated are the modes of intervention in public space. The Muranesi are indeed dominated: by Venice, by the patricians, by a political and social order that the podestà both represents and imposes on them. But, in their daily lives, that does not stop them from working out collective practices, employing forms of action and ways of doing things that are all just as important, if not more so, for defining who they are, as is their subordination.

The inhabitants participate in many fashions in configuring the social and political space of the island. Some Muranesi take on institutional functions that accompany Venice's power and help shape its manifestations. The owners of the glassworks, the glassmakers, the artisans, and perhaps a few richer fishermen, take their turn at the seats of the collegial bodies, to work alongside the podestà to furnish those legislative and judicial structures that the community needs. Complex electoral processes, mixing voting and lottery, and sometimes entailing interviews of candidates, try to guarantee the selection of the most competent and best, while also keeping Murano's families equally represented. Many lower-level functionaries are elected and chosen to serve the government and the community. Far from being second-rank players or power's simple servants, in the eyes of the inhabitants they embody public authority. It is they who announce, defend, and apply the decisions of the podestà and the Thirty. They are the essential intermediaries between the street, where power does its work, and the palace of the podestà, where decisions happen.

Other inhabitants also contribute to the business of governance, in taking on, for the public good, temporary missions, some formal others less so. The fishermen take part in implementing an ecological policy for the Lagoon, the glassworkers help define Murano's economic policy, the boatmen collaborate in broadcasting information, the innkeepers shoulder collecting the wine tax: these are all tasks that integrate the inhabitants into power's deliberations and decisions. The members of guilds and confraternities learn how to negotiate, and to construct a legal, and licit, framework for their collective practices. Their institutions, and, more generally, all places of sociability and labour, become spaces for social-ization and discussion, where the inhabitants develop rules, agree on modes of action and common principles, conventions, and a moral sense, becoming familiar as they do so with collegial modes of action and elaborating a discourse of common good.

In a world dominated by labour and by craft-work, professional competence is a powerful organizer of social hierarchies. The workshop and the guild serve to produce social categories, rights, and customs that give society its shape. The social, political and juridical order is not a mere reflection of decisions made by Venetian institutions; it is in equal measure the result of successive accommodations between law and practices. The legal articulation of the social world – for instance, the definition of citizenship or of the status of foreigners – is also the result of actions by the ordinary people, who, on the basis of the distinctions they know – about wealth, power, honourability, or fame – build society.

The inhabitants participate no less in creating and shaping urban space. The existence of a *piazza* and public buildings (palace of the podestà, the houses of the crier and the *cavaliere*), and of communal infrastructure (bridges, wells, markets, and mill), results from a collective capacity to organize space and to finance, over and over, its planning, construction, and up-keep. In acting upon the territory of the island by their ways of working and living there, the people fashion their framework for living. To inhabit is to construct society.

Participation in civic rituals, in orderly or disorderly way, is one more proof of the role the inhabitants play in the construction of a discourse about society. They recognize the ritual's meaning, often hewing to it, but sometimes contesting it. Their role is neither passive nor secondary. They make the ritual just as much as do those who parade in it; they are its second, indispensable pole, its public, and its reception, and they give sense to the visual display laid on by the patricians. The Muranesi's skill at interpreting power's passage, and in diverting one by one all its codes, attests to their capacity to interpret what politics is, and what gives it sense.

Finally, it is in their relations with justice that the inhabitants reveal their mastery of the stakes that shape their society. Certainly, justice is a very fine example of domination. Both the podestà at Murano and the patrician judges in Venice incarnate the power of the nobles over the folk of the *popolo*; it is they who in the end decide what is just, legitimate, and legal, and who impose on the *popolani* a language of truth. The law and the institutions of justice constrain bodies, words, and deeds. The *cavalier* at Murano and the guards at Venice have recourse to legitimate violence and impose by force the discourse of patrician order. But justice is also a civic and civil space for economic regulation that creates and ballasts confidence, which is an everyday value essential to community life. The inhabitants have need of laws to make rules for transactions, exchanges, and commerce. Murano is a space saturated by law, within which the inhabitants have learned by habit to deploy their moral discourse and justifications to explain their actions. The podestà's tribunal heeds the people and writes down their words. Justice offers them a shared horizon of expectation. It nourishes their political culture and explains their collective capacity, all century long, to negotiate their rights. The people know how to use the machinery of justice to give sense to their actions, but also to justify what they do and what they think. The discourses of justification are essential words that they must take in hand to reconstitute their vision of the world, their fashion of conceiving of society and of the space of politics.

All these forms of action are in no way the people's only. The ordinary inhabitants form social and political space according to models that echo those of the elites. There are in the Middle Ages no popular forms of political action; rather, there are interventions and actions taken up by the *popolo*. Just as there is no purely popular culture, there is no insulated, distinctly popular politics, and in no way does popular action restrict itself to conflict, resistance and violence. The *popolo* contribute in a positive way to the elaboration of order and the configuration of political space. In the construction of social bonds and of all society, they are crucial actors.

# Bibliography

## Manuscript and archival sources

### Archivio di Stato di Venezia

- Avogaria di Comun, Miscellanea Penale
  142, n°17, 1511
  410, n°14, 1517
- Avogaria di Comun, Raspe, reg. 3661 (1508–12)
- Capi del consiglio de' Dieci, Lettere di rettori e di altre cariche, b. 78
- Collegio, Formulari di commissioni, reg. 8
- Consiglio dei Dieci, Deliberazioni, Parti Communi, filza 10
- Dieci Savi alle Decime, 1514,
  b. 15, Sant'Angelo
  b. 49, Santa Maria Zobenigo
  b. 62, San Samuele
  b. 82, Murano
- Milizia da Mar, 219
- Miscellanea Codici, Storia Veneta, Genealogie Barbaro
- Notarile, Testamenti, 191, Girolamo Canal
- Podestà di Murano
  b. 38, Gabriele Venier (1501–2)
  b. 43, Pietro Morosini (1508–9)
  b. 44, Vitale Vitturi (1509–11)
  b. 45, Agostino Suriano (1511–12)
  b. 46, Giacomo Antonio Tiepolo (1512–13)
  b. 48, Gian Giacomo Baffo (1515–16)
  b. 57, Girolamo Morosini (1540–2) and Marco Manolesso (1542–3)
  b. 187, letters to the podestà (1500–60)
  b. 200, *Commissio* of doge Agostino Barbarigo to Francesco Barbarigo (1493)
  b. 203, miscellaneous acts
  b. 204, *scuole* and arts

b. 205, inventories (1495–1679)
b. 212, miscellaneous acts (14th cent. 1559)
b. 229, *registri di cassa*
b. 233, notarial acts
b. 236 bis, *Statuti*
- Podestà di Torcello,
  b. 140, Vincenzo Zantani (1510–11)
- Provveditore alla Sanità, reg. 726

### Biblioteca del Museo Correr

- Mariegole
  2, Luganegheri
  26, Fioleri o verieri de Muran
  IV L 7, Scuola di santo Stefano in Santo Stefano di Murano
  IV L 8, Scuola di san Vincenzo Ferrer in San Pietro martire di Murano
  IV L 10, Confraternita del Santissimo Sacramento in Santo Stefano di Murano
  IV L 17, Scuola dei battuti di San Giovanni Battista di Murano

### Archivio Storico del Patriarcato di Venezia

- Curia vescovile di Torcello, Visite pastorali, reg. 1 (1591 and 1594)

### Archivio parrocchiale di San Donà (Murano)

- Fabbriceria, Atti generali, Prima serie, busta 6, processo n°18 (Avogaria di Comun)

### Archivio parrocchiale di San Pietro (Murano)

- Registro degli ammalati (1510–13)
- Varia 1, Libro XI
- Scuola di San Giovanni Battista dei Battuti, Parti e sentenze

### British library

- Manuscript, Add MS 17046, Register of the Statutes of the Scola di San Zuane Battista di Murano

## Published primary sources (including modern editions)

Leandro Alberti. *Descrittione di tutta l'Italia & isole pertinenti ad essa.* . . . Venice: Gio. Maria Leni, 1577.
Pietro Aretino. *Lettere*. Rome: Salerno Editrice, 2000.

Pietro Aretino. *Sei Giornate. Ragionamento della Nanna e della Antonia* (1534). Giovanni Aquilecchia (ed.), Bari: Laterza, 1969.

Benedetto Bordone. *Libro . . . de tutte l'isole del mondo*. Venice, 1528.

Andrea Calmo. *Le bizzarre, faconde et ingegnose rime pescatorie*. Gino Belloni (ed.), Venice: Marsilio, 2003.

Andrea Calmo. *Le lettere di Messer Andrea Calmo riprodotte sulle stampe migliori, con introduzione ed illustrazioni di Vittorio Rossi*. Turin: Loescher, 1888.

Giacomo Casanova. *Histoire de ma vie*. Paris: R. Laffont, Bouquins, 1993.

Francesco Colonna. *Hypnerotomachia Poliphili*. Giovanni Pozzi & Lucia C. Ciapponi (eds), Padua: Editrice Antenore, 1980 [1499].

Thomas Coryat. *Coryat's Crudities*. Glasgow, UK: James MacLehose and Sons, 1905 [1611].

*Diario di Murano di Francesco Luna* 1625–31. Vincenzo Zanetti (ed.), Venice, 1872.

*Gazzetta di Venezia*. December 1923–February 1924.

*Il Gazzettino*, December 1923–February 1924.

"Gli statuti veneziani di Jacopo Tiepolo del 1242 e le loro glosse". Roberto Cessi (ed.), *Memorie del Reale Istituto Veneto di scienze, lettere ed arti*, 1938, vol. XXX–2, pp. 1–45.

Giovanni Grevembroch. *Gli abiti de Veneziani di quasi ogni età con diligenza raccolti e dipinti nel secolo XVIII*. Venice: Filippi editore, 1981.

*Lettere di XIII Huomini illustri*. Venice: Per Francesco Lorenzini da Turino, 1560.

*Il Libro d'Oro di Murano*. Vincenzo Zanetti (ed.), Venice: Stab. M. Fontana, 1883.

Giovanni Monticolo. *I Capitolari delle Arti Veneziane sottoposte alla giustizia e poi alla giustizia vecchia dalle origini al MCCCXXX*, 1896.

Girolamo Priuli. *I Diarii (1494–1512)*, Roberto Cessi (ed.), Città di Castello/ Bologna: S. Lapi/N. Zanichelli, 1912.

Marino Sanudo. *Cronachetta*. Rinaldo Fulin (ed.). Venice: Visentini, 1880.

Marino Sanudo. *I Diarii*. Rinaldo Fulin *et al.* (ed.). Bologna: Forni, 1969–70 [1879–1903] .

Marino Sanudo il giovane. *De origine, situ et magistratibus urbis Venetae ovvero La città di Venetia (1493–1530)*. Angela Caracciolo Aricò (ed.). Milan: Cisalpino-La Goliardica, 1980.

Francesco Sansovino. *Delle cose notabili della città di Venetia*. Venice: Appresso Felice Valgrisio, 1587.

"Statuto de Muran del 1502". *Statuti della laguna veneta dei secoli XIV–XVI*, Monica Pasqualetto (ed.). Rome: Jouvence, 1989, pp. 207–87.

Giovanni Francesco Straparola. *Le piacevoli notti*. Venice, 1550.

"Summula Statutorum Floridorum di Andrea Dandolo". Luigi Genuardi (ed.). *Nuovo Archivio Veneto*, 21, 1911, pp. 436–67.

Cesare Vecellio's *Habiti Antichi et Moderni, The Clothing of the Renaissance World*. Margaret F. Rosenthal & Ann Rosalind Jones (eds). London: Thames & Hudson, 2008 [Venice, 1590].

*Viaggio a Gerusalemme di Pietro Casola*. Anna Paoletti (ed.). Alessandria: Ed. dell'Orso, 2001.

## Secondary sources

Rather than insert bibliographic comments into my endnotes, which have little more than archival information, I have chosen to lay out a thematic bibliography. For a more complete bibliography, containing both historiographical commentary and, in particular, those French publications that helped me to put this work together, please see the original Fayard edition.

The bibliography below musters the fundamental works (mostly in English and in Italian) that concern the principal questions this book addresses.

## 1 Venice, Murano, and the historical context

### Venice

Dursteler, Eric R. (ed.). *A Companion to Venetian History, 1400–1797.* Leiden: Brill, 2013.

Ferraro, Joanne. *Venice: History of the Floating City.* New York: Cambridge University Press, 2012.

Lane, Frederic C. *Venice: A Maritime Republic.* Baltimore, MD: Johns Hopkins University Press, 1973.

Martin, John & Dennis Romano (eds). *Venice Reconsidered: The History and Civilization of an Italian City-State, 1297–1797.* Baltimore, MD: Johns Hopkins University Press, 2000.

*Storia di Venezia. Dalle origini alla caduta della Serenissima,* 11 vols. Rome: Istituto della Enciclopedia italiana, 1992–98.

### Murano and the Venetian Lagoon

Archivio di Stato di Venezia. *Laguna, lidi, fiumi. Cinque secoli di gestione delle acque.* Venice: Ministero dei lavori pubblici, Magistrato alle acque di Venezia, 1983.

Crouzet-Pavan, Elisabeth. "Murano à la fin du Moyen Âge: spécificité ou intégration dans l'espace vénitien". *Revue historique,* 268–1, 1982, pp. 45–92.

Crouzet-Pavan, Elisabeth. "Toward an Ecological Understanding of the Myth of Venice". In John Martin & Dennis Romano (eds), *Venice Reconsidered: The History and Civilization of an Italian City-State, 1297–1797.* Baltimore, MD: Johns Hopkins University Press, 2000, pp. 39–64.

Goy, Richard. *Chioggia and the Villages of the Venetian Lagoon.* Cambridge: Cambridge University Press, 1985.

*Mostra storica della laguna veneta,* Venice, 1970.

Orlando, Ermanno. *Altre Venezie: Il dogado veneziano nei secoli XIII e XIV (giurisdizione, territorio, giustizia e amministrazione).* Venice: Istituto Veneto di Scienze Lettere ed Arti, 2008.

Ramelli, Silvia. *Murano medievale: urbanistica, architettura, edilizia dal XII al XV secolo.* Padua: Il Poligrafo, 2000.

Sciama, Lidia D. *A Venetian Island: Environment, History, and Change in Burano.* New York & Oxford: Berghahn Books, 2003.

*Statuti della laguna veneta dei secoli XIV–XVI.* Rome: Jouvence, 1989.

Tosi, Andrea (ed.). *La memoria del vetro. Murano e l'arte vetraria nelle storie dei suoi maestri.* Venice: Marsilio, Scuola del Vetro Abate Zanetti, 2006.

Trivellato, Francesca. *Fondamenta dei vetrai: lavoro, tecnologia e mercato a Venezia tra Sei e Settecento.* Rome: Donzelli, 2000.

Zanetti, Vincenzo. *Guida di Murano e delle celebri sue fornaci vetrarie.* Venice, 1866.

Zecchin, Luigi. *Vetro e vetrai di Murano*, 3 vols. Venice: Arsenale Editrice, 1987–90.

### Venetian territorial domination

Maire Vigueur, Jean-Claude (ed.). *I podestà dell'Italia comunale*, 2 vols. Rome: Ecole française de Rome, 2000.

Ventura, Angelo. *Nobiltà e popolo nella società veneta del '400 e '500.* Bari: Laterza, 1964.

Viggiano, Alfredo. *Governanti e governati: legittimità del potere ed esercizio dell'autorità sovrana nello stato veneto della prima età moderna.* Treviso: Fondazione Benetton-Canova, 1993.

### Historical context

Crawshaw, Jane L. Stevens. *Plague Hospitals: Public Health for the City in Early Modern Venice.* Farnham, UK: Ashgate, 2012.

Gilbert, Felix. "Venice in the Crisis of the League of Cambrai". In John R. Hale (ed.), *Renaissance Venice.* London: Faber & Faber, 1973, pp. 274–92.

Mallett, Michael E. & Christine Shaw. *The Italian Wars (1494–1559): War, State and Society in Early Modern Europe.* London: Routledge, 2012.

Mallett, Michael E. & John R. Hale. *The Military Organization of a Renaissance State: Venice, 1400 to 1617.* Cambridge: Cambridge University Press, 1984.

Pellegrini, Marco. *Le guerre d'Italia (1494–1530).* Bologna: Il Mulino, 2009.

## 2 Social history

### The people of Murano and Venice

Chojnacka, Monica. *Working Women of Early Modern Venice.* Baltimore, MD: Johns Hopkins University Press, 2001.

Davis, Robert C. *Shipbuilders of the Venetian Arsenal: Workers and Workplace in the Preindustrial City.* Baltimore, MD: Johns Hopkins University Press, 1991.

Judde de Larivière, Claire & Rosa M. Salzberg. " 'Le peuple est la cité'. L'idée de *popolo* et la condition des *popolani* à Venise (XVᵉ–XVIᵉ siècle)". *Annales HSS*, 4, 2013, pp. 1113–40.

Pullan, Brian S. *Rich and Poor in Renaissance Venice: The Social Institutions of a Catholic State, to 1620.* Oxford: Blackwell, 1971.

Pullan, Brian S. " 'Three Orders of Inhabitants': Social Hierarchies in the Republic of Venice". In Jeffrey Denton (ed.), *Orders and Hierarchies in Late Medieval and Renaissance Europe.* Basingstoke, UK: Macmillan, 1999, pp. 147–68.

Romano, Dennis. *Housecraft and Statecraft: Domestic Service in Renaissance Venice, 1400–1600*. Baltimore, MD: Johns Hopkins University Press, 1996.

Romano, Dennis. *Patricians and Popolani: The Social Foundations of the Venetian Renaissance State*. Baltimore, MD: Johns Hopkins University Press, 1987.

Zago, Roberto. *I Nicolotti: storia di una comunità di pescatori a Venezia nell'età moderna*. Abano Terme: Francisci, 1984.

Zannini, Andrea. "L'identità multipla: essere popolo in una capitale (Venezia, XVI–XVIII secolo)". *Ricerche storiche*. Aurora Savelli & Gérard Dellile (eds). "Essere popolo. Prerogative e rituali d'appartenenza nelle città italiane d'antico regime", 2–3, 2002, pp. 247–62.

## The history of the people

Burke, Peter. *Popular Culture in Early Modern Europe*. Aldershot, UK: Ashgate, 1978; second edition 2009.

Burke, Peter. "We, the People: Popular Culture and Popular Identity in Modern Europe". In Scott Lash & Jonathan Friedman (eds), *Modernity and Identity*. Oxford: Blackwell, 1992, pp. 293–308.

Cohen, Elizabeth S. "Miscarriages of Apothecary Justice: Un-separate Spaces for Work and Family in Early Modern Rome". *Renaissance Studies*, 21, 4, 2007, pp. 480–504.

Cohn, Samuel K. *The Laboring Classes in Renaissance Florence*. New York: Academic Press, 1980.

Mineo, Igor. "States, Orders and Social Distinction". In Andrea Gamberini & Isabella Lazzarini (eds), *The Italian Renaissance State*. Cambridge: Cambridge University Press, 2012, pp. 323–44.

Zorzi, Andrea. "The Popolo". In John M. Najemy (ed.), *Italy in the Age of the Renaissance, 1300–1550*. Oxford: Oxford University Press, 2004, pp. 145–64.

## 3 Rituals, violence, popular action

Atkinson, Niall. *The Noisy Renaissance: Sound, Architecure and Florentine Urban Life*. College Park, PA: Penn State University Press, 2016.

Buc, Philippe. *The Dangers of Ritual: Between Early Medieval Texts and Social Scientific Theory*. Princeton, NJ: Princeton University Press, 2001.

Cohen, Thomas. "Communal Thought, Communal Words, and Communal Rites in a Sixteenth-Century Village Rebellion". In Nicholas Terpstra & Nicholas Eckstein (eds), *Sociability and its Discontents: Civil Society, Social Capital, and their Alternatives in Late Medieval and Early Modern Europe*. Turnhout: Brepols, 2009, pp. 25–50.

Davis, Natalie Zemon. *Society and Culture in Early Modern France: Eight Essays*. London: Duckworth, 1975.

Davis, Natalie Zemon. "Writing 'The Rites of Violence' and Afterward". *Past & Present*, Supplement 7, 2012, pp. 8–29.

Davis, Robert C. *The War of the Fists: Popular Culture and Public Violence in Late Renaissance Venice*. Oxford: Oxford University Press, 1994.

Fenlon, Ian. *The Ceremonial City: History, Memory and Myth in Renaissance Venice*. New Haven, CT, & London: Yale University Press, 2007.

Geertz, Clifford. *The Interpretation of Cultures*. New York: Basic Books, 1973.

Ginzburg, Carlo. "Ritual Pillages: A Preface to Research in Progress". In Edward Muir & Guido Ruggiero (eds), *Microhistory and the Lost Peoples of Europe*. Baltimore, MD: Johns Hopkins University Press, 1991, pp. 20–41.

Johnson, James H. *Venice Incognito: Masks in the Serene Republic*. Berkeley, CA: University of California Press, 2011.

Hunt, John M. "The Conclave from the 'Outside In': Rumor, Speculation, and Disorder in Rome during Early Modern Papal Elections". *Journal of Early Modern History*, 16, 2012, pp. 355–82.

Hunt, John M. *The Vacant See in Early Modern Rome: A Social History of the Papal Interregnum*. Leiden: Brill, 2016.

Mitchell, Bonner. *The Majesty of the State: Triumphal Progresses of Foreign Sovereigns in Renaissance Italy, 1494–1600*. Florence: Leo S. Olschki, 1986.

Muir, Edward. *Civic Ritual in Renaissance Venice*. Princeton, NJ: Princeton University Press, 1981.

Muir, Edward. *Mad Blood Stirring: Vendetta and Factions in Friuli during the Renaissance*. Baltimore, MD: Johns Hopkins University Press, 1993.

Muir, Edward. *Ritual in Early Modern Europe*. Cambridge: Cambridge University Press, 2005.

Partridge, Loren & Randolph Starn. *Arts of Power: Three Halls of State in Italy, 1300–1600*. Berkeley, CA: University of California Press, 1992.

Rosenthal, David. *Kings of the Street: Power, Community, and Ritual in Renaissance Florence*. Turnhout: Brepols, 2015.

Rosenthal, David. "The Spaces of Plebian Ritual and the Boundaries of Transgression". In Roger J. Crum & John T. Paoletti (eds), *Renaissance Florence: A Social History*. Cambridge: Cambridge University Press, 2006, pp. 161–81.

Trexler, Richard C. *Public Life in Renaissance Florence*. New York & London: Academic Press, 1980.

Van Gelder, Maartje. "Ducal Display and the Contested Use of Space in Late Sixteenth-Century Venetian Coronation Festivals". In R. Mulryne, K. De Jonge & R. Morris (eds), *Occasions of State: Early Modern European Festivals and the Negotiation of Power*. New York and London: Routledge, 2017.

## 4 Politics

### Venice, politics, and the people

Burke, Peter. "Early Modern Venice as a Center of Information and Communication". In John Martin & Dennis Romano (eds), *Venice Reconsidered: The History and Civilization of an Italian City-State, 1297–1797*. Baltimore, MD: Johns Hopkins University Press, 2000, pp. 389–419.

Cowan Alexander. "Gossip and Street Culture in Early Modern Venice". *Journal of Early Modern History*, 12, (3–4), 2008, pp. 313–33.

De Vivo, Filippo. *Information and Communication in Venice: Rethinking Early Modern Politics*. Oxford: Oxford University Press, 2007.

Finlay, Robert. *Politics in Renaissance Venice*. London: Benn, 1980.

Muir, Edward. "Was There Republicanism in the Renaissance Republics? Venice after Agnadello". In John Martin & Dennis Romano (eds), *Venice Reconsidered: The History and Civilization of an Italian City-State, 1297–1797*. Baltimore, MD: The Johns Hopkins University Press, 2000, pp. 137–67.

## The people in politics

Challet, Vincent, Jan Dumolyn, Jelle Haemers & Hipólito Rafael Oliva Herrer (eds). *The Voices of the People in Medieval Political Communication.* Turnhout: Brepols, 2014.

Judde de Larivière, Claire (ed.). "Politiques du commun. XVIe–XIXe siècles", *Politix*, 119, 2017.

Poloni, Alma. *Potere al popolo: Conflitti sociali e lotte politiche nell'Italia comunale del Duecento.* Milan: Bruno Mondadori, 2010.

Rospocher, Massimo (ed.). *Beyond the Public Sphere: Opinions, Publics, Spaces in Early Modern Europe (XVI–XVIII).* Bologna: Il Mulino/Duncker & Humbolt, 2012.

Scott, James C. *Domination and the Arts of Resistance: Hidden Transcripts.* New Haven, CT, & London: Yale Universiry Press, 1990.

## Town criers

Judde de Larivière, Claire. "Voicing Popular Politics: The *comandatore* of the Community of Murano in the Sixteenth Century". In Stefano Dall'Aglio, Brian Richardson & Massimo Rospocher (eds), *Voices and Texts in Early Modern Italian Society.* London & New York: Routledge, 2016, pp. 37–51.

Milner, Stephen J. " 'Fanno bandire, notificare, et expressamente comandare': Town Criers and the Information Economy of Renaissance Florence". *I Tatti Studies in the Italian Renaissance*, 16, 1/2, 2013, pp. 107–51.

## Popular revolts and public space

Bourin, Monique, Giovanni Cherubini & Giuliano Pinto (eds). *Rivolte urbane e rivolte contadine nell'Europa del Trecento. Un confronto.* Florence: Firenze University Press, 2008.

Cohen, Thomas V. "The Great Italian Political Shout". In Stefano Dall'Aglio, Brian Richardson & Massimo Rospocher (eds), *Voices and Texts in Early Modern Italian Society.* London & New York: Routledge, 2016, pp. 23–36.

Cohn, Samuel. *Lust for Liberty: The Politics of Social Revolt in Medieval Europe, 1200–1425, Italy, France, and Flanders.* Cambridge MA: Harvard University Press, 2006.

Firnhaber-Baker, Justine & Dirk Schoenaers (eds). *The Routledge History Handbook of Medieval Revolt.* London: Routledge, 2017.

Rospocher, Massimo (ed.). *Oltre la sfera pubblica: Lo spazio della politica nell'Europa moderna.* Bologna: Il Mulino, 2013.

Thompson, Edward P. "The Moral Economy of the English Crowd in the Eighteenth Century". *Past & Present*, 50, 1975, pp. 76–136.

## 5 Justice

### Justice and violence in Venice

Cozzi, Gaetano. "Authority and the Law in Renaissance Venice". In John R. Hale (ed.), *Renaissance Venice.* London: Faber & Faber, 1973, pp. 293–345.

Cozzi, Gaetano (ed.). *Stato, società e giustizia nella Repubblica veneta (sec. XV–XVIII)*, 2 vols. Rome: Jouvence, 1980.

Horodowich, Elizabeth. *Language and Statecraft in Early Modern Venice*. Cambridge: Cambridge University Press, 2008.

Ruggiero, Guido. *Violence in Early Renaissance Venice*. New Brunswick, NJ: Rutgers University Press, 1980.

Setti, Cristina. "L'Avogaria di Comun come magistratura media d'appello". *Il diritto della Regione. Il nuovo cittadino*, 1, 2009, pp. 143–71.

### Medieval justice, violence, and public order

Cohen, Elizabeth S. "Moving Words: Everyday Oralities and Social Dynamics in Roman Trials circa 1600". In Stefano Dall'Aglio, Brian Richardson & Massimo Rospocher (eds), *Voices and Texts in Early Modern Italian Society*. London & New York: Routledge, 2016, pp. 69–83

Cohen, Elizabeth S. & Thomas V. Cohen. *Words and Deeds in Renaissance Rome: Trials before the Papal Magistrates*. Toronto: University of Toronto Press, 1993.

Dean, Trevor. *Crime and Justice in Late Medieval Italy*. Cambridge: Cambridge University Press, 2007.

Sbriccoli, Mario. "Giustizia criminale". In Maurizio Fioravanti (ed.), *Lo stato moderno in Europa. Istituzioni e diritto*. Rome-Bari: Laterza, 2002, pp. 163–205.

Zorzi, Andrea. "Justice". In Andrea Gamberini & Isabella Lazzarini (eds), *The Italian Renaissance State*. Cambridge: Cambridge University Press, 2012, pp. 490–524.

## 6 Method and tools

### Method

Boltanski, Luc & Laurent Thévenot. *On Justification: Economies of Worth*. Princeton, NJ and Oxford: Oxford University Press, 2006 [French edition 1991].

Cohen, Thomas V. "The Macrohistory of Microhistory". *Journal of Medieval and Early Modern History*, 47, 1, 2017, pp. 53–73.

Desrosières, Alain & Laurent Thévenot. *Les catégories socioprofessionnelles*. Paris: La Découverte, 2002.

Ginzburg, Carlo. *The Cheese and the Worms: The Cosmos of a Sixteenth-century Miller*. London: Routledge, 1980 [Italian edition 1976].

Judde de Larivière, Claire & Georges Hanne. "Occupational Naming Conventions: Historicity, Actors, Interactions". *Historical Social Research*, Rainer Diaz-Bone & Robert Salais (eds), special issue 'Conventions and Institutions From a Historical Perspective', 36–4, 2011, pp. 82–102.

Lepetit, Bernard (ed.), *Les formes de l'expérience: une autre histoire sociale*. Paris: Albin Michel, 1995.

Magnússon, Sigurdur G. & Istvan M. Szijártó. *What is Microhistory? Theory and Practice*. London: Routledge, 2013.

"Microhistory Today: A Roundtable Discussion". *Journal of Medieval and Early Modern History*. 47, 1, 2017, pp. 7–52.

Revel, Jacques (ed.). *Giochi di scala: La microstoria alla prova dell'esperienza*. Roma: Viella, 2006.

Sewell, William H. Jr. *Work and Revolution in France*: *The Language of Labor from the Old Regime to 1848*. Cambridge: Cambridge University Press, 1980.

Sewell, William H. Jr. *Logics of History*. *Social Theory and Social Transformation*. Chicago, IL: University of Chicago Press, 2005.

Trivellato, Francesca. "Is There a Future for Italian Microhistory in the Age of Global History?" *California Italian Studies*, Albert R. Ascoli and Randolph Starn (eds.), special Issue 'Italian Futures', 2.1, 2011 (online).

## Tools

Boerio, Giuseppe. *Dizionario del dialetto veneziano*. Venice: Giovanni Cecchini, 1856, new edition, Milan, 1971.

Cortelazzo, Manlio. *Dizionario veneziano della lingua e della cultura popolare nel XVI secolo*. Limena: La Linea Editrice, 2007.

Da Mosto, Andrea. *L'Archivio di Stato di Venezia, indice generale, storico, descrittivo ed analitico*. Rome: Biblioteca d'Arte, 1937.

# Index